Praise for
From the Library of C. S. Lewis

"This is a knowledgeable and inspired selection from what C. S. Lewis called the 'old books' that nurtured his mind, spirit, and imagination. All who love the writings of the master will enjoy these engaging passages from the vast range of Lewis's reading and relish the light that they cast upon his concerns."

> —COLIN DURIEZ, author of *A Field Guide to Narnia, Tolkien and C. S. Lewis,* and *The C. S. Lewis Encyclopedia*

"This is the perfect entrance to the world C. S. Lewis inhabited, and it arrives just when that world of books is under threat of extinction. Thanks to those who have given us such a gold mine."

> —WALTER HOOPER, literary advisor to the C. S. Lewis estate, one of the world's leading authorities on the life and works of C. S. Lewis, and the editor of dozens of Lewis's works

"C. S. Lewis, one of the great men of letters of the twentieth century, loved books. To truly know Lewis, one must become familiar with the body of literature that marked his life. Jim Bell and Tony Dawson give curious students of Lewis a glimpse of the books and authors that informed his life's work and kindled his imagination."

> —JERRY ROOT, assistant professor of Christian Formation and Ministry at Wheaton College, coeditor of *The Quotable C. S. Lewis,* and a C. S. Lewis scholar

"One of the great benefits of reading C. S. Lewis is his singular ability to introduce his own readers to the works of other authors. In this volume, Bell and Dawson have made it easier for us to uncover the literary influences and preferences that characterized Lewis's own reading. The editors have arranged these excerpts around a variety of appealing subjects such as fantasy and imagination, suffering, prayer and contemplation, and God's love. This arrangement invites the reader to enter into the selections devotionally—to enjoy and benefit from these literary treasures much as Lewis himself did. This book is an excellent resource for those interested in meeting new authors, as well as a wonderful way to remind ourselves of favorite texts too long neglected."

—MARJORIE LAMP MEAD, associate director of the Marion E. Wade Center, Wheaton College, and coeditor of *Brothers and Friends: The Diaries of Major Warren Hamilton Lewis* and *C. S. Lewis: Letters to Children*

From the

LIBRARY

of

C. S. LEWIS

Selections from Writers Who
Influenced His Spiritual Journey

Compiled by

JAMES STUART BELL

with Anthony P. Dawson

WATERBROOK
PRESS

From the Library of C. S. Lewis
Published by WaterBrook Press
12265 Oracle Boulevard, Suite 200
Colorado Springs, Colorado 80921

Please see page 387 for complete acknowledgment of copyrighted pieces.

Please note that some of the selections in this book have been condensed from the original work and in some cases wording has been slightly modernized.

Trade Paperback ISBN 978-0-307-73082-4
eBook ISBN 978-0-307-55170-2

Published in the United States by WaterBrook Multnomah, an imprint of the Crown Publishing Group, a division of Penguin Random House LLC, New York.

WaterBrook and its deer colophon are registered trademarks of Penguin Random House LLC.

The Library of Congress cataloged the hardcover edition as follows:
From the library of C. S. Lewis : selections from writers who influenced his spiritual journey / compiled by James Stuart Bell with Anthony Palmer Dawson ; foreword by Lyle W. Dorsett.
   p. cm. — (A writers' palette book)
"A Shaw book."
Includes bibliographical references.
ISBN 0-87788-044-1
1. Lewis, C. S. (Clive Staples), 1898-1963—Religion. 2. Lewis, C. S. (Clive Staples), 1898-1963—Sources. I. Bell, James S. II. Dawson, Anthony P. III. Series.
BX5199.L53F76 2004
230—dc22
                          2004008998

147468846

CONTENTS

FOREWORD

Jim Bell and Tony Dawson have compiled a selection of readings that will nourish the spiritual and intellectual hunger of healthy souls in several ways. First, these readings are in and of themselves a superb tonic to refresh the thirsty soul. Second, these selections reveal much about C. S. Lewis's inner life. Included here are samplings from the massive collection of authors whose writings shaped one of the most influential writers of the twentieth century. Finally, these splendid readings serve as an introduction to a large group of writers whose works enriched Lewis's soul. I would expect many readers to discover for the first time some of the authors who profoundly shaped Professor Lewis's mind and heart. For people who are unfamiliar with many of the authors included here, this book will be the beginning of a delightful educational journey.

In brief, I have found this book to be at once a unique and rich selection of daily readings. It should have a wide audience and a long life.

—Lyle W. Dorsett, professor of Christian Formation and
Ministries, Wheaton College, Wheaton, Illinois

SPECIAL THANKS

Special thanks go to Professor Jerry Root, Lewis scholar at Wheaton College, for his keen insights into Lewis. We would also like to express our gratitude to Corey Thomas, Marjorie Lamp Mead, and the staff of the Marion E. Wade Center for their kind and invaluable assistance as we consulted books from C. S. Lewis's library. We also want to thank Anna Thiel for proofreading the manuscript; her careful attention to detail and insightful comments proved most helpful.

INTRODUCTION

When I wrote my master's thesis on C. S. Lewis twenty-five years ago at University College Dublin, I thought there had already been an exhaustive study of possible spiritual and literary influences on this towering twentieth-century shaper of Christian thought. Yet still today, readers and scholars pour out a perpetual torrent of books, articles, and graduate theses, continuing to speculate on these same influences. This proves there is still much to be learned about the origins of Lewis's intellectual and spiritual backgrounds. Yet, except for the scholars doing the research, most of us are probably not familiar with these sources of his inspiration.

The "Hound of heaven" pursued the self-described "most reluctant convert in England" using the arguments of friends and other factors to draw him, but it was primarily the Christian wisdom of the ages that brought Lewis to his knees and caused him to grow spiritually. Lewis would agree with the statement that great thinkers stand on the shoulders of giants. His conversion to Christianity began by acknowledging respect for those writers he considered truly great (people like George MacDonald, G. K. Chesterton, Samuel Johnson, Edmund Spenser, and John Milton) in spite of the fact that they were Christians.

Lewis would later admit that without these and other profound spiritual influences he could not be the kind of Christian he was, nor could he have the impact on the world with his own writings that he did. If that is so, these writings should have intrinsic value for all of us, as well as help us better understand the spiritual formation of C. S. Lewis himself.

To truly understand Lewis and his works we need to get behind his role as Christian apologist to his interest in philosophy and literature, in reason and romanticism. Lewis was not a one-dimensional reader. His eclectic tastes ranged over a wide variety of genres and time periods. He was a fan of science fiction and fantasy writers as well as Aristotle, Shakespeare, and Augustine. In Lewis's world, myth and allegory mix with precise logic in philosophical debate. Scholars continue to explore how these influences fit together, but there is no magic formula; Lewis was a complex figure who didn't quite fit the trends of his own generation and is able to speak to the needs of each succeeding one.

This volume doesn't attempt to "figure out" C. S. Lewis but to provide a smorgasbord of the content and style of those who have shone forth as messengers of light in his life. In meditating upon these passages we get short impressions of what Lewis valued; these works in many cases affected his thinking, writing, and behavior. They give us a glimpse of the inner world that provided the fuel for his stunning works of theology, poetry, science fiction, fantasy, literary criticism, letters, and children's literature.

Lewis called himself a "dinosaur" who was a repository of the old Western values, one who upheld the legacy of classic Western civilization. In today's postmodern environment this vanishing world is dismissed or vilified. Yet as Lewis knew, the flowering of the best of Christian culture took place prior to the Enlightenment. These writers were in turn influenced by the Greek and Roman cultures that preceded them.

So I believe that from these readings we can obtain clearer insight into C. S. Lewis as well as feed our imaginations and intellects upon those whose talents produced works of theology and literature that contain timeless standards. Many will discover a world they never knew existed and would never enter save for the high recommendation of their trusted friend Lewis. So come along with me and walk the same pilgrim path as our great spiritual mentor and drink from the fountain that blessed those who have gone before us, giving them strength and refreshment for the journey.

—JAMES STUART BELL

NOTE TO READER

Scholars tend to make subjective value judgments about the degree to which various authors influenced Lewis. It is not our purpose to quantify or rank the influence of any of these writers.

At times Lewis in his own writings clearly states that an author had a favorable impression on him. At other times he quotes an author with approval or to support a point. These writers have (to the best of our knowledge) been included in this volume.

In Lewis's professional capacity as literary critic, he dealt with authors who made a positive contribution to the field. Other authors he may have simply enjoyed for his own reading pleasure. With this in mind, we have included writers who are consistent with Lewis's own viewpoint and whose works are found in his personal library, housed at the Marion E. Wade Center in Wheaton, Illinois. Many of these volumes have been annotated and the marginalia betray a positive bias.

We have included some works that played a role in the evolution of his thought that he may, in turn, have left behind. We have not included writers he was familiar with but was either neutral or hostile toward throughout his life. Finally, we have attempted to please those who are aficionados of the complete range of "Lewisiana" as well as those who are familiar only with his popular works.

Please note that we have assigned categories to the selections to help identify some of the themes that would attract Lewis in his reading and research. They are somewhat arbitrary and subjective but will help avoid a random approach and allow readers to gravitate to their initial areas of interest.

1

"FOLLOW AFTER AGAPE"

God's Love

Julian of Norwich

Revelations of Divine Love

He showed me a very lofty spiritual delight in my soul, and in it I was completely filled with everlasting certitude, firmly sustained, without any painful dread. This feeling was so glad and so spiritual that I was entirely at peace, at ease and at rest, so that there was nothing on earth that could have disturbed me.

This lasted only for a while. Then I was transformed and left to myself in depression, weary of my life and irked with myself, so that I kept the patience to go on living only with difficulty. There was no comfort and no ease for me, except faith, hope, and charity, and these I had in reality, though I had very little feeling of them.

And immediately after this our Lord again gave me comfort and rest of soul in delight and certitude, so blessed and so mighty that no dread, no sorrow, no bodily or spiritual pain that could be suffered should have caused me distress.

And then the pain returned to my feelings, again followed by the joy and delight—first the one and then the other, at, I suppose, about twenty different times. In the time of joy I could have said with Saint Paul, "Nothing shall separate me from the love of Christ." And in the pain I could have said, "Lord, save me! I perish!"

This vision was showed to me to teach my understanding that it is profitable for some souls to experience these alterations of mood—sometimes to be comforted and sometimes to fail and to be left to themselves. God wills that we know that he keeps us ever equally safe, in woe as in well-being.

Julian of Norwich (1342–?)—An English Benedictine nun, Julian of Norwich was very ill on May 8–9, 1373, and was visited with sixteen visions of God's love. She became a recluse and spent twenty years meditating on these visions, after which she wrote the Revelations.

GEORGE MacDONALD

Unspoken Sermons

Love is one, and love is changeless.

For love loves unto purity. Love has ever in view the absolute loveliness of that which it beholds. Where loveliness is incomplete, and love cannot love its fill of loving, it spends itself to make more lovely, that it may love more; it strives for perfection, even that itself may be perfected—not in itself, but in the object. As it was love that first created humanity, so even human love, in proportion to its divinity, will go on creating the beautiful for its own outpouring. There is nothing eternal but that which loves and can be loved, and love is ever climbing towards the consummation when such shall be the universe, imperishable, divine.

Therefore all that is not beautiful in the beloved, all that comes between and is not of love's kind, must be destroyed.

And our God is a consuming fire.

George MacDonald (1824–1905)—Scottish Congregationalist pastor, novelist, myth maker, and poet, MacDonald had a profound influence on C. S. Lewis. Lewis said that MacDonald's *Phantastes* "baptized my imagination."

Joy Davidman

Smoke on the Mountain

For many contemporaries God has dwindled into a noble abstraction, a tendency of history, a goal of evolution; has thinned out into a concept useful for organizing world peace—a good thing as an idea. But not the Word made flesh, who died for us and rose again from the dead. Not a Personality that a man can feel any love for. And not, certainly, the eternal Lover who took the initiative and fell in love with *us*.

Is it shocking to think of God as a pursuing lover? Then Christianity is shocking. If we accept the supernatural only as something too weak and passive to interfere with the natural, we had best call ourselves materialists and be done with it—we shall gain in honesty what we lose in respectability. Here's a test to tell if your faith is anything more than faith-and-water. Suppose that tonight the Holy Spirit lifts you high into space, speaks a message to your conscience, then invisibly tucks you back into your safe little bed again. Will you consider the possibility that this experience is genuine? Or will you conclude at once that you must be crazy, and start yelling for a psychiatrist?

And here's a more practical test—since, in all probability, very few of us will be lifted from our beds tonight. Do you think that Christianity is *primarily* valuable as a means of solving our "real" problem—i.e., how to build a permanently healthy, wealthy, and wise society in *this* world? If you do, you're at least half a materialist, and someday the Marxists may be calling you comrade.

So strong is the materialist climate of opinion that even convinced Christians sometimes feel compelled to defend Christianity against the charge of "otherworldliness"—to slight its value as the passport to heaven in favor of its usefulness as a blueprint for remodeling earth. Yet we must not blame our earthiness entirely upon Western scientific progress, as if materialism had waited for Edison to invent it. By no means. The Rome of Lucretius, the Athens of Epicurus—even the Israel of Ecclesiastes—were hardly without their materialist philosophers. Devotion to the prince of this world is one of the ancient temptations, and perhaps our remote ancestors had no sooner invented the slingshot than they reared back on their hind legs and proclaimed that their technical progress had now enabled them to do without religion. The choice before us today is just what it always was—whether to be worldly or otherworldly; whether to live for the unloving self or to live for the love of God.

Joy Davidman (1915–1960)—Poet, author, and the wife of C. S. Lewis, Davidman is the mother of David and Douglas Gresham. C. S. Lewis dedicated his novel *Till We Have Faces* to her and wrote *A Grief Observed* upon her death.

ANDERS NYGREN

Agape and Eros

In the Synoptic Gospels, and still more in Paul, "love" has a definite religious and ethical quality of its own, in itself and quite independently of its object. Hence Paul can say without further qualification: "Follow after Agape" (1 Cor. 14:1). He has no need to specify the object to which this love is to be directed. He knows nothing of any distinction between a true and a false Agape. The moment that love shows itself to be Agape-love its ethical and religious legitimacy is for him beyond doubt. Such love is an outflow of the Divine love whatever its object may be. In John the position is substantially similar. Here also Agape possesses its own definite quality, and we have no need to ask what its object is in order to be able to determine its quality. Hence it can be said of Agape without further qualification: "Agape is of God; and everyone that loves is begotten of God, and knows God. He that loves not knows not God; for God is Agape" (1 John 4:7f.). Here we have the high-water mark of the Johannine conception of Agape. God and Agape are one. Agape as such, regardless of the object to which it is directed, is participation in the life of God: Agape is born of God.

Anders Theodor Samuel Nygren (1890–1978)—Swedish Lutheran minister and educator, Nygren was a prolific author whose works have been translated into ten languages. Nygren served on the World Council of Churches central committee from 1948 to 1954 and was later bishop of Lund.

John Bunyan

Grace Abounding to the Chief of Sinners

I heard one preach a sermon upon those words in the Song 4:1, "Behold you are fair, my love; behold, you are fair." But at that time he made these two words, "My love," his chief and subject matter; from which, after he had a little opened the text, he observed these several conclusions: 1. That the Church, and so every saved soul, is Christ's love, when loveless. 2. Christ's love without a cause. 3. Christ's love when hated of the world. 4. Christ's love when under temptation, and under desertion. 5. Christ's love from first to last. But I got nothing by what he said at present, only when he came to the application of the fourth particular, this was the word he said: If it be so, that the saved soul is Christ's love when under temptation and desertion; then, poor tempted soul, when you are assaulted and afflicted with temptation, and the hidings of God's face, yet think on these two words, "My love," still.

So as I was a-going home, these words came again into my thoughts; and I well remember, as I came in, I said thus in my heart, What shall I get by thinking on these two words? This thought had no sooner passed through my heart, but the words began thus to kindle in my spirit, "You are my love, you are my love," twenty times together; and still as they ran thus in my mind, they waxed stronger and warmer, and began to make me look up; but being as yet between hope and fear, I still replied in my heart, But is it true, but is it true? At which, that sentence fell in upon me, he "knew not that it was true which was done by the angel" (Acts 12:9).

Then I began to give place to the word, which, with power, did over and over make this joyful sound within my soul, You are my love, you are my love; and nothing shall separate you from my love; and with that, Rom. 8:39 came into my mind. Now was my heart filled full of comfort and hope, and now I could believe that my sins should be forgiven me; yea, I was now so taken with the love and mercy of God, that I remember I could not tell how to contain till I got home; I thought I could have spoken of His love, and of His mercy to me, even to the very crows that sat upon the ploughed lands before me, had they been capable to have understood me.

John Bunyan (1628–1675)—Son of a tinker, Bunyan became a Baptist preacher and was imprisoned in Bedford, England, for twelve years for unlicensed preaching. While in prison he wrote *The Pilgrim's Progress*. C. S. Lewis's article on John Bunyan is published in *Selected Literary Essays*.

George MacDonald

Unspoken Sermons

For there can be no unity, no delight of love, no harmony, no good in being, where there is but one. Two at least are needed for oneness; and the greater the number of individuals, the greater, the lovelier, the richer, the diviner is the possible unity.

God is life, and the will-source of life. In the outflowing of that life, I know him; and when I am told that he is love, I see that if he were not love he would not, could not create. I know nothing deeper in him than love, nor believe there is in him anything deeper than love—nay, that there can be anything deeper than love. The being of God is love, therefore creation. I imagine that from all eternity he has been creating. As he saw it was not good for man to be alone, so has he never been alone himself;—from all eternity the Father has had the Son, and the never-begun existence of that Son I imagine an easy outgoing of Father's nature; while to make other beings—beings like us, I imagine the labor of a God, an eternal labor.

George MacDonald (1824–1905)—Scottish Congregationalist pastor, novelist, myth maker, and poet, MacDonald had a profound influence on C. S. Lewis. Lewis said that MacDonald's *Phantastes* "baptized my imagination."

GEORGE HERBERT

Love Bade Me Welcome

Love bade me welcome, yet my soul drew back
    Guilty of dust and sin.
But quick-eyed Love, observing me grow slack
    From my first entrance in,
Drew nearer to me, sweetly questioning
    If I lacked anything.
"A guest," I answered, "worthy to be here";
    Love said, "You shall be he."
"I, the unkind, the ungrateful? Ah my dear,
    I cannot look on thee."
Love took my hand, and smiling did reply,
    "Who made the eyes but I?"
"Truth, Lord, but I have marred them; let my shame
    Go where it doth deserve."
"And know you not," says Love, "who bore the blame?"
    "My dear, then I will serve."
"You must sit down," says Love, "and taste my meat."
    So I did sit and eat.

George Herbert (1593–1633)—Anglican rector of the parish church of Bremerton, near Salisbury, Herbert was one of the seventeenth-century metaphysical poets.

2

"You Have Transfixed My Heart"

Our Love of God

SAINT BERNARD OF CLAIRVAUX

On Loving God

"What shall I render unto the Lord for all His benefits towards me?" (Psalm 116:12). Reason and natural justice alike move me to give up myself wholly to loving Him to whom I owe all that I have and am. But faith shows me that I should love Him far more than I love myself, as I come to realize that He has given me not my own life only, but even Himself. Yet, before the time of full revelation had come, before the Word was made flesh, died on the Cross, came forth from the grave, and returned to His Father; before God had shown us how much He loved us by all this plenitude of grace, the commandment had been uttered, "You shall love the Lord your God with all your heart, and with all your soul and with all your might" (Deuteronomy 6:5), that is, with all your being, all your knowledge, all your powers. And it was not unjust for God to claim this from His own work and gifts. Why should not the creature love his Creator, who gave him the power to love? Why should he not love Him with all his being, since it is by His gift alone that he can do anything that is good? It was God's creative grace that out of nothingness raised us to the dignity of manhood; and from this appears our duty to love Him, and the justice of His claim to that love. But how infinitely is the benefit increased when we think about His fulfillment of the promise, "You, Lord, shall save both man and beast: how excellent is Your mercy, O Lord!" (Psalm 36:6f.).

Saint Bernard of Clairvaux (1090–1153)—Mystic, monastic reformer, and influential figure in the twelfth-century church, Saint Bernard founded the Cistercian Monastery at Clairvaux.

SAINT AUGUSTINE

Confessions

Not with doubtful but with sure knowledge do I love you, O Lord. By your
Word you have transfixed my heart, and I have loved you. Heaven and earth
and all things in them, behold! everywhere they say to me that I should love
you. They do not cease from saying this to all men, "so that they are inex-
cusable." But in a deeper way you will have mercy on him on whom you will
have mercy, and you will show mercy to him to whom you will show mercy,
for otherwise heaven and earth proclaim your praises to the deaf. What is it
then that I love when I love you? Not bodily beauty, and not temporal glory,
not the clear shining light, lovely as it is to our eyes, not the sweet melodies
of many-moded songs, not the soft smell of flowers and ointments and perfumes, not manna and honey, not limbs made for the body's embrace, not
these do I love when I love my God.

Yet I do love a certain light, a certain voice, a certain odor, a certain food,
a certain embrace when I love my God: a light, a voice, an odor, a food, an
embrace for the man within me, where his light, which no place can contain,
floods into my soul; where he utters words that time does not speed away;
where he sends forth an aroma that no wind can scatter; where he provides
food that no eating can lessen; where he so clings that satiety does not sun-
der us. This is what I love when I love my God.

Saint Augustine of Hippo (354–430)—Born in Numidia, a Roman province in North
Africa, to a pagan father and Christian mother, Saint Augustine was consecrated
bishop of Hippo and wrote numerous treatises on Christianity, including *The Confessions*.

BROTHER LAWRENCE

The Practice of the Presence of God

My Reverend Mother,—I have taken this opportunity to communicate to you the thoughts of one of our Society [Brother Lawrence], concerning the wonderful effect and continual succor which he receives from *the Presence of God*.

If sometimes he is a little too much absent from that *Divine Presence*, which happens often when he is most engaged in his outward business, God presently makes Himself felt in his soul to recall him. He answers with exact fidelity to these inward drawings, wither by an elevation of his heart towards God, or by a meek and loving regard to Him, or by such words as love forms upon these occasions, as for instance, My God, *behold me, wholly Yours*: Lord, *make me according to Your heart*. And then it seems to him (as in effect he feels it) that this God of love, satisfied with such few words, reposes again and rests in the depth and center of his soul. The experience of these things gives him such an assurance that God is always deep within his soul, that no doubt of it can arise, whatever may betide.

Judge from this what contentment and satisfaction he enjoys, feeling continually within him so great a treasure: no longer is he in anxious search after it, but he has it open before him, free to take of it what he pleases.

He complains much of our blindness and exclaims often that we are to be pitied, who content ourselves with so little. God's *treasure*, he says, *is like an infinite ocean, yet a little wave of feeling, passing with the moment, contents us. Blind as we are, we hinder God, and stop the current of His graces. But when He finds a soul permeated with a living faith, He pours into it His graces and His favors plenteously; into the soul they flow like a torrent, which, after being forcibly stopped against its ordinary course, when it has found a passage, spreads with impetuosity its pent-up flood.*

Yes, often we stop this torrent, by the little value we set upon it. But let us stop it no longer: let us enter into ourselves and break down the barrier which holds it back. Let us make the most of the day of grace, let us redeem the time that is lost, perhaps we have but little left to us: death follows close, let us be well prepared; for we die but once, and a miscarriage *then* is irretrievable.

Brother Lawrence, or Nicholas Herman of Lorraine (1611–1691)—Low-born Frenchman and Carmelite monk, Brother Lawrence lived a saintly life, which is reflected in his writings.

Saint Augustine

The City of God

But as this divine Master inculcates two precepts—the love of God and the love of our neighbor—and as in these precepts a man finds three things he has to love—God, himself, and his neighbor—and that he who loves God loves himself thereby, it follows that he must endeavor to get his neighbor to love God, since he is ordered to love his neighbor as himself. He ought to make this endeavor in behalf of his wife, his children, his household, all within his reach, even as he would wish his neighbor to do the same for him if he needed it; and consequently he will be at peace, or in well-ordered concord, with all men, as far as in him lies. And this is the order of this concord, that a man, in the first place, injure no one, and, in the second, do good to every one he can reach. Primarily, therefore, his own household are his care, for the law of nature and of society gives him readier access to them and greater opportunity of serving them.

And hence the apostle says, "Now, if any provide not for his own, and specially for those of his own house, he has denied the faith, and is worse than an infidel." This is the origin of domestic peace, or the well-ordered concord of those in the family who rule and those who obey. For they who care for the rest rule—the husband the wife, the parents the children, the masters the servants; and they who are cared for obey—the women their husbands, the children their parents, the servants their masters. But in the family of the just man who lives by faith and is as yet a pilgrim journeying on to the celestial city, even those who rule serve those whom they seem to command; for they rule not from a love of power, but from a sense of the duty they owe to others—not because they are proud of authority, but because they love mercy.

Saint Augustine of Hippo (354–430)—Born in Numidia, a Roman province in North Africa, to a pagan father and Christian mother, Saint Augustine was consecrated bishop of Hippo and wrote numerous treatises on Christianity, including *The Confessions*.

SAINT BERNARD OF CLAIRVAUX

On Loving God

At first, man loves himself for his own sake. That is the flesh, which can appreciate nothing beyond itself. Next, he perceives that he cannot exist by himself, and so begins by faith to seek after God, and to love Him as something necessary to his own welfare. That is the second degree, to love God, not for God's sake, but selfishly. But when he has learned to worship God and to seek Him aright, meditating on God, reading God's Word, praying and obeying His commandments, he comes gradually to know who God is, and finds Him altogether lovely. So, having tasted and seen how gracious the Lord is (Psalm 34:8), he advances to the third degree, when he loves God, not merely as his benefactor but as God. Surely this is the longest state for the one who is growing in God. As to the fourth degree, I know not whether it would be possible to make further progress in this life to that fourth degree and perfect condition wherein man loves himself solely for God's sake. Let any who have attained so far bear record; I confess it seems beyond my powers. Doubtless it will be reached when the good and faithful servant shall have entered into the joy of his Lord (Matthew 25:21), and been satisfied with the plenteousness of God's house (Psalm 36:8). For then in wondrous wise he will forget himself and as if delivered from self, he will grow wholly God's.

Saint Bernard of Clairvaux (1090–1153)—Mystic, monastic reformer, and influential figure in the twelfth-century church, Saint Bernard founded the Cistercian Monastery at Clairvaux.

THOMAS TRAHERNE

Centuries

There are glorious entertainments in this miserable world, could we find them out. What more delightful can be imagined, than to see a Savior at this distance, dying on the Cross to redeem a man from Hell, and to see oneself the beloved of God and all Kingdoms, yea, the admired of ages, and the heir of the whole world? Has not His blood united you and me, cannot we see and love and enjoy each other at a hundred miles distance? In Him is the only sweet and divine enjoyment. I desire but an amiable Soul in any part of all Eternity, and can love it unspeakably: And if love it, enjoy it. For love implies pleasure, because it is ever pleased with what is beloved.

Delight only in the love of Jesus, and direct all your love unto Him. Adore Him, rejoice in Him, admire His love and praise Him, secretly and in the congregation. Enjoy His Saints that are round about you, make yourself amiable that you may be admitted to their enjoyment, by meekness, temperance, modesty, humility, charity, chastity, devotion, cheerfulness, gratitude, joy, thanksgiving. Retire from them that you may be the more precious, and come out unto them the more wise. So shall you make the place wherein you live a nest of sweet perfumes, and every Soul that is round about you will be a bed of Honor, and sweet repose unto you.

Thomas Traherne (1637–1674)—Son of a poor shoemaker, educated at Oxford, and one of the metaphysical poets, Traherne became the Anglican rector of Credenhill in Herefordshire.

SAINT BERNARD OF CLAIRVAUX

On Loving God

And now let us consider what profit we shall have from loving God. Even though our knowledge of this is imperfect, still that is better than to ignore it altogether. I have already said (when it was a question of wherefore and in what manner God should be loved) that there was a double reason constraining us: His right and our advantage. Having written as best I can, though unworthily, of God's right to be loved, I have still to treat of the recompense which that love brings. For although God would be loved without respect of reward, yet He wills not to leave love unrewarded. True charity cannot be left destitute, even though she is unselfish and seeks not her own (1 Corinthians 13:5). Love is an affection of the soul, not a contract: it cannot rise from a mere agreement, nor is it so to be gained. It is spontaneous in its origin and impulse; and true love is its own satisfaction. It has its reward; but that reward is the object beloved. For whatever you seem to love, if it is on account of something else, what you do really love is that something else, not the apparent object of desire. St. Paul did not preach the Gospel that he might earn his bread; he ate that he might be strengthened for his ministry. What he loved was not bread, but the Gospel. True love does not demand a reward, but it deserves one. Surely no one offers to pay for love; yet some recompense is due to one who loves, and if his love endures he will doubtless receive it.

Saint Bernard of Clairvaux (1090–1153)—Mystic, monastic reformer, and influential figure in the twelfth-century church, Saint Bernard founded the Cistercian Monastery at Clairvaux.

JOHN LANGDON-DAVIES

Sex, Sin and Sanctity

Those who have to be ordered to love God usually believe that obedience involves excluding all other loves, to the extent of hating the world, the flesh, and even the self. We therefore find among Christians an inordinate number of haters of life eager to be ordered to love God frigidly and with a stiff upper lip, because, in the first place, they hate the world, the flesh and themselves.

There have always been, however, within the bounds of orthodoxy, those who have never had to be ordered to love God, because they are in love with God. The basis of their erotic ideology is that all love, however mistaken its object, is in essence love of God; and that love of God must, owing to man's fallen nature, begin with self-love. What is wrong with self-love is not the sentiment of love but the object on which it is lavished.

It often follows as a corollary of this view that all love, even the most sensual, is regarded as an attempt to discover the beautiful and the good. It will fail, and by its failure reveal the higher object towards which the love should have been aimed. Although not all have Augustine's honesty to enable them to pray "Make me chaste, but not yet," nevertheless the reformed rake is more likely to learn to love God than the man who is little bothered by any love at all. In the long chain of great men who have expressed this alternative mood we think of Plato, Plotinus, St. Augustine, St. Bernard, Dante.

John Langdon-Davies (1897–1971)—Langdon-Davies was a student at St. John's College, Oxford, a soldier in World War I, and a war correspondent during the Spanish Civil War. His interests and the topics of his works ranged from the atom to Russia to the care of orphaned European children.

3

"How Dearly You Have Paid for Me"

The Life and Sacrifice of Christ

Theologia Germanica

Of a truth we ought to know and believe that there is no life so noble and good and well-pleasing to God as the life of Christ, and yet it is to nature and selfishness the bitterest life. A life of carelessness and freedom is to nature and the self and the me the sweetest and pleasantest life, but it is not the best and in some men may become the worst. But though Christ's life is the most bitter of all, yet it is to be preferred above all. Hereby mark this: There is an inward light which has power to perceive the one true good, and that it is neither this nor that, but that of which St. Paul said: "When that which is perfect is come, then that which is in part shall be done away." By this he meant that the whole and perfect excels all the fragments, and that all which is in part and imperfect is as naught compared to the perfect. Thus all knowledge of the parts is swallowed up when the whole is known; and where that good is known, it cannot but be longed for and loved so greatly that all other love wherewith the man has loved himself and other things fades away. And that inward sight likewise perceives what is best and noblest in all things, and loves it in the one true good and only for the sake of that true good.

———————————————

Theologia Germanica—Of unknown authorship, *Theologia Germanica* was discovered by Martin Luther in 1516. Luther said, "Next to the Bible and St. Augustine, no book has ever come into my hands from which I have learnt more of God and Christ, and man and all things that are."

MARTIN LUTHER

Table Talk

The devil assaults the Christian world with highest power and subtlety, vexing true Christians through tyrants, heretics, and false brethren, and instigating the whole world against them.

On the contrary, Christ resists the devil and his kingdom, with a few simple and contemned people, as they seem in the world, weak and foolish, and yet he gets the victory.

Now, it were a very unequal war for one poor sheep to encounter a hundred wolves, as it befell the apostles, when Christ sent them out into the world, when one after another was made away with and slain. Against wolves we should rather send out lions, or more fierce and horrible beasts. But Christ has pleasure therein, to show his highest wisdom and power in our greatest weakness and foolishness, as the world conceives, and so proceeds that all shall eat their own bane, and go to the devil, who set themselves against his servants and disciples.

For he alone, the Lord of Hosts, does wonders; he preserves his sheep in the midst of wolves, and himself so afflicts them, that we plainly see our faith consists not in the power of human wisdom, but in the power of God, for although Christ permit one of his sheep to be devoured, yet he sends ten or more others in his place.

Martin Luther (1483–1546)—An Augustinian monk who became the father of the Protestant Reformation, Luther was an indefatigable theologian and pastor and champion of the doctrine of justification by "faith alone."

C. F. D. Moule

The Sacrifice of Christ

Yet the sacrifice of Christ, complete and perfect, is nevertheless the historical focus of a continual obedience: the obedience of Christ which must be in all suffering accepted in his name and in all praise and worship and self-dedication whatever. And since this is derived from, focused, and caught up in Christ's sacrifice, it is possible (though only with careful safeguards) to speak *in that sense* of such offerings as a constant reproduction of it—a part of it, and not merely a remembering of it. In Rev. 7:14 there is mention of those who have washed their robes and made them white in the blood of the Lamb. This, of course, is applicable to all Christians as such: we all owe our cleansing to that blood. But if, as is sometimes held, this passage refers specially to martyrs, then I suggest—though this is only a guess—that it is possible that we are confronted with a striking example of the way in which Christ's once-and-for-all sacrifice might be, in certain circumstances, spoken of as repeated in each act of human obedience joined with his. The martyrs' own blood, shed in faithfulness to the Lord, turns out to be the blood of the Lamb. When their blood flowed, behold it was the blood of the Lamb. Their sacrifice was united with his—not as though theirs were independently redemptive or added anything to his, but in the sense that, being united, believer and Lord are, in that sense, one: his blood their blood, their blood his. The blood which is the sacrament of obedience is the Lord's blood: the wine which is the sacrament of obedience is, *in that sense,* the Lord's blood.

Charles Francis Digby Moule (1908–)—Cambridge lecturer and professor of divinity, Moule is an Anglican clergyman, biblical scholar, and prolific author.

RICHARD CRASHAW

Sacred Poems

If I were lost in misery,
What was it to your heaven and thee?
What was it to your precious blood,
If my foul heart call'd for a flood?
What if my faithless soul and I
    Would needs fall in
    With guilt and sin,
What did the Lamb that he should die?
What did the Lamb that he should need,
When the wolf sins, himself to bleed?

    If my base lust
Bargain'd with death and well-beseeming dust,
    Why should the white
    Lamb's bosom write
    The purple name
    Of my sin's shame?

Why should his unstain'd breast make good
My blushes with his own heart-blood?

O my Savior! make me see
How dearly you have paid for me;

That lost again, my life may prove
As then in death, so now in love.

Richard Crashaw (1613?–1649)—A fellow of Peterhouse College, Cambridge, poet, and Roman Catholic convert, Crashaw attended Cambridge University and spent much of his brief adult life in Italy. Crashaw wrote during the period of the metaphysical poets.

G. K. Chesterton

The Everlasting Man

They took the body down from the cross and one of the few rich men among the first Christians obtained permission to bury it in a rock tomb in his garden; the Romans setting a military guard lest there should be some riot and attempt to recover the body. There was once more a natural symbolism in these natural proceedings; it was well that the tomb should be sealed with all the secrecy of ancient eastern sepulture and guarded by the authority of the Caesars. For in that second cavern the whole of that great and glorious humanity which we call antiquity was gathered up and covered over; and in that place it was buried. It was the end of a very great thing called human history; the history that was merely human. The mythologies and the philosophies were buried there, the gods and the heroes and the sages. In the great Roman phrase, they had lived. But as they could only live, so they could only die; and they were dead.

On the third day the friends of Christ coming at daybreak to the place found the grave empty and the stone rolled away. In varying ways they realized the new wonder; but even they hardly realized that the world had died in the night. What they were looking at was the first day of a new creation, with a new heaven and a new earth; and in a semblance of the gardener God walked again in the garden, in the cool not of the evening but the dawn.

Gilbert Keith Chesterton (1874–1936)—Roman Catholic artist, poet, journalist, essayist, and author, Chesterton wrote over one hundred books. C. S. Lewis says, in *Surprised by Joy,* that Chesterton's Christian apologetics had a marked impact on him, and Lewis's own apologetic work owes a debt to Chesterton.

C. G. JUNG

Answer to Job

I would even go so far as to say that the mythical character of a life is just what expresses its universal human validity. It is perfectly possible, psychologically, for the unconscious or an archetype to take complete possession of a man and to determine his fate down to the smallest detail. At the same time objective, non-psychic parallel phenomena can occur which also represent the archetype. It not only seems so, it simply is so, that the archetype fulfills itself not only psychically in the individual, but objectively outside the individual. My own conjecture is that Christ was such a personality. The life of Christ is just what it had to be if it is the life of a god and a man at the same time. It is a *symbolum*, a bringing together of heterogeneous natures, rather as if Job and Yahweh were combined in a single personality. Yahweh's intention to become man, which resulted from his collision with Job, is fulfilled in Christ's life and suffering.

Carl Gustav Jung (1875–1961)—Swiss psychiatrist and one-time collaborator with Freud, Jung founded the school of analytical psychology. Jung's interests in archetypes had an effect on literary interpretations; C. S. Lewis took issue with some of his ideas.

CHARLES KINGSLEY

Discipline and Other Sermons

The scholar and the man of science, studying the wonders of this earth, can trust in him, and say, In the beginning God created the heaven and the earth; and he is full of grace and truth. Many things puzzle me; and the more I learn the less I find I really know: but I shall know as much as is good for me, and for mankind. God is full of grace, and will not grudge me knowledge; and full of truth, and will not deceive me. And I shall never go far wrong as long as I believe, not only in one God, the Father Almighty, Maker of all things visible and invisible, but in one Lord Jesus Christ, his only-begotten Son, light of light, very God of very God, by whom all things are made, who for us men and our salvation came down and died, and rose again; whose kingdom shall have no end; who rules over every star and planet, every shower and sunbeam, every plant and animal and stone, every body and every soul of man; who will teach men, in his good time and way, all that they need to know, in order to multiply and replenish the earth, and subdue it in this life, and attain everlasting life in the world to come. And for the rest, puzzled though I be, shall I not trust him who not only made this world, but so loved it, that he stooped to die for it upon the Cross?

Charles Kingsley (1819–1875)—Anti-Tractarian, Anglican rector at Eversley in Hampshire, novelist, and literary critic, Kingsley was educated at Magdalene College, Cambridge, where C. S. Lewis was later the professor of medieval and renaissance literature. Kingsley is best known for his children's book *The Water Babies,* which Lewis liked very much.

George MacDonald

Unspoken Sermons

Father, into your hand I commend my spirit.

—Luke 23:46.

Neither St. Matthew nor St. Mark tells us of any words uttered by our Lord after the Eloi. They both, along with St. Luke, tell us of a cry with a loud voice, and the giving up of the ghost; between which cry and the giving up, St. Luke records the words, "Father, into your hands I commend my spirit." St. Luke says nothing of the Eloi prayer of desolation. St. John records neither the Eloi, nor the Father into your hands, nor the loud cry. He tells us only that after Jesus had received the vinegar, he said, "It is finished," and bowed his head, and gave up the ghost.

Will the Lord ever tell us why he cried so? Was it the cry of relief at the touch of death? Was it the cry of victory? Was it the cry of gladness that he had endured to the end? Or did the Father look out upon him in answer to his My God, and the blessedness of it make him cry aloud because he could not smile? Was such his condition now that the greatest gladness of the universe could express itself only in a loud cry? Or was it but the last wrench of pain ere the final repose began? It may have been all in one. But never surely in all books, in all words of thinking men, can there be so much expressed as lay unarticulated in that cry of the Son of God. Now had he made his Father Lord no longer in the might of making and loving alone, but Lord in right of devotion and deed of love. Now should inward sonship and the spirit of glad sacrifice be born in the hearts of men; for the divine obedience was perfected by suffering. He had been among his brethren what he would have his brethren be. He had done for them what he would have them do for God and for each other. God was henceforth inside and beneath them, as well as around and above them, suffering with them and for them, giving them all he had, his very life-being, his essence of existence, what best he loved, what best he was. He had been among them, their God-brother. And the mighty story ends with a cry.

Then the cry meant, It is finished; the cry meant, Father, into your hands I commend my spirit. Every highest human act is just a giving back to God of that which he first gave to us. "You God have given me: here again is your gift. I send my spirit home." Every act of worship is a holding up to God of what God has made us. "Here, Lord, look what I have: feel with me in what you have made me, in this your own bounty, my being. I am your child, and know not how to thank you save by uplifting the heave-offering of the overflowing of your life, and calling aloud, 'It is yours: it is mine. I am yours, and therefore I am mine.'" The vast operations of the spiritual as of the physical world, are simply a turning again to the source.

George MacDonald (1824–1905)—Scottish Congregationalist pastor, novelist, myth maker, and poet, MacDonald had a profound influence on C. S. Lewis. Lewis said that MacDonald's *Phantastes* "baptized my imagination."

Andrew Murray

Abide in Christ

Let us hear what the Savior says of the joy of abiding in Him. He promises us *His own joy*: "My joy." As the whole parable refers to the life His disciples should have in Him when ascended to heaven, the joy is that of His resurrection life. This is clear from those other words of His (John 16:22) "I will see you again, and your heart shall rejoice, and your joy shall no man take from you." It was only with the resurrection and its glory that the power of the never-changing life began, and only in it that the never-ceasing joy could have its rise. With it was fulfilled the word: "Therefore your God has anointed you with the oil of gladness above your fellows." The day of His crowning was the day of the gladness of His heart. That joy of His was the joy of a work fully and for ever completed, the joy of the Father's bosom regained, and the joy of souls redeemed. These are the elements of His joy; of them the abiding in Him makes us partakers. The believer shares so fully His victory and His perfect redemption that his faith can without ceasing sing the conqueror's song: "Thanks be to God, who always causes me to triumph."

Andrew Murray (1828–1917)—Evangelical and leader in the South African Dutch Reformed Church, Andrew Murray was educated in Scotland and Holland. He served several pastorates and was six times the moderator of the Reformed Church.

GEORGE MacDONALD

Miracles of Our Lord

St. Luke says that "the fashion of his countenance was altered, and his raiment was white and glistening." St. Matthew says, "His face did shine as the sun, and his raiment was white as the light." St. Mark says, "His raiment became shining, exceeding white as snow, so as no fuller on earth can white them." St. Luke is alone in telling us that it was while he prayed that this change passed upon him. He became outwardly glorious from inward communion with his Father. But we shall not attain to the might of the meaning, if we do not see what was the more immediate subject of his prayer. It is, I think, indicated in the fact, also recorded by St. Luke, that the talk of his heavenly visitors was "of his decease which he should accomplish at Jerusalem." Associate with this the fact that his talk with his disciples, as they came down the mountain, pointed in the same direction, and that all open report of the vision was to be withheld until he should have risen from the dead, and it will appear most likely that the master, oppressed with the thought of that which now drew very nigh, sought the comfort and sympathy of his Father, praying in the prospect of his decease. Let us observe then how, in heaving off the weight of this awful shadow by prayer, he did not grow calm and resigned alone, if he were ever other than such, but his faith broke forth so triumphant over the fear, that it shone from him in physical light. Every cloud of sorrow or dread, touched with such a power of illumination, is itself changed into a glory. The radiance goes hand in hand with the coming decay and the three day's victory of death. It is as a foretaste of his resurrection, a putting on of his new glorified body for a moment while he was yet in the old body and the awful shadow yet between. It may be to something like this as taking place in other men that the apostle refers when he says: "We shall not all sleep, but we shall all be changed." That coming death was to be but as the overshadowing cloud, from which the glory should break anew and for ever. The transfiguration then was the divine defiance of the coming darkness.

George MacDonald (1824–1905)—Scottish Congregationalist pastor, novelist, myth maker, and poet, MacDonald had a profound influence on C. S. Lewis. Lewis said that MacDonald's *Phantastes* "baptized my imagination."

SAINT ATHANASIUS

On the Incarnation of the Word of God

It is, indeed, in accordance with the nature of the invisible God that He should be thus known through His works; and those who doubt the Lord's resurrection because they do not now behold Him with their eyes, might as well deny the very laws of nature. They have ground for disbelief when works are lacking; but when the works cry out and prove the fact so clearly, why do they deliberately deny the risen life so manifestly shown? Even if their mental faculties are defective, surely their eyes can give them irrefragable proof of the power and Godhead of Christ. A blind man cannot see the sun, but he knows that it is above the earth from the warmth which it affords; similarly, let those who are still in the blindness of unbelief recognize the Godhead of Christ and the resurrection which He has brought about through His manifested power in others. Obviously He would not be expelling evil spirits and despoiling idols, if He were dead, for the evil spirits would not obey one who was dead. If, on the other hand, the very naming of Him drives them forth, He clearly is not dead; and the more so that the spirits, who perceive things unseen by men, would know if He were so and would refuse to obey Him. But, as a matter of fact, what profane persons doubt, the evil spirits *know*—namely that He is God; and for that reason they flee from Him and fall at His feet, crying out even as they cried when He was in the body, "We know You Who You are, the Holy One of God," and, "Ah, what have I in common with You, You Son of God? I implore You, torment me not."

Both from the confession of the evil spirits and from the daily witness of His works, it is manifest, then, and let none presume to doubt it, that the Savior has raised His own body, and that He is very Son of God, having His being from God as from a Father, Whose Word and Wisdom and Whose Power He is. He it is Who in these latter days assumed a body for the salvation of us all, and taught the world concerning the Father. He it is Who has destroyed death and freely graced us all with incorruption through the promise of the resurrection, having raised His own body as its first-fruits, and displayed it by the sign of the cross as the monument to His victory over death and its corruption.

Saint Athanasius (ca. 296–373)—Architect of the Nicene Creed (325) and champion of Trinitarian orthodoxy, Saint Athanasius was bishop of Alexandria. A defender of the faith and a prolific author, Saint Athanasius is considered a father of the church.

Evelyn Underhill

The Mystery of Sacrifice

It is the "offered Christ which is distributed among us," as the ancient Liturgies say; communion is the fruit of sacrifice. The will of man, secretly incited by grace, moves to the altar and is expressed in oblation. The love of God, brooding upon the offering, consecrates and transforms. Both are needed. Our limited love and effort rise to their height, that they may be met and fulfilled by the unlimited Divine Love.

Thus that communion of the faithful which is indeed the climax of the Liturgy should never be detached from the total Eucharistic movement of which it is a part. Its deepest, most sacred meaning is only understood by us when we perceive it to be the inevitable culmination of a close-knit act of sacrificial worship; an act which can never be that of individual fervor, but always that of the whole Christian family, transcending yet including in itself the separate movements and longings of each of its members. How completely the liturgic pattern here rebukes those who come to religion for the sake of their own souls; and, valuing its sacraments as means to the satisfaction of their own spiritual needs, ignore both their corporate responsibility in respect of the whole Eucharistic action, and the place of that whole action in the vast economy of God. For here the small self-offering of man in his wholeness is met by the Divine generosity, and transformed to His supernatural purpose; and the separate experiences of individual devotion are to be esteemed only as fragments of this one sublime experience of the Bride of Christ. Thus it is only when costly and humble adoration, lost in the tide of worship and bowed down before that which it can never understand, has reached its height, that the soul can draw near to receive the food of Eternal Life.

Evelyn Underhill (1875–1941)—Anglican mystic and philosopher of religion, Underhill was the first woman granted lecture status at Oxford University; she was also a fellow of King's College, London. Underhill authored thirty-nine books on church history and Christian mysticism.

Saint Athanasius

On the Incarnation of the Word of God

The incorporeal and incorruptible and immaterial Word of God comes to our realm, howbeit He was not far from us before. For no part of Creation is left void of Him: He has filled all things everywhere, remaining present with His own Father. But He comes in condescension to show loving-kindness upon us, and to visit us. And seeing the race of rational creatures in the way to perish, and death reigning over them by corruption; seeing, too, that the threat against transgression gave a firm hold to the corruption which was upon us, and that it was monstrous that before the law was fulfilled it should fall through: seeing, once more, the unseemliness of what was come to pass: that the things whereof He Himself was Artificer were passing away: seeing, further, the exceeding wickedness of men, and how by little and little they had increased it to an intolerable pitch against themselves: and seeing, lastly, how all men were under penalty of death: He took pity on our race, and had mercy on our infirmity, and condescended to our corruption, and, unable to bear that death should have the mastery—lest the creature should perish, and His Father's handiwork in men be spent for naught—He takes unto Himself a body, and that of no different sort from ours.

For He did not simply will to become embodied, or will merely to appear. For if He willed merely to appear, He was able to affect His divine appearance by some other and higher means as well. But He takes a body of our kind, and not merely so, but from a spotless and stainless virgin, knowing not a man, a body clean and in very truth pure from intercourse of men. For being Himself mighty, and Artificer of everything, He prepares the body in the Virgin as a temple unto Himself, and makes it His very own as an instrument, in it manifested, and in it dwelling.

Saint Athanasius (ca. 296–373)—Architect of the Nicene Creed (325) and champion of Trinitarian orthodoxy, Saint Athanasius was bishop of Alexandria. A defender of the faith and a prolific author, Saint Athanasius is considered a father of the church.

JULIAN OF NORWICH

Revelations of Divine Love

As the body wears clothes and the bones are covered with skin with our heart inside, so are we, soul and body, clad in the goodness of God.

Our soul is so wonderfully loved of Him that no one can comprehend it. That is to say, no creature can fully comprehend how much, and how sweetly, and how tenderly our Maker loves us. Therefore we may with grace and His help stand in awe of this love, and forever marvel at this high, over-passing, inestimable Love that Almighty God has toward us of His goodness.

He that made all things for love, by the same love keeps them, and shall keep them forever.

So that I would better understand, this blessed word came to me: "Lo, how I loved you! Behold and see that I loved you so much that I died for you and suffered willingly. And now is all my bitter pain and all my hard travail turned to endless joy and bliss to me and to you. Now it shall be that if you pray for anything that pleases me I will gladly give it. For my pleasing is your holiness and your endless joy and bliss with me."

In love He sustains us within Himself. In love He travailed when He suffered the sharpest throes and the most grievous pains that ever were or ever shall be, and finally died. All this was to bring us to Himself, and only because of His marvelous love. He said to me, "If I would have had to suffer more to bring you to myself, I would have done so."

Julian of Norwich (1342–?)—An English Benedictine nun, Julian of Norwich was very ill on May 8–9, 1373, and was visited with sixteen visions of God's love. She became a recluse and spent twenty years meditating on these visions, after which she wrote the *Revelations*.

SAINT ATHANASIUS

On the Incarnation of the Word of God

The Word perceived that corruption could not be got rid of otherwise than through death; yet He Himself, as the Word, being immortal and the Father's Son, was such as could not die. For this reason, therefore, He assumed a body capable of death, in order that it, through belonging to the Word Who is above all, might become in dying a sufficient exchange for all, and, itself remaining incorruptible through His indwelling, might thereafter put an end to corruption for all others as well, by the grace of the resurrection. It was by surrendering to death the body which He had taken, as an offering and sacrifice free from every stain, that He forthwith abolished death for His human brethren by the offering of the equivalent. For naturally, since the Word of God was above all, when He offered His own temple and bodily instrument as a substitute for the life of all, He fulfilled in death all that was required. Naturally also, through this union of the immortal Son of God with our human nature, all men were clothed with incorruption in the promise of the resurrection. For the solidarity of mankind is such that, by virtue of the Word's indwelling in a single human body, the corruption which goes with death has lost its power over all. You know how it is when some great king enters a large city and dwells in one of its house; because of his dwelling in that single house, the whole city is honored, and enemies and robbers cease to molest it. Even so is it with the King of all; He has come into our country and dwelt in one body amidst the many, and in consequence the designs of the enemy against mankind have been foiled, and the corruption of death, which formerly held them in its power, has simply ceased to be. For the human race would have perished utterly had not the Lord and Savior of all, the Son of God, come among us to put an end to death.

Saint Athanasius (ca. 296–373)—Architect of the Nicene Creed (325) and champion of Trinitarian orthodoxy, Saint Athanasius was bishop of Alexandria. A defender of the faith and a prolific author, Saint Athanasius is considered a father of the church.

C. F. D. MOULE

The Sacrifice of Christ

If, then, the Gospel is more than a declaration, if it is something which we do not merely know about but experience, essentially God's action to reconcile estranged man to himself, then it follows that the uniqueness and finality of his action in Jesus Christ is not the uniqueness of discontinuity, nor the finality of a dead and static thing. There can never be an end absolutely to this reconciliation, for it is the living God at work and it is part and parcel of the fellowship which issues from his work and in which it is perpetuated. And thus it was that the physical body of Christ, given up to death and raised from death, brought with it that fellowship which we call the Church, the Body of Christ. "Destroy this temple, and in three days I will raise it up again." He spoke of the temple of his body. And in a sense, too, the Church was continuous with the People of God of the old dispensation. The unique incarnation, for all its uniqueness and finality, is found to be the center of history—not discontinuous; a great flowing stream, not a separate draught of water; the apex of a pyramid, not an unattached point in mid-air.

Charles Francis Digby Moule (1908–)—Cambridge lecturer and professor of divinity, Moule is an Anglican clergyman, biblical scholar, and prolific author.

The Burning Glass and Other Poems

Out of a Dream

Out of a dream I came—
Woeful with sinister shapes,
Hollow sockets aflame,
The mouth that gapes
With cries, unheard, of the dark;
The bleak, black night of the soul;
Sweating, I lay in my bed,
Sick of the wake for a goal.

And lo—Earth's close-shut door,
Its panels a cross, its key
Of common and rusting iron,
Opened, and showed to me
A face—found; lost—of old:
Of a lifetime's longing the sum;
And eyes that assuaged all grief:
    "Behold! I am come."

Walter de la Mare (1873–1956)—A graduate of St. Paul's Cathedral Choir School, London, and a clerk in the statistics department of the Anglo-American Standard Oil Company, de la Mare published stories and poetry. A government pension and the success of his works enabled him to focus on literary pursuits after 1908.

4

"I Will Seek You"

Knowing God

Thomas Aquinas

Summa Theologiae

God is not just supremely good within a particular genus or order of reality; he is the absolutely supreme good. For we saw that God was called good as being the first source of every perfection things desire. And these perfections, as we have shown, flow out from God not as from an agent in the same genus, but as from an agent agreeing neither in species nor in genus with its effects. Now an agent in the same genus mirrors its effects with unchanged form, but an agent not in the same genus mirrors them more perfectly, the heat of the sun, for example, excelling that of fire. So, since it is as first source of everything not himself in a genus that God is good, he must be good in the most perfect manner possible. And for this reason we call him supremely good.

Hence: 1. What supreme goodness adds to goodness is something not absolute but merely relative. Now the relations that God is said to bear to creatures, though represented mentally as existing in God, really exist not in God but in the creatures, just as things are called objects of knowledge not because they are related to knowledge, but because knowledge is related to them. So the supreme good does not have to be composite, but other good things must fall short of him.

2. The assertion that *good is what everything desires* does not mean that every good is desired by everything, but that whatever is desired is good. And the assertion that *no one is good but God alone*, means "good by nature" as we shall see.

3. There is no way of comparing things not in the same genus, when they are actually in different genera. But we say God is not in the same genus as other goods, not because he belongs to another genus but because he

exists outside all genera and initiates them all. And so he is related to other things by surpassing them; and this is the comparison implied by supreme goodness.

———————————————————————

Thomas Aquinas (1225–1274)—Roman Catholic saint, theologian, mystic, and scholar, Aquinas was educated by Benedictine monks at Monte Cassino and at the University of Naples. He became a Dominican friar at age seventeen. He is perhaps best known for his major work, the *Summa Theologiae*.

JOHN DONNE

Donne's Sermons

Did God satisfy himself with the *visible* and discernible world; with all on earth, and all between that, and him? Were those *four Monarchies*, the *four Elements*, and all the subjects of those four Monarchies (if all the four Elements have Creatures) company enough for God? Was that *Heptarchie*, the *seven kingdoms* of the *seven Planets*, conversation enough for him? Let every Star in the firmament, be (so some take them to be) a several world, was all this enough? We see, God drew persons nearer to him, than Sun, or Moon, or Stars, or anything, which is *visible*, and discernible to us, he created *Angels*; How many, how great? Arithmetic lacks *numbers* to express them, proportion lacks *Dimensions* to figure them; so far was God from being *alone*.

And yet God had not shed himself far enough; he had the *Leviathan*, the Whale in the Sea, and *Behemoth* and the *Elephant* upon the land; and all these great *heavenly bodies* in the way, and *Angels* in their infinite numbers, and manifold offices, in heaven; but, because *Angels*, could not propagate, nor make more *Angels*, he enlarged his love, in making *man*, that so he might enjoy all natures at once, and have the nature of *Angels*, and the nature of *earthly Creatures*, in one Person. God would not be without man, nor he would not come single, not alone to the making of man; but it is *Faciamus hominem, Let us, us, make man;* God, in his whole council, in his whole College, in his whole society, in the whole Trinity, makes man, in whom the whole nature of all the world should meet.

John Donne (1572–1631)—One of the metaphysical poets, John Donne was raised a Roman Catholic and converted to Anglicanism. He was ordained in 1615 and eventually became the dean of St. Paul's Cathedral, London.

Richard Hooker

Ecclesiastical Polity

The Being of God is a kind of Law to his working; for that perfection which God is, gives perfection to that he does. Those natural, necessary, and internal operations of God, the Generation of the Son, the Proceeding of the Spirit, are without the compass of my present intent; which is to touch only such operations as have their beginning and being by a voluntary purpose, wherewith God has eternally decreed when and how they should be: which eternal decree is that we term an eternal Law. Dangerous it were for the feeble brain of man to wade far into the doings of the Most High; whom although to know be life, and joy to make mention of his name; yet our soundest knowledge is, to know that we know him not as indeed he is, neither can know him; and our safest eloquence concerning him, is our silence, when we confess without confession, that his glory is inexplicable, his greatness above our capacity and reach. He is above, and we upon earth; therefore it behooves our words to be wary and few. Our God is one, or rather very Oneness, and mere unity, having nothing but Itself in Itself, and not consisting (as all things do besides God) of many things. In which essential Unity of God, a Trinity personal nevertheless subsists, after a manner far exceeding the possibility of man's conceit. The works which outwardly are of God, they are in such sort of him being One, that each person has in them somewhat peculiar and proper. For being Three, and they all subsisting in the essence of one Deity, from the Father, by the Son, through the Spirit, all things are. That which the Son does hear of the Father, and which the Spirit does receive of the Father and the Son, the same we have at the hands of the Spirit, as being the last; and therefore the nearest unto us in order, although in power the same with the second and the first.

Richard Hooker (ca. 1554–1600)—Theologian and defender of the Church of England during the reign of Queen Elizabeth, Hooker wrote *The Laws of Ecclesiastical Politie*. C. S. Lewis believed this book to be well written and full of wisdom and good sense.

George Herbert

The Country Parson

Oh Almighty and ever-living Lord God! Majesty, and Power, and Brightness, and Glory! How shall we dare to appear before your face, who are contrary to you, in all we call you? For we are darkness, and weakness, and filthiness, and shame. Misery and sin fill our days: yet are you our Creator, and we your work: Your hands both made us, and also made us Lords of all your creatures; giving us one world in ourselves, and another to serve us: then did you place us in Paradise, and were proceeding still on in your Favors, until we interrupted your Counsels, disappointed your Purposes, and sold our God, our glorious, our gracious God for an apple. Oh write it! Oh brand it in our foreheads forever: for an apple once we lost our God, and still lose him for no more; for money, for meat, for diet: But you Lord, are patience and pity, and sweetness, and love; therefore we sons of men are not consumed. You have exalted your mercy above all things; and have made our salvation, not our punishment, your glory: so that then where sin abounded, not death, but grace superabounded; accordingly, when we had sinned beyond any help in heaven or earth, then you said, Lo, I come! then did the Lord of life, unable of himself to die, contrive to do it. He took flesh, he wept, he died; for his enemies he died; even for those that derided him then, and still despise him. Blessed Savior! many waters could not quench your love! nor no pit overwhelm it. But though the streams of your blood were current through darkness, grave, and hell; yet by these your conflicts, and seemingly hazards, did you arise triumphant, and therein made us victorious.

George Herbert (1593–1633)—Anglican rector of the parish church of Bremerton, near Salisbury, Herbert was one of the seventeenth-century metaphysical poets.

Edward Young

Night Thoughts

O You, who does permit these ills to fall,
For gracious ends, and would'st that man should mourn!
O You, whose hands this goodly fabric framed,
Who know'st it best, and would'st that man should know!
What is this sublunary world? A vapor;
A vapor all it holds; itself, a vapor;
From the damp bed of chaos, by Your beam
Exhaled, ordain'd to swim its destined hour
In ambient air, then melt, and disappear.
Earth's days are number'd, nor remote her doom;
As mortal, though less transient, than her sons;
Yet they dote on her, as the world and they
Were both eternal, solid; You, a dream.
They dote!—on what? Immortal views apart,
A region of outsides! a land of shadows!
A fruitful field of flowery promises!
A wilderness of joys! perplex'd with doubts,
And sharp with thorns! a troubled ocean, spread
With bold adventurers, their all on board!

Edward Young (1683–1765)—English politician, clergyman, satirist, playwright, and poet, Young served as royal chaplain and rector of Welwyn. His best-known work is the Christian apologetic *The Complaint,* also entitled *Night Thoughts,* which he wrote after the death of his wife and stepdaughter.

DOROTHY L. SAYERS

Introductory Papers on Dante

Although the unity of Christ's mystical body is such that the blessed dead are deeply concerned with the living, whether to help, pity, pray for them, or to feel indignation at their sins, yet in Heaven the powers of anger and pity are experienced *pure*, and not bound up with a whole complex of confused personal feelings. When God and His Saints are angry, anger does not tear them to pieces, distort their judgment and poison their lives: they pity, but pity does not ravage them with helpless torments and put them at the mercy of the blackmailing egotism which thrives by exploiting and playing upon the feelings of the tender-hearted; in C. S. Lewis's admirable phrase: "The action of pity will live for ever, but the passion of pity will not."

Dorothy L. Sayers (1893–1957)—Translator of Dante's *The Divine Comedy,* literary critic, playwright, and detective novelist, Sayers was a friend and correspondent of C. S. Lewis.

SAINT AUGUSTINE

Confessions

"Great are you, O Lord, and greatly to be praised; great is your power, and infinite is your wisdom." And man desires to praise you, for he is a part of your creation; he bears his mortality about with him and carries the evidence of his sin and the proof that you resist the proud. Still he desires to praise you, this man who is only a small part of your creation. You have prompted him, that he should delight to praise you, for you have made us for yourself and restless is our heart until it comes to rest in you. Grant me, O Lord, to know and understand whether first to invoke you or to praise you; whether first to know you or call upon you. But who can invoke you, knowing you not? For he who knows you not may invoke you as another than you are. It may be that we should invoke you in order that we may come to know you. But "how shall they call on him in whom they have not believed? Or how shall they believe without a preacher?" Now, "they shall praise the Lord who seek him," for "those who seek shall find him," and, finding him, shall praise him. I will seek you, O Lord, and call upon you. I call upon you, O Lord, in my faith which you have given me, which you have inspired in me through the humanity of your Son, and through the ministry of your preacher.

Saint Augustine of Hippo (354–430)—Born in Numidia, a Roman province in North Africa, to a pagan father and Christian mother, Saint Augustine was consecrated Bishop of Hippo and wrote numerous treatises on Christianity, including *The Confessions*.

Proving the Unseen

We ought to know something of God. We ought to have heard enough of God to know Christ as He came to us. "Well, but," you say, "I am not sure that I should know Him." Well, I grant you I am afraid that I should not, either. I do not know, but I am sure of this—that I never shall know Him if I do not obey Him. I am sure of that. And if you want to know Him, so that He cannot escape you, and you would find Him anywhere, wherever He was, in the midst of a crowd or on the hilltop, do what He tells you, and He will go on helping you on and on, till at last you shall see His very self.

"And tell them that I am going up to God, to my Father and your Father." We do not know Him as Christ did. God is more His Father in that way, because Christ knows all about His Father, and we are poor little children, and cannot know what our great Brother knows. Oh, we may know Him with the whole of our nature, for we need Him as much, and no more or less, in that way, than Jesus Christ did.

The whole of the universe was nothing to Jesus without His Father. The day will come when the whole universe will be nothing to us without the Father, but with the Father an endless glory of delight. Observe that the Lord is "My Father and your Father." But He is not quite content with that, and remember that He never speaks unnecessary words. He says, "And to My God and your God." Because, after all that the word "father" could teach those of us who have had the very best of fathers, "God" means more and more, and better and better, for ever and ever, than even that best of words signifies to me. "My God and your God," for God is more than a father in the same direction—further and further in the same direction. It is as if the Father could but take you to His bosom, but God takes you inside Him, into

His very soul. If you have lower thoughts of God than these, it is pitiful, and you do God no honor, and you do yourself much wrong.

———————————————

George MacDonald (1824–1905)—Scottish Congregationalist pastor, novelist, myth maker, and poet, MacDonald had a profound influence on C. S. Lewis. Lewis said that MacDonald's *Phantastes* "baptized my imagination."

Beowulf

Then brave Beowulf of the Geats made a boastful speech, ere he lay down in bed: "I count myself no less in fighting-power, in battle-deeds, than Grendel does himself and therefore by the sword I will not kill him—rid him of life— though I have the power. He knows not of these noble arts—to strike back at me and hew my shield, brave though he be in hostile deeds. But we two at night shall not make use of swords, if he dare seek a combat without arms; and then may the wise God, the holy Lord, decree the triumph to whichever side seems meet to Him!"

Then the warrior brave in battle lay down, the pillow received the hero's face, and around him many a bold sea-warrior sank upon his couch in hall. Not one of them supposed that he would ever revisit his dear home, his people and the noble dwelling in which he was brought up; and they had learned that in time past murderous death had taken off far too many of the Danish people, in the wine-hall. But to the people of the Geats, the Lord gave the weaved destiny of success in war—help and support, so that they should all overcome their enemy through the power of one man, through his own strength. It is known for certain that the mighty God has always ruled over the race of men.

———————————————

Beowulf—Perhaps the most important poem in Old English, *Beowulf* is the medieval legend of a warrior who fights and kills the dragon Grendel and, years later, Grendel's mother when she seeks to avenge her son. The poem survives in a tenth-century manuscript but was certainly written earlier.

ANICIUS BOETHIUS

The Consolation of Philosophy

The two seem clean contrary and opposite, God's universal foreknowledge and freedom of the will. If God foresees all things and cannot be mistaken in any way, what Providence has foreseen as a future event must happen. So that if from eternity Providence foreknows not only men's actions but also their thoughts and desires, there will be no freedom of will. No action or desire will be able to exist other than that which God's infallible Providence has foreseen. For if they can be changed and made different from how they were foreseen, there will be no sure foreknowledge of the future, only an uncertain opinion; and this I do not think can be believed of God.

What I am trying to show is that, whatever the order of the causes, the coming to pass of things foreknown is necessary even if the foreknowledge of future events does not seem to impose the necessity on them.

If a man is sitting, it is necessary that the opinion which concludes that he is sitting is true; and on the other hand, if the opinion about the man is true, because he is sitting, it is necessary that he is sitting. There is necessity, therefore, in both statements; in the one that the man is sitting, and in the other that the opinion is true. But it is not because the opinion is true, that the man sits; rather, the opinion is true because it is preceded by the man's act of sitting. So although the cause of the truth proceeds from the one side, there is, nevertheless, a common necessity in either side. Clearly the same reasoning applies to Providence and future events.

Anicius Boethius (ca. 480–524)—Philosopher, statesman, and Christian, Boethius was an advisor to the Ostrogothic king Theodoric after the sack of Rome. His *Consolation of Philosophy* was second only to the Bible as an influence on medieval thought and literature.

THOMAS TRAHERNE

Centuries

O how do Your affections extend like the sunbeams unto all stars in heaven and to all the kingdoms in the world. Yours at once enlighten both hemispheres: quicken us with life, enable us to digest the nourishment of our Souls, cause us to see the greatness of our nature, the Love of God, and the joys of heaven: melt us into tears, comfort and enflame us, and do all in a celestial manner, that the Sun can do in a terrene and earthly. O let me so long eye You, till I be turned into You, and look upon me till You are formed in me, that I may be a mirror of Your brightness, a habitation of Your love, and a temple of Your glory. That all Your Saints might live in me, and I in them: enjoying all their felicities, joys, and treasures.

Thomas Traherne (1637–1674)—Son of a poor shoemaker, educated at Oxford, and one of the metaphysical poets, Traherne became the Anglican rector of Credenhill in Herefordshire.

5

"MUTUALLY CHRIST'S"

Community and Loving Others

George MacDonald

Unspoken Sermons

Nor is there anything we can ask for ourselves that we may not ask for another. We may commend any brother, any sister, to the common fatherhood. And there will be moments when, filled with that spirit which is the Lord, nothing will ease our hearts of their love but the commending of all men, all our brothers, all our sisters, to the one Father. Nor shall we ever know that repose in the Father's hands, that rest of the Holy Sepulchre, which the Lord knew when the agony of death was over, when the storm of the world died away behind his retiring spirit, and he entered the regions where there is only life, and therefore all that is not music is silence, (for all noise comes of the conflict of Life and Death)—we shall never be able, I say, to rest in the bosom of the Father, till the fatherhood is fully revealed to us in the love of the brothers. For he cannot be our father save as he is their father; and if we do not see him and feel him as their father, we cannot know him as ours. Never shall we know him aright until we rejoice and exult for our race that he is *the* Father. He that loves not his brother whom he has seen, how can he love God whom he has not seen? To rest, I say, at last, even in those hands into which the Lord commended his spirit, we must have learned already *to love our neighbor as ourselves.*

George MacDonald (1824–1905)—Scottish Congregationalist pastor, novelist, myth maker, and poet, MacDonald had a profound influence on C. S. Lewis. Lewis said that MacDonald's *Phantastes* "baptized my imagination."

COVENTRY PATMORE

The Rod, the Root, and the Flower

Theologians teach that our ultimate felicity will consist in the development
of a single divine humanity made up of innumerable unique and sympathetic individualities or "members," each one shining with its proper and
peculiar luster, which shall be as unlike any other luster as that of sapphire is
from that of a ruby or an emerald; and they further teach that the end of this
life is the awakening and growth of such individualities through a faithful following of the peculiar good which is each individual's "ruling love"; since
each has his ruling love, if he knew it, that is, his peculiar and partial way of
discerning and desiring the absolute good, which no created being is capable
of discerning and desiring in its fullness and universality. Every man who is
humanly alive—and it must be admitted that there are a good many to
whom such life can only be attributed by a charitable surmisal—is conscious
that the bond of man with man consists, not in similarity, but in dissimilar-
ity; the happiness of love, in which alone is happiness, residing, as again the
theologians say, not in union but conjunction, which can only be between
spiritual dissimilars. That man is created in the capacity for uniqueness of
character is shown by the human face, which is never at all alike in any two
persons, and of which the peculiarity is nothing but an expression of the
latent inherent difference which it is the proper work of life to bring into
actuality.

Coventry Patmore (1823–1896)—The works of this Victorian poet, who is best
known for *The Angel in the House, The Unknown Eros,* and *The Root and the Flower,* are
a mixture of the homey, erotic mysticism, and spirituality. C. S. Lewis expressed
appreciation for Patmore in his letters.

CHRISTOPHER DAWSON

Religion and Culture

Any religious movement which adopts a purely critical and negative attitude to culture is therefore a force of destruction and disintegration which mobilizes against it the healthiest and most constructive elements in society—elements which can by no means be dismissed as worthless from the religious point of view. On the other hand, the identification of religion with the particular cultural synthesis which has been achieved at a definite point of time and space by the action of historical forces is fatal to the universal character of religious truth. It is indeed a kind of idolatry—the substitution of an image made by man for the eternal transcendent reality. If this identification is carried to its extreme conclusion, the marriage of religion and culture is equally fatal to either partner, since religion is so tied to the social order that it loses its spiritual character, and the free development of culture is restricted by the bonds of religious tradition until the social organism becomes as rigid and lifeless as a mummy.

Christopher Dawson (1889–1970)—An Oxford scholar of Trinity College, a Roman Catholic, author, sociologist, and historian, Dawson specialized in the study of religion and culture.

WILLIAM LANGLAND

Piers the Ploughman

Love is first among the company of the Lord of Heaven; He is a mediator between God and man, as a Mayor is between king and people.

And so that one can recognize love by natural instinct, it begins by some power whose source and center is in the heart of man. For every virtue springs from a natural knowledge in the heart, implanted there by the Father who created us—He who looked upon us with love and let His Son die for our sins, wishing no evil to those who tortured Him and put Him to death, but praying for their forgiveness.

From this you may see an example in His own person, that He was mighty yet gentle, and granted mercy to those that hanged Him on the Cross and pierced His heart.

So I advise you who are rich to have pity on the poor; and though you have power to summon them before the courts, be merciful in what you do. For "with what measure you mete"—whether well or ill—you shall be measured with that when you leave this world.

For though you speak the truth and are honest in your dealings, and as chaste as an innocent child that weeps at its baptism, unless you love men truly, and give to the poor, generously sharing the goods God has given you, you shall have no more merit from your Masses and Hours than old Molly from her maidenhead, that no man wants.

William Langland (ca. 1332–ca. 1400)—Author of *The Vision of William Concerning Piers the Ploughman,* an allegorical poem of social satire and exposition of the Christian life, Langland took minor orders in the church, which allowed him to make a living by singing masses and copying documents. *Piers the Ploughman* is considered to be the greatest poem of Middle English prior to Chaucer and was much loved by C. S. Lewis.

John Woolman

Journal

This morning in the meeting the Indian who came with the Moravian, being also a member of that Society, prayed, and then the Moravian spoke a short time to the people. And in the afternoon, they coming together and my heart being filled with a heavenly care for their good, I spoke to them awhile by interpreters, but none of them being perfect in the work. And I, feeling the current of love run strong, told the interpreters that I believed some of the people would understand me, and so proceeded, in which exercise I believe the Holy Ghost wrought on some hearts to edification, where all the words were not understood. I looked upon it as a time of divine favor, and my heart was tendered and truly thankful before the Lord. And after I sat down one of the interpreters seemed spirited up to give the Indians the substance of what I said.

Before our first meeting this morning, I was led to meditate on the manifold difficulties of these Indians, who by the permission of the Six Nations dwell in these parts, and a near sympathy with them was raised in me; and my heart being enlarged in the love of Christ, I thought that the affectionate care of a good man for his only brother in affliction does not exceed what I then felt for that people.

I came to this place through much trouble, and though through the mercies of God I believed that if I died in the journey it would be well with me, yet the thoughts of falling into the hands of Indian warriors was in times of weakness afflicting me; and being of a tender constitution of body, the thoughts of captivity among them was at times grievous, as supposing that they, being strong and hardy, might demand service of me beyond what I could well bear. But the Lord alone was my helper, and I believed if I went into captivity it would be for some good end. And thus from time to time my mind was centered in resignation, in which I always found quietness. And now this day, though I had the same dangerous wilderness between me and home, I was inwardly joyful that the Lord had strengthened me to come on this visit and manifested a fatherly care over me in my poor lowly condition, when in my own eyes I appeared inferior to many among the Indians.

John Woolman (1720–1772)—American Quaker preacher and reformer, Woolman traveled throughout the American colonies and England preaching and promoting the abolition of slavery. He is best known for his *Journal,* which was published after his death.

C. E. M. JOAD

Philosophy

In a properly ordered soul no one desire is allowed to dominate the rest, or to prejudice the well-being of the whole, since, tamed by reason, the various desires have learnt to stand back and refrain from interfering with one another's satisfaction. Thus, the reasonable man, precisely because he is dominated by reason, is also a satisfied man. Plato transfers his conclusion from the stage of the soul to that of the State. Ordinary people, as we have seen, are those in whom the third part of the soul is predominant. Left to themselves, they are not capable of philosophy; they do not, that is to say, strive to know the principles of reality, they have little wisdom and are concerned only to satisfy their desires. It is for this reason that they crave money and power. The life of the ordinary man is forever restless and discontented, unless he finds some positive reason for contentment. And so he tries to discover positive reasons, in women or in wine, in sport or in competitions, or even in war, and in pursuit of these will strive with his fellows. Such, too, is the condition of democracy, the condition of free competition, in which every man is as good as his neighbor…and equally entitled with him both to govern and to be satisfied. Finding the resultant insecurity intolerable, democracies tend to develop into tyrannies, an absolute ruler being appointed to put an end to competition and party strife and to discipline the people for their own good and for the good of the community.

Cyril Edwin Mitchinson Joad (1891–1953)—Educated at Oxford, professor at Birkbeck College, London, popular philosopher, and controversialist, C. E. M. Joad was best known for his appearances on the BBC's *Brains Trust* radio program. He became a Christian in later life.

Poems and Plays

A Woman's Last Word

I. Let's contend no more, Love,
    Strive nor weep:
  All be as before, Love,
    —Only sleep!

II. What so wild as words are?
    I and thou
  In debate, as birds are,
    Hawk on bough!

III. See the creature stalking
    While we speak!
  Hush and hide the talking,
    Cheek on cheek!

IV. What so false as truth is,
    False to thee?
  Where the serpent's tooth is
    Shun the tree—

V. Where the apple reddens
    Never pry—
  Lest we lose our Edens,
    Eve and I.

VI.   Be a god and hold me
          With a charm!
      Be a man and fold me
          With thine arm!

VII.   Teach me, only teach, Love!
          As I ought
      I will speak thy speech, Love,
          Think thy thought—

VIII. Meet, if thou require it,
          Both demands,
      Laying flesh and spirit
          In thy hands.

IX.   That shall be to-morrow,
          Not to-night:
      I must bury sorrow
          Out of sight.

X.   —Must a little weep, Love,
          (Foolish me!)
      And so fall asleep, Love,
          Loved by thee.

Robert Browning (1812–1889)—Browning was a Victorian poet and the husband of Elizabeth Barrett Browning. His massive poem *The Ring and the Book* was much loved by C. S. Lewis.

SIR THOMAS BROWNE

The Religio Medici

I have a private method which others observe not; I take the opportunity of myself to do good; I borrow occasion of Charity from my own necessities, and supply the wants of others, when I am in most need myself: for it is an honest stratagem to take advantage of ourselves, and so to husband the acts of virtue, that, where they are defective in one circumstance, they may repay their want and multiply their goodness in another. I have a competence, and ability to perform those good works to which He has inclined my nature. He is rich, who has enough to be charitable; and it is hard to be so poor, that a noble mind may not find a way to this piece of goodness. *He that gives to the poor lends to the* LORD: there is more truth in that one sentence, than in a Library of Sermons; and indeed, if those Sentences were understood by the Reader, with the same Emphasis as they are delivered by the Author, we needed not those Volumes of instructions, but might be honest by an Epitome. Upon this motive only I cannot behold a Beggar without relieving his Necessities with my Purse, or his Soul with my Prayers; these scenical and accidental differences between us, cannot make me forget that common and untouched part of us both: there is under these *Centoes* and miserable outsides, these mutilate and semi-bodies, a soul of the same alloy with our own, whose Genealogy is GOD as well as ours, and in as fair a way to Salvation as ourselves. Statists that labor to contrive a Common-wealth without poverty, take away the object of charity, not understanding only the Common-wealth of a Christian, but forgetting the prophecy of CHRIST.

Sir Thomas Browne (1605–1682)—Educated at Oxford and a medical doctor, Browne was a Royalist in the Civil War and received a knighthood for his loyalty. *The Religio Medici* was a confession of faith, revealing deep insight into the mysteries of Christianity.

JOHN DONNE

Poetry and Prose

A Defense of Women's Inconstancy

That Women are *Inconstant,* I with any man confess, but that *Inconstancy* is a bad quality, I against any man will maintain: For everything as it is one better than another, so is it fuller of *change;* the *Heavens* themselves continually turn, the *Stars* move, the *Moon* changes; *Fire* whirls, *Air* flies, *Water* ebbs and flows, the face of the *Earth* alters her looks, *Time* stays not; the Color that is most light will take most dyes: so in Men, they that have the most reason are the most alterable in their designs, and the darkest or most ignorant, do most seldom change; therefore Women changing more than Men, have also more *Reason.* They cannot be immutable like stocks, like stones, like the Earth's dull Center; Gold that lies still, rusts; Water corrupts; Air that moves not, poisons; then why should that which is the perfection of other things be imputed to Women as the greatest imperfection?

John Donne (1572–1631)—One of the metaphysical poets, John Donne was raised a Roman Catholic and converted to Anglicanism. He was ordained in 1615 and eventually became the dean of St. Paul's Cathedral, London.

Joy Davidman

Smoke on the Mountain

"Provoke not your children to wrath." Easily said; but how are we to avoid it? Strife between old and young seems inevitable. Today the world changes fast and inconceivably fast; in pastoral and agricultural times, what a man knew was of use to his son, but in the industrial age Father's knowledge is out of date before the son is half grown up. We should be more than human if the result were not bitterness and conflict. Then too there are just too many people on this teeming and screaming earth for us to welcome a new man with whole-souled enthusiasm. Our God-given biologic nature, which rejoices in parenthood, and our fallen self-seeking nature, which hates it as the creator of responsibilities, are at war with each other; and if we cannot make peace with ourselves, how shall we make peace with our children?

The ideal solution, of course, would be to remake our jerry-built, precarious society into a sound and safe one. But, let's admit it, we don't know how; and if we knew, we have not the power; and if we had the power, as long as we are sinners we should lack the love. There is only one thing a man can really remake—himself—and that only with the aid of God's grace. Laws and organizations and schools are good things, crèches and social services and youth groups may be admirable things. Yet—a reminder obvious, trite, but necessary—none of them can replace the love and guidance of father and mother. Our problem, then, pending reconstruction of the world, is to reconstruct our own lives so that we give our children as much warmth and attention and time and teaching as the present world will allow.

At least we might give them our leisure. Let us drop the disastrous cant that persuades women, often against their own hearts, that they have a "duty" to neglect their children for civic affairs, or broadening cultural activities, or even, heaven help us, for "realizing their creative potentialities through self-expression in a rewarding career." Let us drop too the curious theory that the care and teaching of children are entirely women's work, and that their father should have as little to do with them as possible. Most of all, let us remind the innumerable Americans who don't seem to know it that begetting and rearing a family are far more real and rewarding than making and spending money.

Joy Davidman (1915–1960)—Poet, author, and the wife of C. S. Lewis, Davidman is the mother of David and Douglas Gresham. C. S. Lewis dedicated his novel *Till We Have Faces* to her and wrote *A Grief Observed* upon her death.

MARTIN LUTHER

Ninety-five Theses

Faith's object is not to lay men under obligations, nor does it distinguish between friends and enemies, or look to gratitude or ingratitude, but most freely and willingly spends itself and its goods, whether it loses them through ingratitude, or gains goodwill. For thus did its Father, distributing all things to all men abundantly and freely, making His sun to rise upon the just and the unjust. Thus, too, the child does and endures nothing except from the free joy with which it delights through Christ in God, the Giver of such great gifts.

You see, then, that, if we recognize these great and precious gifts, as Peter says, which have been given to us, love is quickly diffused in our hearts through the Spirit, and by love we are made free, joyful, all-powerful, active workers, victors over all our tribulations, servants to our neighbor, and nevertheless lords of all things. But for those who do not recognize the good things given to them through Christ, Christ has been born in vain; such persons walk by works, and will never attain the taste and feeling of these great things. Therefore just as our neighbor is in want, and has need of our abundance, so we too in the sight of God were in want and had need of His mercy. And as our heavenly Father has freely helped us in Christ, so ought we freely to help our neighbor by our body and works, and each should become to other a sort of Christ, so that we may be mutually Christ's, and that the same Christ may be in all of us; that is, that we may be truly Christians.

Martin Luther (1483–1546)—An Augustinian monk who became the father of the Protestant Reformation, Luther was an indefatigable theologian and pastor and champion of the doctrine of justification by "faith alone."

GEORGE MacDONALD

Annals of a Quiet Neighborhood

All through the slowly-fading afternoon, the autumn of the day, when the colors are richest and the shadows long and lengthening, I paced my solemn old-thoughted church. Sometimes I went up in to the pulpit and sat there, looking on the ancient walls which had grown up under men's hands that men might be helped to pray by the visible symbol of unity which the walls gave, and that the voice of the Spirit of God might be heard exhorting men to forsake the evil and choose the good. And I thought how many witnesses to the truth had knelt in those ancient pews. For as the great church is made up of numberless communities, so is the great shining orb of witness-bearers made up of millions of lesser orbs. All men and women of true heart bear individual testimony to the truth of God, saying, "I have trusted and found Him faithful." And the feeble light of the glowworm is yet light, pure and good, and with a loveliness of its own. "So, O Lord," I said, "let my light shine before men." And I felt no fear of vanity in such a prayer, for I knew that the glory to come of it is to God only—"that men may glorify their Father in heaven." And I knew that when we seek glory for ourselves, the light goes out, and the Horror that dwells in darkness breathes cold upon our spirits.

George MacDonald (1824–1905)—Scottish Congregationalist pastor, novelist, myth maker, and poet, MacDonald had a profound influence on C. S. Lewis. Lewis said that MacDonald's *Phantastes* "baptized my imagination."

BARON FRIEDRICH VON HUGEL

Man of God

Like all living realities, living Religion possesses a sovereign spontaneity and rich simplicity which seem to render all attempts at analysis an insult. Indeed, Religion in particular possesses three essentials, which continually bring expansion and simplicity to its tension and complexity.

Religion is essentially Social *horizontally;* in the sense that each several soul is *therefore* unique because intended to realize just *this* post, function, joy, effect within the total organism of all souls. Hence no soul is expected to be a "jack-of-all-trades," but only to develop fully its own special gifts and *attraits,* within and through, and for, that larger organism of the human family, in which other souls are as fully to develop their own differing gifts and *attraits,* as so many supplements and compensations to the others.

And Religion is essentially Social *vertically*—indeed here is its deepest root. It is unchangeably a faith in God, a love of God, an intercourse with God; and though the soul cannot abidingly abstract itself from its fellows, it can and ought frequently to recollect itself in a simple sense of God's presence. Such moments of direct preoccupation with God alone bring a deep refreshment and simplification to the soul.

And Religion, in its fullest development, essentially requires, not only this our little span of earthly years, but a life beyond. Neither an Eternal Life that is already fully achieved here below, nor an Eternal Life to be begun and known solely in the beyond, satisfies these requirements. But only an Eternal Life already begun and truly known in part here, though fully to be achieved and completely to be understood hereafter, corresponds to the deepest longings of man's spirit as touched by the prevenient Spirit, God.

Baron Friedrich von Hugel (1853–1925)—A Roman Catholic philosopher of religion, von Hugel was considered too Protestant for some Catholics and too Catholic for some Protestants. Beloved by many from both parties, he was a mystic with a wise and broad intellectual grasp.

Joseph Butler

The Analogy of Religion

Whatsoever you would that men should do unto you, do you even so unto them.

All this is indeed no more than that we should have a real love to our neighbor: but then, which is to be observed, the words, *as yourself,* express this in the most distinct manner, and determine the precept to relate to the affection itself. The advantage, which this principle of benevolence has over other remote considerations, is, that it is itself the temper of virtue: and likewise, that it is the chief, nay the only effectual security of our performing the several offices of kindness we owe to our fellow-creatures. When from distant considerations men resolve upon anything to which they have no liking, or perhaps an averseness, they are perpetually finding out evasions and excuses; which need never be wanting, if people look for them: and they equivocate with themselves in the plainest cases in the world. This may be in respect to single determinate acts of virtue: but it comes in much more, where the obligation is to a general course of behavior; and most of all, if it be such as cannot be reduced to fixed determinate rules. This observation may account for the diversity of expression, in that known passage of the prophet Micah: *to do justly, and to love mercy.* A man's heart must be formed to humanity and benevolence, he must *love mercy,* otherwise he will not act mercifully in any settled course of behavior. As consideration of the future sanctions of religion is our only security of persevering in our duty, in cases of great temptations: so to get our heart and temper formed to a love and liking of what is good is absolutely necessary in order to our behaving rightly in the familiar and daily intercourses among mankind.

Joseph Butler (1692–1752)—An Oxford scholar and Anglican minister, Joseph Butler was, during his career, bishop of Bristol, dean of St Paul's Cathedral, and bishop of Durham. The *Analogy of Religion* is Butler's major contribution to moral philosophy.

James Moffatt

The Theology of the Gospels

Jesus prohibits any restriction of love and pity to those who are unkind to ourselves. The doctrine sounds heroic to ordinary human nature, but Jesus does not present it as heroic. He grounds His demand upon the natural attitude of the Father, upon what Francis of Assisi called "the great courtesy of God." He assumes that men enjoy the benefits of rain and sunshine from the hand of the Father and argues that a similar generosity must stream out from their hearts upon the undeserving. Love is the absolute character of God, love even for the undeserving. The Most High is *kind to the thankless and the evil.* *Be pitiful, even as your Father is perfect*, as your love extends even to your enemies. The moral claim is that the sons of the kingdom must reproduce in their own lives the spirit of their royal Father, especially towards those who have wronged them.

James Moffatt (1870–1944)—Scottish scholar, theologian, professor at Mansfield College, Oxford, and Union Theological Seminary, New York, Moffatt is best known for his English translation of the Bible.

G. K. CHESTERTON

Heretics

We make our friends; we make our enemies; but God makes our next-door neighbor. Hence he comes to us clad in all the careless terrors of nature; he is as strange as the stars, as reckless and indifferent as the rain. He is Man, the most terrible of the beasts. That is why the old religions and the old scriptural language showed so sharp a wisdom when they spoke, not of one's duty towards humanity, but one's duty towards one's neighbor. The duty towards humanity may often take the form of some choice which is personal or even pleasurable. That duty may be a hobby; it may even be a dissipation. We may work in the East End because we are peculiarly fitted to work in the East End, or because we think we are; we may fight for the cause of international peace because we are very fond of fighting. The most monstrous martyrdom, the most repulsive experience may be the result of choice or a kind of taste. We may be so made as to be particularly fond of lunatics or specially interested in leprosy.... But we have to love our neighbor because he is *there*—a much more alarming reason for a much more serious operation. He is the sample of humanity which is actually given us. Precisely because he may be anybody he is everybody. He is a symbol because he is an accident.

Gilbert Keith Chesterton (1874–1936)—Roman Catholic artist, poet, journalist, essayist, and author, Chesterton wrote over one hundred books. C. S. Lewis says, in *Surprised by Joy*, that Chesterton's Christian apologetics had a marked impact on him, and Lewis's own apologetic work owes a debt to Chesterton.

Sir Thomas More

Selections from His English Works

I would that every man would know there were but one man in all the whole world, and that that one were himself; and that he would thereupon go about to mend that one, and thus would all wax well. Which thing we should shortly do, if we would once turn our wallet that I told you of, and the bag with other folks' faults cast at our back, and cast the bag that bears our own faults, cast it once before us at our breast: it would be a goodly thing for us to look on our own faults a while. And I dare boldly say, both they and we should much the better amend, if we were so ready each to pray for the other, as we be ready to seek each other's reproach and rebuke.

Sir Thomas More (1478–1535)—An Oxford scholar, humanist, lawyer, author, and statesman, More resigned from his post as lord chancellor to protest King Henry VIII's break with the Roman Catholic Church. More was beheaded for his refusal to recognize Henry as the head of the Church of England and was canonized as a Roman Catholic saint in 1935.

J. R. R. TOLKIEN

Letters

From a letter to Anne Barrett, Houghton Mifflin Co.
30 August 1964

C. S. L. [Lewis] of course had some oddities and could sometimes be irritating. He was after all and remained an Irishman of Ulster. But he did nothing for effect; he was not a professional clown, but a natural one, when a clown at all. He was generous-minded, on guard against all prejudices, though a few were too deep-rooted in his native background to be observed by him. That his literary opinions were ever dictated by envy (as in the case of T. S. Eliot) is a grotesque calumny. After all it is possible to dislike Eliot with some intensity even if one has no aspirations to poetic laurels oneself.

Well of course I could say more, but I must draw the line. Still I wish it could be forbidden that after a great man is dead, little men should scribble over him, who have not and must know they have not sufficient knowledge of his life and character to give them any key to the truth. Lewis was not "cut to the quick" by his defeat in the election to the professorship of poetry: he knew quite well the cause. I remember that we had assembled soon after in our accustomed tavern and found C. S. L. sitting there, looking (and since he was no actor at all probably feeling) much at ease. "Fill up!" he said, "and stop looking so glum. The only distressing thing about this affair is that my friends seem to be upset."

John Ronald Reuel Tolkien (1892–1973)—An Oxford scholar, etymologist, translator, and close friend of C. S. Lewis, J. R. R. Tolkien is best known as the author of *The Hobbit* and *The Lord of the Rings*. Although he was born in South Africa, Tolkien spent most of his life in England, serving as professor of Anglo Saxon at Merton College.

George Fox

Journal of George Fox

All my dear friends in the noble Seed of God, who have known His power, life, and presence among you, let it be your joy to hear or see the springs of life break forth in any: through which you may have all unity in the same, feeling life and power. And above all things, take heed of judging any one openly in your meetings, except they be openly profane or rebellious, such as be out of the truth; that by the power, life and wisdom you may stand over them, and by it answer the witness of God in the world, that such, whom you bear your testimony against, are none of you: so that therein the truth may stand clear and single. But such as are tender, if they should be moved to bubble forth a few words, and speak in the Seed and Lamb's power, suffer and bear that; that is, the tender. And if they should go beyond their measure, bear it in the meeting for peace and order's sake, and that the spirits of the world be not moved against you. But when the meeting is done, then if any be moved to speak to them, between you and them, one or two of you that feel it in the life, do it in the love and wisdom that is pure and gentle from above: for love is that which does edify, bears all things, suffers long, and does fulfill the law. So in this you have order and edification, you have wisdom to preserve you all wise and in patience; which takes away the occasion of stumbling the weak, and the occasion of the spirits of the world to get up: but in the royal Seed, the heavy stone, you keep down all that is wrong; and by it answer that of God in all. For you will hear, see, and feel the power of God preaching, as your faith is all in it (when you do not hear words), to bind, to chain, to limit, to frustrate; that nothing shall rise nor come forth but what is in the power: for with that you will hold back, and with that you will let up, and open every spring, plant, and spark; in which will be your joy and refreshment in the power of God.

George Fox (1624–1691)—Religious mystic, reformer, and founder of the Society of Friends (Quakers), Fox wrote his *Journal*, which was edited by a committee supervised by William Penn. Fox rejected formal sacraments in favor of the belief that all of life is a sacrament.

GEORGE MacDONALD

Donal Grant

His heart was so full of love and the joy of love, that they had made him very still: now the delight of love awoke. He took her in his arms like a child, rose, and went walking about the room with her, petting and soothing her. He held her close to his heart; her head was on his shoulder, and his face was turned to hers.

"I love you," he said, "and love you to all eternity! I have love enough now to live upon, if you should die to-night, and I should tarry till he come. O God, you are too good to me! It is more than my heart can bear! To make men and women, and give them to each other, and not be one moment jealous of the love wherewith they love one another, is to be a God indeed!"

So said Donal—and spoke the high truth. But alas for the love wherewith men and women love each other! There were small room for God to be jealous of *that!* It is the little love with which they love each other, the great love with which they love themselves, that hurts the heart of their father.

George MacDonald (1824–1905)—Scottish Congregationalist pastor, novelist, myth maker and poet, George MacDonald had a profound influence on C. S. Lewis. Lewis said that MacDonald's *Phantastes* "baptized my imagination."

6

"Constant Dying"

Self and the Soul

AUSTIN FARRER

Saving Belief

Every sparrow is an individual, unlike every other; and the special thing God makes in that sparrow is the product of all the special circumstances concurrent in her production. Most of us have little insight into the singularity of sparrows. We can do better with the human case. For you to be what you are involves a universe; and if your being what you are is the work of God, then an infinity of events was under his hand. It was his skill to draw you out of the genetic pattern of your ancestry, the culture of your time, and the complex of relationships surrounding you. This is not to deny that had your ancestors been more temperate, your parents wiser, your teachers more conscientious and your school-fellows not such little beasts, you would have been a better person than you are. Yet, such as you are, God made you; and the supreme prerogative of the divine art is to draw good even from evil. Not a greater good, no; we do not help God to produce better things by offering him worse materials. But what he makes is always a unique good. You are you, and no one just like you. The defects, as well as the advantages, of your background have gone into the composition of the mixture.

Austin Farrer (1904–1968)—Doctor of Divinity and fellow of Trinity College, Oxford, and later warden of Keble College, Oxford, Austin Farrer was a member of the Inklings, a literary discussion group that included C. S. Lewis and J. R. R. Tolkien. Farrer was one of the witnesses at the civil marriage ceremony of C. S. Lewis and Joy Davidman, and he preached the sermon at Joy's funeral.

Andrew Murray

Abide in Christ

How little understood how great His need, but also how perfect His claim to my emptiness! Let me, in its beautiful light, study the wondrous union between Jesus and His people, until it becomes to me the guide into full communion with my beloved Lord. Let me listen and believe, until my whole being cries out, "Jesus is indeed to me the True Vine, bearing me, nourishing me, supplying me, using me, and filling me to the full to make me bring forth fruit abundantly." Then shall I not fear to say, "I am indeed a branch to Jesus, the True Vine, abiding in Him, resting on Him, waiting for Him, serving Him, and living only that through me, too, He may show forth the riches of His grace, and give His fruit to a perishing world."

It is when we try thus to understand the meaning of the parable, that the blessed command spoken in connection with it will come home to us in its true power. The thought of what the Vine is to the branch, and Jesus to the believer, will give new force to the words, "Abide in me!" It will be as if He says, "Think, soul, how completely I belong to you. I have joined myself inseparably to you; all the fullness and fatness of the Vine are yours in very deed. Now you once are in me, be assured that all I have is wholly yours. It is my interest and my honor to have you a fruitful branch; only *Abide in me.* You are weak, but I am strong; you are poor, but I am rich. Only abide in me; yield yourself wholly to my teaching and rule; simply trust my love, my grace, my promises. Only believe I am wholly yours; I am the Vine, you are the branch."

Andrew Murray (1828–1917)—Evangelical and leader in the South African Dutch Reformed Church, Andrew Murray was educated in Scotland and Holland. He served several pastorates and was six times the moderator of the Reformed Church.

F. H. BRADLEY

The Principles of Logic

Every individual is in some sense perfect, we may be assured, in its own rank and place; and, in its very striving for perfection, it is already, beyond our vision, itself unique and complete. But, when you ask to be shown exactly what each individual itself is—that detailed understanding remains in the end unattainable. For religious faith doubtless the case here is otherwise, but even for such faith the detail is, again, at a certain point unknown. How much of each individual self is the realization of its own perfect and unique being, and how much in any case must fall somewhere outside, we are unable to see. And no true religion, we may add, will seek to justify, whether in this world or in any other world, the perfection of the individual, if taken by himself; nor will it anywhere think to escape from the grace of God and from the life gained only through constant dying.

Francis Herbert Bradley (1846–1924)—A fellow of Merton College, Oxford, and a philosopher influenced by Kant and Hegel, Bradley was a pivotal figure in the British idealist movement. His most influential work is *Appearance and Reality*.

SAMUEL TAYLOR COLERIDGE

Aids to Reflection

Life is the one universal soul, which, by virtue of the enlivening BREATH, and
the informing WORD, all organized bodies have in common, each *after its
kind*. This, therefore, all animals possess, and man as an animal. But, in
addition to this, God transfused into man a higher gift, and specially
inbreathed:—even a living (that is, self-subsisting) soul, a soul having its life
in itself. "And man became a living soul." He did not merely *possess* it, he
became it. It was his proper *being*, his truest *self, the* man *in* the man. None
then, not one of human kind, so poor and destitute, but there is provided for
him, even in his present state, *a house not built with hands.* Aye, and spite of
the philosophy (falsely so called) which mistakes the causes, the conditions,
and the occasions of our becoming *conscious* of certain truths and realities for
the truths and realities themselves—a house gloriously furnished. Nothing is
wanted but the eye, which is the light of this house, the light which is the eye
of this soul. This *seeing* light, this *enlightening* eye, is Reflection. It is more,
indeed, than is ordinarily meant by that word; but it is what a *Christian*
ought to mean by it, and to know too, whence it first came, and still continues to come—of what light even this light is *but* a reflection. This, too, is
THOUGHT; and all thought is but unthinking that does not flow out of this,
or tend towards it.

Samuel Taylor Coleridge (1772–1834)—Poet, literary critic, and philosopher,
Coleridge was best known for his *The Rime of the Ancient Mariner* and *Biographia
Literaria.* Lewis, in *The Abolition of Man,* recounts the story of Coleridge at the Falls of
the Clyde in Scotland.

Francis Quarles

Emblems

My Soul is like a Bird; my Flesh, the Cage;
Wherein, she wears her weary Pilgrimage
Of hours as few as evil, daily fed
With sacred Wine, and Sacramental Bread;
The keys that lock her in, and lets her out,
Are Birth, and Death; 'twixt both, she hops about
From perch to perch; from Sense to Reason; then,
From higher Reason, down to Sense again:
From Sense she climbs to Faith; where, for a season,
She sits and sings; then, down again to Reason;
From Reason, back to Faith; and straight, from thence
She rudely flutters to the Perch of Sense;
From Sense, to Hope; then hops from Hope to Doubt;
From Doubt, to dull Despair; there, seeks about
For desperate Freedom; and at every Grate,
She wildly thrusts, and begs the untimely date
Of unexpired thraldom, to release
The afflicted Captive, that can find no peace:
Thus am I cooped within this fleshly Cage,
I wear my youth, and waste my weary Age,
Spending that breath which was ordained to chant
Heaven's praises forth, in sighs and sad complaint:
While happier birds can spread their nimble wing
From Shrubs to Cedars, and there chirp and sing,
In choice of raptures, the harmonious story
Of man's Redemption and his Maker's Glory:

You glorious Martyrs; you illustrious Troops,
That once were cloistered in your fleshly Coops.
Great LORD of souls, to whom should prisoners fly,
But You? You had your Cage, as well as I:
And, for my sake, your pleasure was to know
The sorrows that it brought, and felt them too;
O set me free, and I will spend those days,
Which now I waste in begging, in Your praise.

Francis Quarles (1592–1644)—Educated at Christ's College, Cambridge, Quarles was a Royalist, poet, pamphleteer, and literary critic. He wrote in the metaphysical poetic tradition and is best known for his collection of poems entitled *Emblems*.

George MacDonald

Unspoken Sermons

If there be a God, and I am his creature, there may be, there should be, there must be some communication open between him and me. If any one allow a God, but one scarce good enough to care about his creatures, I will yield him that it were foolish to pray to such a God; but the notion that, with all the good impulses in us, we are the offspring of a cold-hearted devil, is so horrible in its inconsistency, that I would ask that man what hideous and cold-hearted disregard to the truth makes him capable of the supposition! To such a one God's terrors, or, if not his terrors, then God's sorrows yet will speak; the divine something in him will love, and the love be left moaning.

If I find my position, my consciousness, that of one from home, nay, that of one in some sort of prison; if I find that I can neither rule the world in which I live nor my own thoughts or desires; that I cannot quiet my passions, order my likings, determine my ends, will my growth, forget when I would, or recall what I forget; that I cannot love where I would, or hate where I would; that I am no king over myself; that I cannot supply my own needs, do not even always know which of my seeming needs are to be supplied, and which treated as impostors; if, in a word, my own being is everyway too much for me; if I can neither understand it, be satisfied with it, nor better it—may it not well give me pause—the pause that ends in prayer?

When my own scale seems too large for my management; when I reflect that I cannot account for my existence, have had no poorest hand in it, neither, should I not like it, can do anything towards causing it to cease; when I think that I can do nothing to make up to those I love, any more than to those I hate, for evils I have done them and sorrows I have caused them; that in my worst moments I disbelieve in my best, in my best loathe my worst; that there is in me no wholeness, no unity; that life is not a good to me, for

I scorn myself—when I think all or any such things, can it be strange if I think also that surely there ought to be somewhere a being to account for me, one to account for himself, and make the round of my existence just; one whose very being accounts and is necessary to account for mine; whose presence in my being is imperative, not merely to supplement it, but to make to myself my existence a good?

George MacDonald (1824–1905)—Scottish Congregationalist pastor, novelist, myth maker, and poet, MacDonald had a profound influence on C. S. Lewis. Lewis said that MacDonald's *Phantastes* "baptized my imagination."

H. Richard Niebuhr

The Responsible Self

To some of us it seems that in the cross of Jesus Christ, in the death of such a man who trusts God and is responsible to him as a son, we face the great negative instance or the negation of the premise that God is love, and that unless this great negative instance—summarizing and symbolizing all the negative instances—is faced, faith in the universal power as God must rest on quicksand; in facing it, however, we have the demonstration in this very instance of a life-power that is not conquered, not destroyed. Reality maintains and makes powerful such life as this. The ultimate power does manifest itself as the Father of Jesus Christ through his resurrection from death. The resurrection is not manifest to us in physical signs but in his continuing Lordship—his session at the right hand of power, as the old creeds put it. So we apprehend the way of God as manifested not in creation and destruction but in these *and* resurrection, in the raising of the temporal to the eternal plane.

However adequate or inadequate our theories of at-onement or reconciliation may be, the fact remains: the movement beyond resignation to reconciliation is the movement inaugurated and maintained in Christians by Jesus Christ. By Jesus Christ men have been and are empowered to become sons of God—not as those who are saved out of a perishing world but as those who know that the world is being saved. That its being saved from destruction involves the burning up of an infinite amount of tawdry human works, that it involves the healing of a miasmic ocean of disease, the resurrection of the dead, the forgiveness of sins, the making good of an infinite number of irresponsibilities, that such making good is not done except by suffering servants who often do not know the name of Christ though they bear his image—all this Christians know. Nevertheless, they move toward their end and all endings as those who, knowing defeats, do not believe in defeat.

Helmut Richard Niebuhr (1894–1962)—An American Protestant theologian, professor of theology at Yale University, and author, Niebuhr combined in his works the study of Christianity and social science. His brother was the theologian Reinhold Niebuhr.

SAINT ATHANASIUS

On the Incarnation of the Word of God

For the searching and right understanding of the Scriptures there is need of a good life and a pure soul, and for Christian virtue to guide the mind to grasp, so far as human nature can, the truth concerning God the Word. One cannot possibly understand the teaching of the saints unless one has a pure mind and is trying to imitate their life. Anyone who wants to look at sunlight naturally wipes his eye clear first, in order to make, at any rate, some approximation to the purity of that on which he looks; and a person wishing to see a city or country goes to the place in order to do so. Similarly, anyone who wishes to understand the mind of the sacred writers must first cleanse his own life, and approach the saints by copying their deeds. Thus united to them in the fellowship of life, he will both understand the things revealed to them by God and, thenceforth escaping the peril that threatens sinners in the judgment, will receive that which is laid up for the saints in the kingdom of heaven. Of that reward it is written: "Eye has not seen nor ear heard, neither has entered into the heart of man the things that God has prepared" for them that live a godly life and love the God and Father in Christ Jesus our Lord, through Whom and with Whom be to the Father Himself, with the Son Himself, in the Holy Spirit, honor and might and glory to ages of ages. Amen.

Saint Athanasius (ca. 296–373)—Architect of the Nicene Creed (325) and champion of Trinitarian orthodoxy, Saint Athanasius was bishop of Alexandria. A defender of the faith and a prolific author, Saint Athanasius is considered a father of the church.

BROTHER LAWRENCE

The Practice of the Presence of God

I renounced, for the love of Him, everything that was not His; and I began to live, as if there was none but He and I in the world. Sometimes I considered myself before Him, as a poor criminal at the feet of his judge; at other times, I beheld Him in my heart as my Father, as my God; I worshiped Him the oftenest that I could, keeping my mind in His Holy Presence, and recalling it as often as I found it wandering from Him. I found no small trouble in this exercise, and yet I continued it, notwithstanding all the difficulties that I encountered, without troubling or disquieting myself when my mind had wandered involuntarily. I made this my business, as much all the day long as at the appointed times of prayer; for at all times, every hour, every minute, even in the height of my business, I drove away from my mind everything that was capable of interrupting my thought of God.

Such has been my common practice ever since I entered into religion; and though I have done it very imperfectly, yet I have found great advantages by it. These, I well know, are to be imputed solely to the mercy and goodness of God, because we can do nothing without Him; and *I* still less than any. But when we are faithful to keep ourselves in His Holy Presence, and set Him always before us; this not only hinders our offending Him, and doing anything that may displease Him, at least willfully, but it also begets in us a holy freedom, and, if I may so speak, a familiarity with God, wherewith we ask, and that successfully, the graces we stand in need of. In fine, by often repeating these acts, they become *habitual,* and the *Presence of* God is rendered as it were *natural* to us. Give him thanks, if you please, with me for His great goodness towards me, which I can never sufficiently marvel at, for the many favors He has done to so miserable a sinner as I am.

Brother Lawrence, or Nicholas Herman of Lorraine (1611–1691)—Low-born Frenchman and Carmelite monk, Brother Lawrence lived a saintly life, which is reflected in his writings.

Baron Friedrich von Hugel

Letters to a Niece

I am struck too at how the little regarded, the very simple, unbrilliant souls—souls treated by impatient others as more or less wanting, are exactly pretty often specially enlightened by God and specially near to Him. And there, no doubt, is the secret of this striking interconnection between an apparent minimum of earthly gifts and a maximum of heavenly light. The cause is not that gifts of quick-wittedness, etc., are bad, or are directly obstacles to Grace. No, no. But that quite ordinary intelligence—real slowness of mind—will quite well do as reflections of God's light, and that such limitations are more easily accompanied by simplicity, naiveness, recollection, absence of self-occupation, gratefulness, etc., which dispositions are necessary for the soul's union with God. Such souls more easily approach action—and more easily escape activity.

A wonderful thoughtful friend insisted to me that the soul's health and happiness depended upon a maximum of *zest* and as little as possible of excitement. *Zest* is the pleasure which comes from thoughts, occupation, etc., that fit into, that are continuous, applications, etc., of extant habits and interests of a good kind—duties and joys that steady us and give us balance and centrality. *Excitement* is the pleasure which comes from breaking loose, from fragmentariness, from losing our balance and centrality. Zest is natural warmth—excitement is fever heat. For zest—to be relished—requires much self-discipline and recollection—much spaciousness of mind: whereas the more distracted we are, the more racketed and impulse-led, the more we thirst for excitement and the more its sirocco air dries up our spiritual sap and makes us long for more excitement.

Baron Friedrich von Hugel (1853–1925)—A Roman Catholic philosopher of religion, von Hugel was considered too Protestant for some Catholics and too Catholic for some Protestants. Beloved by many from both parties, he was a mystic with a wise and broad intellectual grasp.

ANDERS NYGREN

Agape and Eros

Eros is essentially and in principle self-love. It is not too much to say that self-love is the basic form of all love that bears the stamp of Eros. Love for God and love for one's neighbor (or for any other object than God) can alike be reduced to self-love. Neighborly love, for which there would seem to be no room in the realm of Eros, is none the less provided with a satisfactory motive in the thought that it represents a stage in one's own ascent to higher things. And love for God is firmly founded on the conviction that He is the satisfaction of all man's needs and desires.

Agape, on the other hand, excludes all self-love. Christianity does not recognize self-love as a legitimate form of love. Christian love moves in two directions, towards God and towards its neighbor; and in self-love it finds its chief adversary, which must be fought and conquered. It is self-love that alienates man from God, preventing him from sincerely giving himself up to God, and it is self-love that shuts up a man's heart against his neighbor. When, quite early in the history of Christianity, self-love began to be spoken of as a third form of Christian love, and as the true basis of love for God and one's neighbor, this meant nothing else but a compromise between Eros-love and Agape-love. Agape was being accommodated to the essential principles of Eros, and was assuming its characteristic traits. The result of this compromise could only be that Agape succumbed to Eros; for a love towards God and one's neighbor that is based on self-love cannot be anything else but Eros-love.

Anders Theodor Samuel Nygren (1890–1978)—Swedish Lutheran minister and educator, Nygren was a prolific author whose works have been translated into ten languages. Nygren served on the World Council of Churches central committee from 1948 to 1954 and was later bishop of Lund.

Blaise Pascal

Pensées

Self-love.—The nature of self-love and of this human Ego is to love self only and consider self only. But what will man do? He cannot prevent this object that he loves from being full of faults and wants. He wants to be great, and he sees himself small. He wants to be happy, and he sees himself miserable. He wants to be perfect, and he sees himself full of imperfections. He wants to be the object of love and esteem among men, and he sees that his faults merit only their hatred and contempt. This embarrassment in which he finds himself produces in him the most unrighteous and criminal passion that can be imagined; for he conceives a mortal enmity against that truth which reproves him and which convinces him of his faults. He would annihilate it, but, unable to destroy it in its essence, he destroys it as far as possible in his own knowledge and in that of others; that is to say, he devotes all his attention to hiding his faults both from others and from himself, and he cannot endure either that others should point them out to him, or that they should see them.

Truly it is an evil to be full of faults; but it is a still greater evil to be full of them and to be unwilling to recognize them, since that is to add the further fault of a voluntary illusion. We do not like others to deceive us; we do not think it fair that they should be held in higher esteem by us than they deserve; it is not, then, fair that we should deceive them and should wish them to esteem us more highly than we deserve.

Thus, when they discover only the imperfections and vices which we really have, it is plain they do us no wrong, since it is not they who cause them; they rather do us good, since they help us to free ourselves from an evil, namely, the ignorance of these imperfections. We ought not to be angry at their knowing our faults and despising us; it is but right that they should know us for what we are and should despise us, if we are contemptible.

Blaise Pascal (1623–1662)—Philosopher, physicist, mathematician, inventor, and one of the most formidable intellects of seventeenth-century France, Pascal developed the laws of hydraulics and probability and is one of the fathers of the modern computer. His *Provincial Letters* are considered high French prose, and his *Pensées* (thoughts) were the beginnings of an apology for the Christian faith. Lewis's copies of Pascal's works are heavily annotated.

John Calvin

Institutes of the Christian Religion

1. Without knowledge of self there is no knowledge of God

Our wisdom, in so far as it ought to be deemed true and solid Wisdom, consists almost entirely of two parts: the knowledge of God and of ourselves. But as these are connected together by many ties, it is not easy to determine which of the two precedes and gives birth to the other. For, in the first place, no man can survey himself without forthwith turning his thoughts towards the God in whom he lives and moves; because it is perfectly obvious, that the endowments which we possess cannot possibly be from ourselves; nay, that our very being is nothing else than subsistence in God alone. In the second place, those blessings which unceasingly distill to us from heaven, are like streams conducting us to the fountain. Here, again, the infinitude of good which resides in God becomes more apparent from our poverty. In particular, the miserable ruin into which the revolt of the first man has plunged us, compels us to turn our eyes upwards; not only that while hungry and famishing we may ask what we want, but being aroused by fear may learn humility. For as there exists in man something like a world of misery, and ever since we were stripped of the divine attire our naked shame discloses an immense series of disgraceful properties every man, being stung by the consciousness of his own unhappiness, in this way necessarily obtains at least some knowledge of God. Thus, our feeling of ignorance, vanity, want, weakness, in short, depravity and corruption, reminds us that in the Lord, and none but He, dwell the true light of wisdom, solid virtue, exuberant goodness. We are accordingly urged by our own evil things to consider the good things of God; and, indeed, we cannot aspire to Him in earnest until we have begun to be displeased with ourselves.

John Calvin (1509–1564)—French Reformer and political leader in Geneva, Switzerland, Calvin published *The Institutes of the Christian Religion* when he was twenty-seven years old. Apart from Luther, Calvin is considered the most notable of the Protestant Reformers.

Joseph Addison

The Spectator

But a man can never have taken in his full measure of Knowledge, has not time to subdue his Passions, establish his Soul in Virtue, and come up to the Perfection of his Nature, before he is hurried off the Stage. Would an infinitely wise Being make such glorious Creatures for so mean a Purpose? Can he delight in the Production of such abortive Intelligences, such short-lived reasonable Beings? Would he give us Talents that are not to be exerted? Capacities that are never to be gratified? How can we find that Wisdom, which shines through all his Works, in the Formation of Man, without looking on this World as only a Nursery for the next, and believing that the several Generations of rational Creatures, which rise up and disappear in such quick Successions, are only to receive their first Rudiments of Existence here and afterwards to be transplanted into a more friendly Climate, where they may spread and flourish to all Eternity?

There is not, in my Opinion, a more pleasing and triumphant Consideration in Religion than this of the perpetual Progress which the Soul makes towards the Perfection of its Nature, without ever arriving at a Period in it. To look upon the Soul as going on from Strength to Strength, to consider that she is to shine for ever with new Accessions of Glory, and brighten to all Eternity; that she will be still adding Virtue to Virtue, and Knowledge to Knowledge; carries in it something wonderfully agreeable to that Ambition which is natural to the Mind of Man. Nay, it must be a prospect pleasing to God himself, to see his Creation for ever beautifying in his Eyes and drawing nearer to him, by greater degrees of semblance.

The Soul considered with its Creator, is like one of those Mathematical Lines that may draw nearer to another for all Eternity without a Possibility of touching it: And can there be a Thought so transporting, as to consider our selves in these perpetual Approaches to him, who is not only the Standard of Perfection but of Happiness!

Joseph Addison (1672–1719)—English man of letters and Chief Secretary of Ireland under the Whigs, Addison was educated at Magdalen College, Oxford, where C. S. Lewis later studied and taught. A path surrounding the College is named in Addison's honor, and Lewis walked this path while he said his prayers.

C. G. JUNG

Answer to Job

But the indwelling of the Holy Ghost, the third Divine Person, in man, brings about a Christification of many, and the question then arises whether these many are all complete God-men. Such a transformation would lead to insufferable collisions between them, to say nothing of the unavoidable inflation to which the ordinary mortal, who is not freed from original sin, would instantly succumb. In these circumstances it is well to remind ourselves of St. Paul and his split consciousness: on one side he felt he was the apostle directly called and enlightened by God, and, on the other side, a sinful man who could not pluck out the "thorn in the flesh" and rid himself of the Satanic angel who plagued him. That is to say, even the enlightened person remains what he is, and is never more than his own limited ego before the One who dwells in him, whose form has no knowable boundaries, who encompasses him on all sides, fathomless as the abysms of the earth and as vast as the sky.

Carl Gustav Jung (1875–1961)—Swiss psychiatrist and one-time collaborator with Freud, Jung founded the school of analytical psychology. Jung's interests in archetypes had an effect on literary interpretations; C. S. Lewis took issue with some of his ideas.

AUSTIN FARRER

The Glass of Vision

Our psychological make-up is admittedly an instrument of the most baffling complexity, liable to all sorts of disorders, and certain to color whatever passes through it. There will be something for the psychologist to study in Shakespeare and in Jeremiah: and indeed the province has not been neglected. But are we to conclude that the waywardness of our psyche prevents reality from exerting any real pressure or constraint upon us, except in so far as we bully and regiment her by hard logic and hard practicality? Does the reality of our friends not shine through our free emotional reactions to them? Do we see men most really when we let ourselves love them, and even poetize a bit about them, when we let our minds free to respond to them, or when we take them to pieces with analytical exactitude? If there is objective reality in the poetizing of love, in spite of all its riot of subjectivity, then there seems no reason why the apparent greatness of Shakespeare's poetry should not have something to do with realities of human existence pressing and constraining his fictions: nor is the question of the reality of the divine constraint on Jeremiah's mind excluded by anything we know.

Austin Farrer (1904–1968)—Doctor of Divinity and fellow of Trinity College, Oxford, and later warden of Keble College, Oxford, Austin Farrer was a member of the Inklings, a literary discussion group that included C. S. Lewis and J. R. R. Tolkien. Farrer was one of the witnesses at the civil marriage ceremony of C. S. Lewis and Joy Davidman, and he preached the sermon at Joy's funeral.

BARON FRIEDRICH VON HUGEL

Letters to a Niece

I want, then, to wish you a very rich, deep, true, straight and simple growth in the love of God, accepted and willed gently but greatly, *at the daily, hourly, cost of self.* I have to try my little old best more than ever at this, now; for I find that any and all brooding or sulking or useless self-occupation—any pride or vanity at once disturbs or dries up my incubation-work.

I am so glad you are trying to work the *Imitation* [*of Christ*] into your life: it is the only way to read it which is really worthy of what itself is so intensely alive. Now *there* is a book written as should be all religious books; they should be the quintessence of a long experience and fight in suffering and self-transformation. Also the twenty Huvelin sayings—they sprang straight from a life penetrated by God and the deepest love of Him.

I always feel the situation is different from more ordinary reading. I mean that religious reading should always be select, slow, ruminating, and given to comparatively few books or papers. So we will, when you are again ready, get on with our Greek things—plenty of *them*—and, alongside, and behind them all, will be our few deepest readings, full of prayer, full of self-humiliation, full of gentle attempts gently to will whatever suffering God may *kindly* send us. A Jesuit novice once told me, with kindling countenance, how grand he had found the practice of *at once* meeting suffering with joy. God alone can help us succeed in this; but what, Child, is Christianity, if it be not something like that?

Baron Friedrich von Hugel (1853–1925)—A Roman Catholic philosopher of religion, von Hugel was considered too Protestant for some Catholics and too Catholic for some Protestants. Beloved by many from both parties, he was a mystic with a wise and broad intellectual grasp.

7

"The Lack of the Divine"

Sin and Temptation

Austin Farrer

Lord, I Believe

Delight is naturally kindled by delight and God, who loves his children's love, delights in their delighting. How, then, is he disposed towards the causes of unwholesome sadness? The flame of happiness would run and spread, but for the obstacles my words and acts and attitudes oppose to it. How then is God disposed towards these acts and attitudes of mine? Does not he detest them? And what is the fate of things which earn the detestation of almighty love? Is it not that they should be abolished? God's hatred or wrath is, indeed, nothing but this, a simple desire for the abolition of its object; it is not, like mine, a passion. Surely, then, God's will is set to wither the tentacles of my unkindness, when they are twisted round my neighbor's throat.

He strikes at my unkindness, I tell myself, and not at me; he hates the sin, but loves the sinner. Here is a saying which must be true in substance, if there is to be any hope for sinful men; yet it is misleading and dangerous, if it suggests to me that my sin is not myself, but somehow detachable. For this is what Satan most wishes me to believe, and commonly makes me believe. According to Satan, and according to me, my sins occur during moral holidays, when my sober, working self is off the job. If he finds me gullible enough, the devil even tells me that I am not really involved at all, my sin is not the act even of a holiday self; it is a play of moral mice harmlessly tolerated, while I, the lordly cat, pretend to be asleep.

Austin Farrer (1904–1968)—Doctor of Divinity and fellow of Trinity College, Oxford, and later warden of Keble College, Oxford, Austin Farrer was a member of the Inklings, a literary discussion group that included C. S. Lewis and J. R. R. Tolkien. Farrer was one of the witnesses at the civil marriage ceremony of C. S. Lewis and Joy Davidman, and he preached the sermon at Joy's funeral.

Revelations of Divine Love

Often I wondered why, in the great foreseeing wisdom of God, the beginning of sin was not hindered, for then, I thought, all would have been well. Then the Lord spoke, "Sin has a part to play, but all shall be well"

After this the Lord reminded me of the longing that I had to him beforehand, and I saw that nothing held me back but sin. Then I looked upon the rest of mankind, and I thought, "If sin had not been, we should all have been clean like our Lord, just as he originally made us."

Thus, in my folly, I often wondered why the great foreseeing wisdom of God did not prevent sin from entering the world, for then, I thought, all should have been well. However, this line of reasoning only led to mourning and sorrow, not to a solution to the problem, and I should have left it behind.

But Jesus spoke to me all that I needed to understand, and here is what he said, "Sin has a part to play in my plan, but all shall be well, and all shall be well, and all manner of thing shall be well."

In this naked word, *sin,* our Lord brought to my mind all that is evil and shameful, and the utter wickedness which he bore for us both in his spirit and his body in the course of his life, passion, and death. All of this was showed me in a moment, for our good Lord did not desire to frighten me at this terrible sight.

So pain endures for a time. Its role is to purge us, make us to know ourselves, and it drives us to the Lord to plead for mercy. The passion of our Lord and the knowledge that his will will indeed be done gives us strength to bear up to all this.

Julian of Norwich (1342–?)—An English Benedictine nun, Julian of Norwich was very ill on May 8–9, 1373, and was visited with sixteen visions of God's love. She became a recluse and spent twenty years meditating on these visions, after which she wrote the *Revelations*.

Rudolph Otto

Religious Essays

Sin is the lack of the divine itself, it is not-to-have-God and not-to-wish-to-have-God; it is a very turning away from the Eternal as it reveals and imparts itself; in general terms it is the reluctance of the creature to be drawn to God, and lastly, the "natural man's" resistance against grace itself.

And thus the battle of the flesh against the spirit, in its highest sense, is determined by entirely different characteristics from those in the third stage. It is the difference between mere "conversion" of the will and the mystical "rebirth" of the soul. This being born again is no longer the active transfer of our will from the realm of inclination into that of obedience. It is, in the sense of the third chapter of the Gospel according to St. John, the conquest of the resistance of the natural man, to...overcome the natural aversion, indeed the horror, against that "entirely other" to which after all he is called. It is the complete giving up of the natural sphere of existence in favor of the divine spiritual, and accordingly the laying oneself open to receive divine grace, salvation, and blessedness itself. It is becoming faithful, and therefore not an act of will. One cannot of one's self enter upon faith. As has already been said, faith, in the deepest sense of the word, cannot be enjoined, it can only be "kindled," that is "given." It is *conversio passiva* in the scriptural sense: "Convert us, then we are converted" (Lamentations 5:3). And it is only here that the mysterious experience of the redemptive "struggle of conversion" appears, for this does not arise from antipathy to the law, being occasioned rather by the wholly mysterious resistance of the fleshly creature to the dominating, selective, searching, rescuing, forgiving, self-imparting *grace* of God.

Rudolph Otto (1869–1937)—German Protestant theologian, philosopher, and educator, Otto studied non-Christian religions, focusing particularly on religious experience.

Hilaire Belloc

The Green Overcoat

He was turning round irresolutely to seek once again for that Inverness, which he was now more confident than ever was not there, when the Devil, who has great power in these affairs, presented to his eyes, cast negligently over a chair, a GREEN OVERCOAT of singular magnificence....

Now the Devil during all Professor Higginson's life had had but trifling fun with him until that memorable moment. The opportunity, as the reader will soon discover, was (from the Devil's point of view) remarkable and rare. More, far more, than Professor Higginson's somewhat sterile soul was involved in the issue.

The Green Overcoat appeared for a few seconds seductive, then violently alluring, next—and in a very few seconds—irresistible.

Professor Higginson shot a sin-laden and frightened glance towards the light and the noise and the music within. No one was in sight. Through the open door of the rooms, whence the sound of the party came loud and fairly drunken, he saw no face turned his way. The hall itself was deserted. Then he heard a hurl of wind, a dash of rain on the hall window. With a rapidity worthy of a greater game, and to him most unusual, he whisked the garment from the chair, slipped into the shadow of the door, struggled into the Green Overcoat with a wriggle that seemed to him to last five weeks—it was, as a fact, a conjurer's trick for smartness—and it was on! The Devil saw to it that it fitted.

Hilaire Belloc (1870–1953)—Belloc was born in Paris, studied at Balliol College, Oxford, and became a British subject in 1906. He served in Parliament and then retired to full-time journalism and writing, during which time he edited several publications and wrote over one hundred works, many devoted to Catholic thought. He was a great friend of G. K. Chesterton's.

Blaise Pascal

Pensées

The Christian religion, then, teaches men these two truths; that there is a God whom men can know, and that there is a corruption in their nature which renders them unworthy of Him. It is equally important to men to know both these points; and it is equally dangerous for man to know God without knowing his own wretchedness, and to know his own wretchedness without knowing the Redeemer who can free him from it. The knowledge of only one of these points gives rise either to the pride of philosophers, who have known God, and not their own wretchedness, or to the despair of atheists, who know their own wretchedness, but not the Redeemer.

And, as it is alike necessary to man to know these two points, so is it alike merciful of God to have made us know them. The Christian religion does this; it is in this that it consists.

Let us herein examine the order of the world and see if all things do not tend to establish these two chief points of this religion: Jesus Christ is the end of all, and the center to which all tends. Whoever knows Him knows the reason of everything.

Those who fall into error err only through failure to see one of these two things. We can, then, have an excellent knowledge of God without that of our own wretchedness and of our own wretchedness without that of God. But we cannot know Jesus Christ without knowing at the same time both God and our own wretchedness.

The God of Abraham, the God of Isaac, the God of Jacob, the God of Christians, is a God of love and of comfort, a God who fills the soul and heart of those whom He possesses, a God who makes them conscious of their inward wretchedness, and His infinite mercy, who unites Himself to their inmost soul, who fills it with humility and joy, with confidence and love, who renders them incapable of any other end than Himself.

Blaise Pascal (1623–1662)—Philosopher, physicist, mathematician, inventor, and one of the most formidable intellects of seventeenth-century France, Pascal developed the laws of hydraulics and probability and is one of the fathers of the modern computer. His *Provincial Letters* are considered high French prose, and his *Pensées* (thoughts) were the beginnings of an apology for the Christian faith. Lewis's copies of Pascal's works are heavily annotated.

The Cloud of Unknowing

Sensuality is the faculty of our soul which affects and controls all our bodily reactions, and through which we know and experience the physical creation, both pleasant and unpleasant. It has two functions, one which looks after our physical needs, and one which provides for our physical appetites. It is the one and the same faculty that will grumble when the body is lacking essential requirements, yet when the need is met, will move it to take more than it requires to maintain and further our desires. It grumbles when its likes are not met, and it is highly delighted when they are.

Before man sinned, sensuality was so obedient to will, its master as it were, that it never led it into perverted physical pleasure or pain, or any pretended spiritual pleasure or pain, induced by the enemy of souls into our earthly minds. But it is not so now. Unless it is ruled by grace in the will, so that it is prepared to suffer humbly and wholly the consequences of original sin (which it feels when it is deprived of its wonted pleasures, and can only have those irritating things that are so good for it!), and unless it will control both its strong desires when it has its wonted pleasures, and its greedy delight when the improving irritations are gone, it will wallow, like some pig in the mire, so wretchedly and wildly in all the wealth of the world, and the filth of the flesh, that the whole of its life will be animal and physical rather than human and spiritual.

My spiritual friend, to such degradation as you see here have we fallen through sin. Can we be surprised then that we are totally and easily deceived when we seek to understand the meaning of spiritual words and actions, especially if we do not yet know the faculties of our soul and the way they work?

The Cloud of Unknowing is a late fourteenth-century mystical, contemplative work of Christian devotion. Though unknown, the author was probably a Dominican monk.

John Woolman

Essays

These poor Africans were people of a strange language and not easy to converse with, and their situation as slaves too generally destroyed that brotherly freedom which frequently subsists between us and inoffensive strangers. In this adverse condition, how reasonable is it to suppose that they would revolve in their distressed minds the iniquities committed against them and mourn!—mourn without any to comfort them?

Though through gradual proceedings in unrighteousness dimness has come over many minds, yet the nature of things are not altered. Long oppression has not made oppression consistent with brotherly love, nor length of time through several ages made recompense to the posterity of those injured strangers. Many of them lived and died without having their suffering case heard, and determined according to equity; and under a degree of sorrow on account of the wantonness, the vanity, and superfluity too common among us as a civil society, even while a heavy load of unrighteous proceedings lies upon us, do I now under a feeling of universal love and in a fervent concern for the real interest of my fellow members in society, as well as the interest of my fellow creatures in general, express these things.

Suppose an inoffensive youth, forty years ago, was violently taken from Guinea, sold here as a slave, labored hard till old age, and had children who are now living. Though no sum may properly be mentioned as an equal reward for the total deprivation of liberty, yet if the sufferings of this man be computed at no more than fifty pounds, I expect candid men will suppose it within bounds, and that his children have an equitable right to it.

Now when our minds are thoroughly divested of all prejudice in relation to the difference of color, and the love of Christ in which there is no partiality prevails upon us, I believe it will appear that a heavy account lies against us as a civil society for oppressions committed against people who did not injure us, and that if the particular case of many individuals were fairly stated, it would appear that there was considerable due to them.

I conclude with the words of that righteous judge in Israel: "Behold here I am; witness against me before the Lord and before his anointed: whose ox have I taken? or whose ass have I taken? or whom have I defrauded? whom have I oppressed? or of whose hand have I received any bribe to blind my eyes therewith? and I will restore it to you" (1 Samuel 12:3).

John Woolman (1720–1772)—American Quaker preacher and reformer, Woolman traveled throughout the American colonies and England preaching and promoting the abolition of slavery. He is best known for his *Journal*, which was published after his death.

Jakob Boehme

Dialogues

Do but think on the Words of our Lord Jesus Christ, when He said, "Except you be converted, and become as little Children, you shall not enter into the Kingdom of Heaven." There is no shorter Way than this; neither can there be a better Way found. Truly, Jesus says unto you, Unless you turn and become as a Child, hanging upon Him for All Things, you shall not see the Kingdom of God. This do, and Nothing shall hurt you; for you shall be at Friendship with all the Things that are, as you depend on the Author and Fountain of them, and become like Him, by such Dependence, and by the Union of your Will with His Will. But mark what I have further to say; and be not startled at it, though it may seem hard for you at first to conceive. If you will be like All Things, you must forsake All Things; you must turn your Desire away from them All, and not desire or hanker after any of them; you must not extend your Will to possess that for your own, or as your own, which is *Something,* whatever that Something is.

For as soon as ever you take Something into your Desire, and receive it into yourself for your OWN, or in Propriety, then this very Something (of whatever Nature it is) is the same with yourself; and this works with you in your Will, and you are then bound to protect it, and to take Care of it even as of your own Being. But if you do receive no Thing into your Desire, then you are free from All Things, and rule over all Things at once, as a Prince of God. For you have received Nothing for your own, and are Nothing to all Things; and all Things are as Nothing to you. You are as a Child, which understands not what a Thing is, and though you do perhaps understand it, yet you understand it without mixing with it, and without it sensibly affecting or touching your Perception, even in that Manner where God does rule and see all Things; He comprehending All, and yet Nothing comprehending Him.

Jakob Boehme (1575–1624)—A German Lutheran and mystic, Boehme was not formally educated and worked all of his life as a shoemaker. He read widely and wrote and published with considerable influence among the Pietists, Romantics, Idealists, and Cambridge Platonists.

BOETHIUS

The Consolation of Philosophy

The more varied your precious possessions, the more help you need to protect them, and the old saying is proved correct, he who has much, wants much. And the contrary is true as well, he needs least who measures wealth according to the needs of nature, and not the excesses of ostentation.

When a being endowed with a godlike quality in virtue of his rational nature thinks that his only splendor lies in the possession of inanimate goods, it is the overthrow of the natural order. Other creatures are content with what is their own, but you, whose mind is made in the image of God, seek to adorn your superior nature with inferior objects, oblivious of the great wrong you do your Creator. It was His will that the human race should rule all earthly creatures, but you have degraded yourself to a position beneath the lowest of all. If every good is agreed to be more valuable than whatever it belongs to, then by your own judgement when you account the most worthless of objects as goods of yours, you make yourself lower than those very things, and it is no less than you deserve. Indeed, the condition of human nature is just this; man towers above the rest of creation so long as he recognizes his own nature, and when he forgets it, he sinks lower than the beasts. For other living things to be ignorant of themselves, is natural; but for man it is a defect.

Anicius Boethius (ca. 480–524)—Philosopher, statesman, and Christian, Boethius was an advisor to the Ostrogothic king Theodoric after the sack of Rome. His *Consolation of Philosophy* was second only to the Bible as an influence on medieval thought and literature.

RICHARD ROLLE

Selected Works

Those that dwell in temporal plenty are beguiled by five things that they love: by riches, by dignity, by will, by power, and by worship. These bind them in sin and constrain them in faults; they are overcome by these lusts and never released but by death—but their release is too late, when there is nothing more but endless pain.

These things hinder them from despising the world, from the love of God, from knowledge of themselves and from the desire of the heavenly kingdom. No man may be saved unless he cease to love the world.

Let it be enough for you, therefore, having despised all other things, to love God, to praise God, to be with God, to rejoice in God, not to part from Him but to draw unto Him with unquenched desire. Compel yourself to despise the world that is so full of wretchedness, in which is abiding malice, destroying persecution, swelling wrath and devouring lust, false blame for sins, bitterness of slander; where all things are confused without order, where neither righteousness is loved nor truth approved, where faithfulness is unfaithful and friendship cruel, that stands in prosperity and falls in adversity.

There are yet other things that should move us to the despising of the world: the changing of the times, shortness of this present life, certain death, the uncertain chance of death, stability of everlasting things and vanity of present things, truth of the joys to come. Choose which you will: if you love the world, you shall perish with it; if you love Christ, with him shall you reign.

Richard Rolle of Hampole (ca. 1295–1349)—Rolle was born in Yorkshire and educated at Oxford, but he lived as a hermit and contemplative. He broke with the scholars of his day and wrote in the vernacular to reach those not formally trained in the gospel.

8

"Fatherly and Forgiving Goodness"

Grace and Redemption

John Bunyan

The Pilgrim's Progress

Now I could see in my dream that the High-way Christian was to travel on was protected on either side by a Wall, and the Wall was called Salvation. Burdened Christian began to run up the High-way, but not without great difficulty because of the load he was carrying on his back.

He ran this way until he came to a place on somewhat higher ground where there stood a Cross. A little way down from there was an open Grave. And I saw in my dream that just as Christian approached the Cross, his Burden came loose from his shoulders, fell from his back, and began to roll downward until it tumbled into the open Grave to be seen no more.

After this, Christian was glad and light. He exclaimed with a joyful heart, "Through His sorrows He has given me rest, and through His death He has given me life." Then he stood still for awhile to examine and ponder the Cross; for it was very surprising to him that the sight of the Cross alone had brought him complete deliverance from his Burden. So he continued to look and watch until springs of tears welled up in his eyes and came pouring down his cheeks.

Then, as he stood watching and weeping, three Shining Ones suddenly appeared and greeted him. "Be at peace!" The first announced. "Your sins are forgiven!" The second one stripped off his tattered clothing and dressed him in bright, new garments. After this, the third one set a mark upon his forehead and handed him a Scroll with a seal on it. He directed Christian to study the Scroll as he traveled and to present it upon his arrival at the Celestial Gate.

John Bunyan (1628–1675)—Son of a tinker, Bunyan became a Baptist preacher and was imprisoned in Bedford, England, for twelve years for unlicensed preaching. While in prison he wrote *The Pilgrim's Progress*. C. S. Lewis's article on John Bunyan is published in *Selected Literary Essays*.

GEORGE HERBERT

The Country Parson

The Country Parson, when any of his cure is sick, or afflicted with loss of friend, or estate, or any ways distressed, fails not to afford his best comforts, and rather goes to them, than sends for the afflicted, though they can, and otherwise ought to come to him. To this end he has thoroughly digested all the points of consolation, as having continual use of them, such as are from God's general providence extended even to lilies; from his particular, to his Church; from his promises, from the examples of all Saints, that ever were; from Christ himself, perfecting our Redemption no other way, than by sorrow; from the Benefit of affliction, which softens, and works the stubborn heart of man; from the certainty both of deliverance, and reward, if we faint not; from the miserable comparison of the moment of griefs here with the weight of joys hereafter. Besides this, in his visiting the sick, or otherwise afflicted, he follows the Church's counsel, namely, in persuading them to particular confession, laboring to make them understand the great good use of this ancient and pious ordinance, and how necessary it is in some cases: he also urges them to do some pious charitable works, as a necessary evidence and fruit of their faith, at that time especially: the participation of the holy Sacrament, how comfortable, and Sovereign a Medicine it is to all sin-sick souls; what strength, and joy, and peace it administers against all temptations, even to death itself, he plainly, and generally intimates to the disaffected, or sick person, that so the hunger and thirst after it may come rather from themselves, than from his persuasion.

George Herbert (1593–1633)—Anglican rector of the parish church of Bremerton, near Salisbury, Herbert was one of the seventeenth-century metaphysical poets.

JAMES MOFFATT

The Theology of the Gospels

Anticipations of the divine nature as implying self-sacrifice and sympathy had been already voiced here and there both within Judaism and Hellenism, by the fifty-third chapter of Isaiah, *e.g.*, by sayings like *In all their afflictions he was afflicted*—which the finer faith of the rabbis dwelt upon with emphasis, and also, throughout the higher reaches of Greek and Oriental thought, by the contemporary belief in the dying and suffering god of the cults. These are glimpses of the light that was coming into the world in full splendor through the person of Jesus Christ. But how difficult it was to believe that the higher life came through dying to self, and that it is divine to bear suffering willingly for the sake of others, is shown by Peter's blunt remonstrance. He was shocked at the notion of the son of God actually dreaming of anything so humiliating and unworthy as pain and self-sacrifice. The pageant of apocalyptic eschatology dazzled his eyes till they failed as yet to recognize where the true glory of life lay. It required the facts of the passion and the cross and the resurrection to convince the disciples that Jesus was right in His reading of God's character, and therefore He revealed the nature of the Father, not simply by telling men of His intuitions, but by acting as He believed in the line of God and pointing men, through what He did and suffered, to the essential spirit and motives of the Father. The parables enshrine with unrivalled clearness the fatherly and forgiving goodness of God.

James Moffatt (1870–1944)—Scottish scholar, theologian, professor at Mansfield College, Oxford, and Union Theological Seminary, New York, Moffatt is best known for his English translation of the Bible.

George MacDonald

Sir Gibbie

Doubtless Gibbie, as well as many a wiser man, might now and then make a mistake in the embodiment of his obedience, but even where the action misses the command, it may yet be obedience to him who gave the command, and by obeying one learns how to obey. I hardly know, however, where Gibbie blundered, except it was in failing to recognize the animals before whom he ought not to cast his pearls—in taking it for granted that, because his guardian was a minister, and his wife a minister's wife, they must therefore be disciples of the Jewish carpenter, the eternal Son of the Father of us all. Had he had more of the wisdom of the serpent, he would not have carried them the New Testament as an ending of strife, the words of the Lord as an enlightening law; he would perhaps have known that to try too hard to make people good, is one way to make them worse; that the only way to make them good is to be good—remembering well the beam and the mote; that the time for speaking comes rarely, the time for being never departs.

George MacDonald (1824–1905)—Scottish Congregationalist pastor, novelist, myth maker, and poet, MacDonald had a profound influence on C. S. Lewis. Lewis said that MacDonald's *Phantastes* "baptized my imagination."

Martin Luther

The Bondage of the Will

So it is not irreligious, idle, or superfluous, but in the highest degree wholesome and necessary, for a Christian to know whether or not his will has anything to do in matters pertaining to salvation. Indeed, let me tell you, this is the hinge on which our discussion turns, the crucial issue between us; our aim is, simply, to investigate what ability "free-will" has, in what respect it is the subject of Divine action and how it stands related to the grace of God. If we know nothing of these things, we shall know nothing whatsoever of Christianity, and shall be in worse case than any people on earth! He who dissents from that statement should acknowledge that he is no Christian; and he who ridicules or derides it should realize that he is the Christian's chief foe. For if I am ignorant of the nature, extent and limits of what I can and must do with reference to God, I shall be equally ignorant and uncertain of the nature, extent and limits of what God can and will do in me—though God, in fact, works all in all (cf. 1 Cor. 12:6). Now, if I am ignorant of God's works and power, I am ignorant of God himself; and if I do not know God, I cannot worship, praise, give thanks or serve Him, for I do not know how much I should attribute to myself and how much to Him. We need, therefore, to have in mind a clear-cut distinction between God's power and ours, and God's work and ours, if we would live a godly life.

So, you see, this point is a further item in any complete summary of Christianity. Self-knowledge, and the knowledge and glory of God, are bound up with it.

Martin Luther (1483–1546)—An Augustinian monk who became the father of the Protestant Reformation, Luther was an indefatigable theologian and pastor and champion of the doctrine of justification by "faith alone."

WALTER HILTON

The Scale of Perfection

Do not be surprised that the awareness of grace is sometimes withdrawn from the lover of God, for Holy Scripture says of the spouse: I sought Him and did not find Him; I called Him and He did not answer. That is, when I sink back into my natural weakness, grace is withdrawn; and if it is withdrawn, my failure is the cause, and not because He has departed from me. But His absence makes me feel my misery. I seek Him with great desire of heart, and He gives me no answer that I can recognize. And then I cry with all my soul: Return again, my Beloved. And yet it seems as though He did not hear me. The painful consciousness of self, the assaults of sensible love and fear, and my lack of spiritual strength, form as it were a continual cry from my soul to God. And yet He estranges Himself for a time and does not come, however much I cry to Him. And the reason is that He is sure of His lover; He knows he will not turn again fully to the love of the world, because he has no taste for it, and so He holds Himself aloof.

But at last, in His own good time, He returns, full of grace and truth, and visits the soul which is languishing with desire and sighing lovingly after His presence.

Happy is the soul that is ever nourished by the experience of love when He is present, and is upheld by desire of Him when He is absent. He is wise and well instructed in the love of God who keeps himself temperately and reverently in His presence, who contemplates Him lovingly without careless levity, and is patient and at ease in His absence without harmful despair and sore bitterness.

Walter Hilton (d. 1396)—Hilton was an English mystic and hermit and became the Augustinian Canon of Thurgarton in Nottinghamshire.

WILLIAM MORRIS

The Hollow Land

But one of those knights said: "Be not angry with me, Sir Florian, but do you think you will go to Heaven?"

"The saints! I hope so," I said, but one who stood near him whispered to him to hold his peace, so I cried out:

"O friend! I hold this world and all therein so cheap now, that I see not anything in it but shame which can any longer anger me; wherefore speak out."

"Then, Sir Florian, men say that at your christening some fiend took on him the likeness of a priest and strove to baptize you in the Devil's name, but God had mercy on you so that the fiend could not choose but baptize you in the name of the most holy Trinity: and yet men say that you hardly believe any doctrine such as other men do, and will at the end only go to Heaven round about as it were, not at all by the intercession of our Lady; they say too that you can see no ghosts or other wonders, whatever happens to other Christian men."

I smiled.—"Well, friend, I scarcely call this a disadvantage, moreover what has it to do with the matter in hand?"

How was this in Heaven's name? We had been quite still, resting, while this talk was going on, but we could hear the hawks chattering from the rocks, we were so close now.

And my heart sunk within me, there was no reason why this should not be true; there was no reason why anything should not be true.

"This, Sir Florian," said the knight again, "how would you feel inclined to fight if you thought that everything about you was mere glamour; this earth here, the rocks, the sun, the sky? I do not know where I am for certain, I do not know that it is not midnight instead of undern: I do not know if I have been fighting men or only *simulacra*—but I think, we all think, that we have been led into some devil's trap or other, and—and—may God forgive me my sins!—I wish I had never been born."

There now! he was weeping—they all wept—how strange it was to see those rough, bearded men blubbering there, and sniveling till the tears ran over their armor and mingled with the blood, so that it dropped down to the earth in a dim, dull, red rain.

My eyes indeed were dry, but then so was my heart; I felt far worse than weeping came to, but nevertheless I spoke cheerily.

"Dear friends, where are your old men's hearts gone to now? See now! This is a punishment for our sins, is it? well, for our forefathers' sins or our own? if the first, O brothers, be very sure that if we bear it manfully God will have something very good in store for us hereafter; but if for our sins, is it not certain that He cares for us yet, for note that He suffers the wicked to go their own ways pretty much; moreover brave men, brothers, ought to be the masters of *simulacra*—come, is it so hard to die once for all?"

William Morris (1834–1896)—An artist and poet who was educated at Exeter College, Oxford, Morris was a member of the Pre-Raphaelite Brotherhood. C. S. Lewis's piece on Morris in his *Selected Literary Essays* reveals his deep appreciation for Morris's writing, especially his fantasy.

RICHARD HOOKER

The Certainty and Perpetuity
of Faith in the Elect

It is true, such is our weak and wavering nature, we have no sooner received grace, but we are ready to fall from it: we have no sooner given our assent to the law, that it cannot fail, but the next conceit which we are ready to embrace is, that it may, and that it does fail. Though we find in ourselves a most willing heart to cleave unseparably unto God, even so far as to think unfeignedly with Peter, "Lord, I am ready to go with you into prison and to death;" yet how soon and how easily, upon how small occasions are we changed, if we be but a while let alone and left unto ourselves? The Galatians today, for their sakes which teach them the truth of Christ, content, if need were, to pluck out their own eyes, and the next day ready to pluck out theirs which taught them. The love of the Angel of the Church of Ephesus, how greatly inflamed, and how quickly slacked.

The higher we flow, the nearer we are unto an ebb, if men be respected as mere men, according to the wonted course of their alterable inclination, without the heavenly support of the Spirit.

Again, the desire of our ghostly enemy is so uncredible, and his means so forcible to overthrow our faith, that whom the blessed Apostle knew betrothed and made hand-fast unto Christ, to them he could not write but with great trembling: "I am jealous over you with a godly jealousy, for I have prepared you to one husband to present you a pure virgin unto Christ: but I fear, lest as the serpent beguiled Eve through his subtlety, so your minds should be corrupted from the simplicity which is in Christ." The simplicity of faith which is in Christ takes the naked promise of God, his bare word, and on that it rests.

Richard Hooker (ca. 1554–1600)—Theologian and defender of the Church of England during the reign of Queen Elizabeth, Hooker wrote *The Laws of Ecclesiastical Politie*. C. S. Lewis believed this book to be well written and full of wisdom and good sense.

CHARLES KINGSLEY

Discipline and Other Sermons

About justice and honesty we cannot deceive ourselves; for they are sanctification itself, righteousness itself, true holiness itself, the very likeness of God, and the very grace of God.

But if so, they come from God; they are God's gift, and not any natural product of our own hearts: and for that very reason we can and must keep them alive in us by prayer. As long as we think that the sentiment of justice and truth is our own, so long shall we be in danger of forgetting it, paltering with it, playing false to it in temptation, and by some injustice or meanness grieving (as St. Paul warns us) the Holy Spirit of God, who has inspired us with that priceless treasure.

But if we believe that from God, the fount of justice, comes all our justice; that from God, the fount of truth, comes all our truthfulness, then we shall cry earnestly to him, day by day, as we go about this world's work, to be kept from all injustice, and from all falsehood. We shall entreat him to cleanse us from our secret faults, and to give us truth in the inward parts; to pour into our hearts that love to our neighbor which is justice itself, for it works no ill to its neighbor, and so fulfils the law. We shall dread all meanness and cruelty, as sins against the very Spirit of God; and our most earnest and solemn endeavor in life will be, to keep innocence, and take heed to the thing that is right; for that will bring us peace at the last.

Charles Kingsley (1819–1875)—Anti-Tractarian, Anglican rector at Eversley in Hampshire, novelist, and literary critic, Kingsley was educated at Magdalene College, Cambridge, where C. S. Lewis was later the professor of medieval and renaissance literature. Kingsley is best known for his children's book *The Water Babies,* which Lewis liked very much.

Sir Gawain and the Green Knight

She lightly took her leave and left our hero,
Who had for her no further entertainment.
When she's gone, at once Sir Gawain's up,
Arrays himself in rich robed elegance,
Puts away with care his lover's keepsake,
Hiding it where handily he'll find it.
To the castle's chapel then he came,
Approached a priest in private, and he prayed him
To hear how he had lived and better lead him
To save his soul when he resumed his journey.
With fair intent he there confessed his faults,
His sins both great and small, and sought God's mercy
And asked for absolution of that man.
And he absolved and cleansed him so securely
The next day should have been the day of doom.
Afterwards he entertained the ladies,
Scintillating so with song and story,
High in spirits, as he'd seldom done there since his stay.

> When daytime drew to night
> They felt it fair to say
> He'd never shone so bright
> As he had shone that day.

Sir Gawain and the Green Knight—This popular fourteenth-century English poem comes from the Arthurian cycle and tells of Sir Gawain's quest to fulfill a vow made to a mysterious green knight. J. R. R. Tolkien translated and edited a version of this work.

9

"YOU SHALL FIND YOUR GROUND IN GOD"

Suffering

C. F. D. MOULE

The Sacrifice of Christ

St. Paul rejoices that his sufferings help to complete what is lacking of the afflictions of Christ. This seems to mean two things. First, that the Christian's sufferings (in this case the Apostle's) are a share in Christ's sufferings, because the Christian and Christ are somehow connected. To be in Christ is of course to share Christ's sufferings, and there are always more of them in the future for each of us. Secondly it means that there is a quota of sufferings which the whole Church, the corporate Christ, has to exhaust before God's plan of salvation is complete; and the Apostle rejoices to take his share—or more than his share—of these. Thus "the afflictions of Christ" are both Christ's historical sufferings, mystically shared and entered into in each Christian's sufferings, and the corporate Christ's, the Christian Church's afflictions. The two are in that sense one. There is plenty of evidence that the Christians took over the Jewish apocalyptic idea of the Messianic woes; and there was a certain quota of these to be completed before the end could come. So the afflictions of the (corporate) Christ, the Messianic community, were a necessary prelude to the consummation, and their endurance was cause for rejoicing. But also there is this more mystical conception of sharing Christ's Cross.

Charles Francis Digby Moule (1908–)—Cambridge lecturer and professor of divinity, Moule is an Anglican clergyman, biblical scholar, and prolific author.

JOHN DONNE

Devotions

No man is an island, entire of itself; every man is a piece of the continent, a part of the main. If a clod is washed away by the sea, Europe is the less, as well as if a promontory were, as well as if a manor of your friend's or of your own were: any man's death diminishes me, because I am involved in mankind, and therefore never send to know for whom the bells tolls; it tolls for you. Neither can we call this a begging of misery, or a borrowing of misery, as though we were not miserable enough of ourselves, but must fetch in more from the next house, in taking upon us the misery of our neighbors. Truly it were an excusable covetousness if we did, for affliction is a treasure, and scarce any man has enough of it. No man has affliction enough that is not matured and ripened by it, and made fit for God by that affliction. If a man carry treasure in bullion, or in a wedge of gold, and have none coined into current money, his treasure will not defray him as he travels. Tribulation is treasure in the nature of it, but it is not current money in the use of it, except we get nearer and nearer our home, heaven, by it. Another man may be sick too, and sick to death, and this affliction may lie in his bowels, as gold in a mine, and be of no use to him; but this bell, that tells me of his affliction, digs out and applies that gold to me: if by this consideration of another's danger I take my own into contemplation, and so secure myself, by making my recourse to my God, who is our only security.

John Donne (1572–1631)—One of the metaphysical poets, John Donne was raised a Roman Catholic and converted to Anglicanism. He was ordained in 1615 and eventually became the dean of St. Paul's Cathedral, London.

Thomas à Kempis

The Imitation of Christ

Whatever I can desire or imagine for my own comfort I look for not here but hereafter. For if I alone should have all the world's comforts and could enjoy all its delights, it is certain that they could not long endure. Therefore, my soul, you cannot enjoy full consolation or perfect delight except in God, the Consoler of the poor and the Helper of the humble. Wait a little, my soul, wait for the divine promise and you will have an abundance of all good things in heaven. If you desire these present things too much, you will lose those which are everlasting and heavenly. Use temporal things but desire eternal things. You cannot be satisfied with any temporal goods because you were not created to enjoy them.

Even if you possessed all created things you could not be happy and blessed; for in God, Who created all these things, your whole blessedness and happiness consists—not indeed such happiness as is seen and praised by lovers of the world, but such as that for which the good and faithful servants of Christ wait, and of which the spiritual and pure of heart, whose conversation is in heaven, sometime have a foretaste.

Vain and brief is all human consolation. But that which is received inwardly from the Truth is blessed and true. The devout man carries his Consoler, Jesus, everywhere with him, and he says to Him: "Be with me, Lord Jesus, in every place and at all times. Let this be my consolation, to be willing to forego all human comforting. And if Your consolation be wanting to me, let Your will and just trial of me be my greatest comfort. For You will not always be angry, nor will You threaten forever."

When consolation is taken away, do not at once despair but wait humbly and patiently for the heavenly visit, since God can restore to you more abundant solace.

This is neither new nor strange to one who knows God's ways, for such change of fortune often visited the great saints and prophets of old. Thus there was one who, when grace was with him, declared: "In my prosperity I said: 'I shall never be moved.'" But when grace was taken away, he adds what he experienced in himself: "You hid Your face, and I was troubled." Meanwhile he does not despair; rather he prays more earnestly to the Lord, saying: "To You, O Lord, will I cry; and I will make supplication to my God." At length, he receives the fruit of his prayer, and testifying that he was heard, says, "The Lord has heard, and has had mercy on me: the Lord became my helper." And how was he helped? "You have turned," he says, "my mourning into joy, and have surrounded me with gladness."

Thomas à Kempis (ca. 1380–1471)—Born at Kempin (thus the surname à Kempis) near Cologne, Germany, Thomas Hämmerlien entered the Augustinian monastery at Mount Saint Agnes, where he worked as a copyist and spiritual director. He was a mystic, and his *Imitation of Christ* is thought by many to be second only to the Bible in its spiritual influence on readers. It was highly valued by C. S. Lewis.

George Herbert

Life of Herbert by Izaak Walton

A Letter of Mr. George Herbert to his Mother, in her Sickness

But perhaps, being above the common people, our credit and estimation calls on us to live in a more splendid fashion: but, O God! how easily is that answered, when we consider that the blessings in the holy Scripture are never given to the rich, but to the poor. I never find "Blessed be the rich," or "Blessed be the noble"; but "Blessed be the meek," and, "Blessed be the poor," and, "Blessed be the mourners, for they shall be comforted." —And yet, O God! most carry themselves so, as if they not only desired, but even feared to be blessed. —And for afflictions of the body, dear Madam, remember the holy Martyrs of God, how they have been burned by thousands, and have endured such other tortures, as the very mention of them might beget amazement: but their fiery trials have had an end; and yours—which, praised be God, are less, are not like to continue long. I beseech you, let such thoughts as these moderate your present fear and sorrow; and know that if any of yours should prove a Goliath-like trouble, yet you may say with David, "That God, who has delivered me out of the paws of the lion and bear, will also deliver me out of the hands of this uncircumcised Philistine." —Lastly, for those afflictions of the soul; consider that God intends that to be as a Sacred Temple for himself to dwell in, and will not allow any room there for such an inmate as grief; or allow that any sadness shall be his competitor. And, above all, if any care of future things molest you, remember those admirable words of the Psalmist: "Cast your care on the Lord, and he shall nourish you." To which join that of St. Peter, "Casting all your care on the Lord, for he cares for you." What an admirable thing is this, that God puts his shoulder to our burden, and entertains our care for us, that we may the more quietly intend his service. To conclude, let me commend only one place more to you: Phillip. iv. 4. St. Paul says there, "Rejoice in the Lord always: and again I say, rejoice." He doubles it to take away the scruple of those that might say, What, shall we rejoice in afflictions? Yes. I say again, rejoice; so that it is not left to us to rejoice, or not rejoice; but, whatsoever befalls us, we must always, at all times, rejoice in the Lord, who takes care for us. And it follows in the next verse: "Let your moderation appear to all men: The Lord is at hand: Be careful for nothing." What can be said more comfortably? Trouble not yourselves; God is at hand, to deliver us from all, or in all. —Dear Madam, pardon my boldness, and accept the good meaning of

Your most obedient son,

George Herbert

George Herbert (1593–1633)—Anglican rector of the parish church of Bremerton, near Salisbury, Herbert was one of the seventeenth-century metaphysical poets.

Izaak Walton (1593–1683)—This English author wrote about the lives of John Donne, Richard Hooker, and George Herbert—authors included in this volume—but Walton is best known for *The Compleat Angler,* a book on fishing and moral reflection.

Emblems

What sullen star ruled my untimely birth,
That would not lend my days one hour of mirth?
How oft have these bare knees been bent to gain
The slender alms of one poor smile in vain!
How often, tired with the fastidious light,
Have my faint lips implored the shades of night!
How often have my nightly torments pray'd
For ling'ring twilight, glutted with the shade!
Day worse than night, night worse than day appears;
In fears I spend my nights, my day in tears:
I moan unpitied, groan without relief,
There is no end or measure of my grief.
The smiling flow'r salutes the day; it grows
Untouch'd with care; it neither spins nor sows:
Oh that my tedious life were like this flow'r,
Or freed from grief, or finish'd with an hour.

Francis Quarles (1592–1644)—Educated at Christ's College, Cambridge, Quarles was a Royalist, poet, pamphleteer, and literary critic. He wrote in the metaphysical poetic tradition and is best known for his collection of poems entitled *Emblems*.

JULIAN OF NORWICH

Revelations of Divine Love

The highest point that may be seen in the Passion is to think and know who He is that suffered. And in this He brought in part to mind the height and nobleness of the glorious Godhead, and therewith the preciousness and the tenderness of the blessed Body, which are together united; and also the degree to which mankind is loath to suffer pain. For as much as He was most tender and pure, so He was most strong and mighty to suffer.

And for every man's sin that shall be saved He suffered: and every man's sorrow and desolation He saw, and sorrowed for kindness and love. For as long as He was capable of feeling, He suffered for us and sorrowed for us; and now He is risen, yet still He suffers with us.

And I, beholding all this by His grace, saw that His love for our souls was so strong that willingly He chose suffering with great desire, and mildly He suffered it with well-pleasing. And the soul that beholds it, when it is touched by grace, shall see that the pains of Christ's Passion pass all pains: all pains, that is to say, which shall be turned into everlasting, surpassing joys by the virtue of Christ's Passion.

Julian of Norwich (1342–?)—An English Benedictine nun, Julian of Norwich was very ill on May 8–9, 1373, and was visited with sixteen visions of God's love. She became a recluse and spent twenty years meditating on these visions, after which she wrote the *Revelations*.

Martin Luther

Table Talk

The Scriptures show two manner of sacrifices acceptable to God. The first is called a sacrifice of thanks or praise, and is when we teach and preach God's Word purely, when we hear and receive it with faith, when we acknowledge it, and do everything that tends to the spreading of it abroad, and thank God from our hearts for the unspeakable benefits which through it are laid before us, and bestowed upon us in Christ, when we praise and glorify him, etc. "Offer unto God thanksgiving." "He that offers thanks praises me." "Thank the Lord, for he is gracious, because his mercy endures for ever." "Praise the Lord, O my soul, and all that is within me praise his holy name. Praise the Lord, O my soul, and forget not all his benefits."—Psalms.

Secondly, when a sorrowful and troubled heart in all manner of temptations has his refuge in God, calls upon him in a true and upright faith, seeks help of him, and waits patiently upon him. Hereof the Psalms, "In my trouble I called upon the Lord, and he heard me at large." "The Lord is nigh unto them that are of a contrite heart, and will save such as be of an humble spirit." "The sacrifice of God is a troubled spirit; a broken and contrite heart, O God, shall you not despise." And again: "Call upon me in the time of need, so will I deliver you, and you shall praise me."

Martin Luther (1483–1546)—An Augustinian monk who became the father of the Protestant Reformation, Luther was an indefatigable theologian and pastor and champion of the doctrine of justification by "faith alone."

John Donne

Donne's Sermons

Every man might justly say, "I am the man that has seen affliction," and come to say, with the Apostle Paul, "Who is weak, and I am not weak too? Who is offended, and I am not affected with it?"

The strongest, the most powerful of men are noted in the Scriptures. They, the strongest, the mightiest, they that thought themselves safest and sorrow-proof, are afflicted. The dearest beloved of God, and those of whose service God may have use in his Church, they are apt to be hindered in their service by these afflictions. Nothing makes a man so great among men, nothing makes a man so necessary to God that he can escape afflictions. These afflictions are his, the Lord's.

Christ saw his afflictions. Afflictions did not blind him, not stupefy him. Affliction did not make him insensible of affliction (which is a frequent, but a desperate condition). He saw it. And he maintained the dignity of his station. Still he played the man; still he survived to glorify God and to be an example to other men of patience under God's corrections, and of thankfulness in God's deliverance.

It is a particular comfort that our afflictions are from the Lord.

In the first treason against ourselves, in Adam's rebellion, who was not in his loins? And in the second treason, in the treason against Christ Jesus, all our sins were upon his shoulders. In those two treasons we have had no exception, no exemption. That penalty for our first treason in Adam we do bear. And would any wish to be excepted from imitation of Jesus' passion and fulfilling his sufferings in his body, in bearing cheerfully the afflictions and tribulations of this life?

John Donne (1572–1631)—One of the metaphysical poets, John Donne was raised a Roman Catholic and converted to Anglicanism. He was ordained in 1615 and eventually became the dean of St. Paul's Cathedral, London.

Many say they have no peace nor rest, but so many crosses and trials, afflictions and sorrows, that they know not how they shall ever get through them. Now he who in truth will perceive and take note, perceives clearly, that true peace and rest lie not in outward things; for if it were so, the Evil Spirit also would have peace when things go according to his will which is nowise the case; for the prophet declares, "There is no peace, says my God, to the wicked." And therefore we must consider and see what is that peace which Christ left to His disciples at the last, when He said: "My peace I leave with you, My peace I give unto you." We may perceive that in these words Christ did not mean a bodily and outward peace; for His beloved disciples, with all His friends and followers, have ever suffered, from the beginning, great affliction, persecution, nay, often martyrdom, as Christ Himself said: "In this world you shall have tribulation." But Christ meant that true, inward peace of the heart, which begins here, and endures forever hereafter. Therefore He said: "Not as the world gives," for the world is false, and deceives in her gifts. She promises much, and performs little. Moreover there lives no man on earth who may always have rest and peace without troubles and crosses, with whom things always go according to his will; there is always something to be suffered here, turn which way you will. And as soon as you are quit of one assault, perhaps two come in its place. Wherefore yield yourself willingly to them, and seek only that true peace of the heart, which none can take away from you, that you may overcome all assaults. Thus then, Christ meant that inward peace which can break through all assaults and crosses of oppression, suffering, misery, humiliation and what more there may be of the like, so that a man may be joyful and patient therein, like the beloved disciples and followers of Christ.

Theologia Germanica—Of unknown authorship, *Theologia Germanica* was discovered by Martin Luther in 1516. Luther said, "Next to the Bible and St. Augustine, no book has ever come into my hands from which I have learnt more of God and Christ, and man and all things that are."

CHARLES KINGSLEY

Discipline and Other Sermons

He has time, and he has will. No human being so mean, no human sorrow too petty, but what he has the time and the will, as well as the power, to have mercy on it, because he is the Son of Man. Therefore he will turn aside even to you, whoever you are, who are weary and heavy laden, and can find no rest for your soul, at the very moment, and in the very manner, which is best for you. When you have suffered long enough, he will establish, strengthen, settle you. He will bind up your wounds, and pour in the oil and the wine of his spirit—the Holy Ghost, the Comforter; and will carry you to his own inn, whereof it is written, He shall hide you secretly in his own presence from the provoking of men; he shall keep you in his tabernacle from the strife of tongues. He will give his servants charge over you to keep you in all your ways; and when he comes again, he will repay them, and fetch you away, to give you rest in that eternal bosom of the Father, from which you, like all human souls, came forth at first, and to which you shall at last return, with all human souls who have in them that spirit of humanity, which is the spirit of God, and of Christ, and of eternal life.

Charles Kingsley (1819–1875)—Anti-Tractarian, Anglican rector at Eversley in Hampshire, novelist, and literary critic, Kingsley was educated at Magdalene College, Cambridge, where C. S. Lewis was later the professor of medieval and renaissance literature. Kingsley is best known for his children's book *The Water Babies,* which Lewis liked very much.

JOHN DONNE

Words of Consolation

Let no man be disheartened nor discouraged if he have brought a good conscience and faithful labor to the service of the Lord. Let him not think his wages the worse paid if God do mingle bodily sickness, temporal losses, personal disgraces, with his labors. Let him not think that God should not do thus to them that wear out themselves in his service, for the best part of our wages is adversity, because that gives us a true fast and a right value of our prosperity. The prophet Jeremiah had it; the best of his rank must.

No man is excused of subsequent afflictions by precedent, nor of falling into more by having borne some already. Elijah reckoned too hastily when he told God, "Lord, take away my life." God had more to lay upon him. A last year's fever prevents not this, nor a sickness in the fall another in the spring. Men are not such as a grove of trees, that being felled now stand safe from the axe for a dozen years after. But our afflictions are as beggars; they tell others and send more after them. Sickness does but usher in poverty, and poverty contempt, and contempt dejection of spirit. No man may refuse a warrant demanding a loan because he has lent before. And though afflictions be not of God's revenue (for afflictions borne grudgingly are not real service to God), yet they are of his subsidies, and he has additional glory out of our afflictions. The more afflictions he sends us, the more glory may we return to him.

John Donne (1572–1631)—One of the metaphysical poets, John Donne was raised a Roman Catholic and converted to Anglicanism. He was ordained in 1615 and eventually became the dean of St. Paul's Cathedral, London.

GEORGE HERBERT

The Pulley

When God at first made man,
Having a glass of blessings standing by;
"Let us," said he, "pour on him all we can;
Let the world's riches, which dispersed lie,
    Contract into a span."

So strength first made a way;
Then beauty flow'd, then wisdom, honor, pleasure;
When almost all was out, God made a stay,
Perceiving that alone of all his treasure,
    Rest in the bottom lay.

"For if I should," said he,
"Bestow this jewel also on my creature,
He would adore my gifts instead of me,
And rest in Nature, not the God of Nature:
    So both should losers be.

"Yet let him keep the rest,
But keep them with repining restlessness;
Let him be rich and weary, that at least,
If goodness lead him not, yet weariness
    May toss him to my breast."

George Herbert (1593–1633)—Anglican rector of the parish church of Bremerton, near Salisbury, Herbert was one of the seventeenth-century metaphysical poets.

Thomas à Kempis

The Imitation of Christ

When comfort is withdrawn, do not be cast down, but humbly and patiently await the visitation of God, for He is able and powerful to give you more grace and more spiritual comfort than you first had. Such alteration of grace is no new thing and no strange thing to those who have had experience in the way of God. Such alteration was found many times in the great saints and the holy prophets, and so the prophet David says: "I have said in my abundance, I shall not be moved forever." That is to say, when David had abundance of spiritual comfort, he said to our Lord that he trusted he would never be deprived of such comfort. But afterwards, when grace withdrew itself, David said: "You have withdrawn your face from me, and I am perturbed." That is to say: O Lord, You have withdrawn Your spiritual comfort from me, and I am left in great trouble and depression. Yet David did not despair because of this, but prayed heartily to our Lord and said: "To You shall I cry, O Lord, and I shall make petition to my God." That is, I shall busily cry to You, O Lord, and I shall humbly pray for Your grace and comfort. And soon he had the effect of his prayer, as he himself bears witness, saying: "Our Lord has heard my prayer and has had mercy on me and has now again sent me spiritual help and comfort." And therefore he said afterwards: "Lord, You have turned my joy into sorrow and You have encompassed me about with heavenly gladness."

Thomas à Kempis (ca. 1380–1471)—Born at Kempin (thus the surname à Kempis) near Cologne, Germany, Thomas Hämmerlien entered the Augustinian monastery at Mount Saint Agnes, where he worked as a copyist and spiritual director. He was a mystic, and his *Imitation of Christ* is thought by many to be second only to the Bible in its spiritual influence on readers. It was highly valued by C. S. Lewis.

10

"INEXPRESSIBLE SWEETNESS"

Prayer and Contemplation

SAMUEL JOHNSON

Dr. Johnson's Prayers

Almighty and most merciful Father, who loves those whom You punish, and turns away your anger from the penitent, look down with pity upon my sorrows, and grant that the affliction which it has pleased You to bring upon me, may awaken my conscience, enforce my resolutions of a better life and impress upon me such conviction of your power and goodness, that I may place in You my only felicity, and endeavor to please You in all my thoughts, words, and actions. Grant, O Lord, that I may not languish in fruitless and unavailing sorrow, but that I may consider from whose hand all good and evil is received, and may remember that I am punished for my sins, and hope for comfort only by repentance. Grant, O merciful God, that by the assistance of your Holy Spirit I may repent, and be comforted, obtain that peace which the world cannot give, pass the residue of my life in humble resignation and cheerful obedience; and when it shall please You to call me from this mortal state, resign myself into your hands with faith and confidence, and finally obtain mercy and everlasting happiness, for the sake of Jesus Christ our Lord. *Amen.*

Samuel Johnson (1709–1784)—A lexicographer and literary critic, Johnson is considered by some, including Malcolm Muggeridge, to be among the greatest Englishmen of letters. Nevill Coghill compared C. S. Lewis to Samuel Johnson in terms of his physical stature and his scholarship and wit.

MARTIN LUTHER

Table Talk

Our Savior Christ as excellently as briefly comprehends in the Lord's prayer all things needful and necessary. Except under troubles, trials, and vexations, prayer cannot rightly be made. God says: "Call on me in the time of trouble"; without trouble it is only a bald prattling, and not from the heart; 'tis a common saying: "Need teaches to pray." And though the papists say that God well understands all the words of those that pray, yet St. Bernard is far of another opinion, who says: God hears not the words of one that prays, unless he that prays first hears them himself. The pope is a mere tormenter of the conscience. The assemblies of his greased crew, in prayer, were altogether like the croaking of frogs, which edified nothing at all; mere sophistry and deceit, fruitless and unprofitable. Prayer is a strong wall and fortress of the church; it is a godly Christian's weapon, which no man knows or finds, but only he who has the spirit of grace and of prayer.

The three first petitions in our Lord's prayer comprehend such great and celestial things, that no heart is able to search them out. The fourth contains the whole policy and economy of temporal and house government, and all things necessary for this life. The fifth fights against our own evil consciences, and against original and actual sins, which trouble them. Truly that prayer was penned by wisdom itself; none but God could have done it.

Martin Luther (1483–1546)—An Augustinian monk who became the father of the Protestant Reformation, Luther was an indefatigable theologian and pastor and champion of the doctrine of justification by "faith alone."

SAINT BERNARD OF CLAIRVAUX

On Loving God

You whom the Holy Spirit is urging to act that your soul may become the Bride of God, must... "sit alone and keep silence" as the prophet says.... Get away then I tell you, not physically but in mind and in intention, in spirit and devotion; for the Lord Christ is Himself a Spirit, and it is spiritual solitude that He requires of you, though bodily withdrawal is not without its uses, when it may be had, especially in a time of prayer. You have His own commandment in the matter, "When you pray, enter into your room and when you have shut the door, pray." He, Himself practiced what He preached. He would spend all night in prayer, not only hiding from the crowds, but not allowing any even of His closest friends to come with Him. Even at the last, when He was hastening to His willing death, though He had taken three with Him, He withdrew even from them when He desired to pray. You must do likewise, when you want to pray.

He who would pray must choose the best time to do so as well as the best place. A time of leisure is the fittest and most suitable, especially the silence of the night; for prayer is freer in the night and purer too. How confidently does prayer mount up, unknown to any except God and the holy angel who receives it on the heavenly altar! How acceptable and clear it is in its modesty then, how peaceful and serene with no noise or interruption to disturb it!

Saint Bernard of Clairvaux (1090–1153)—Mystic, monastic reformer, and influential figure in the twelfth-century church, Saint Bernard founded the Cistercian Monastery at Clairvaux.

RICHARD BAXTER

The Saint's Everlasting Rest

Concerning *the fittest place* for heavenly contemplation, it is sufficient to say that the most convenient is *some private retirement*. Our spirits need every help, and to be freed from every hindrance in the work. If, in private prayer, Christ directs us to "enter into our closet and shut the door, that our Father may see us in secret," so should we do this in meditation. How often did Christ himself retire to some mountain, or wilderness, or other solitary place! I give not this advice for occasional meditation, but for that which is set and solemn. Therefore withdraw yourself from all society, even that of godly men, that you may awhile enjoy the society of your Lord. If a student cannot study in a crowd, who exercises only his invention and memory, much less should you be in a crowd, who are to exercise all the powers of your soul, and upon an object so far above nature. We are fled so far from superstitious solitude, that we have even cast off the solitude of contemplative devotion. We seldom read of God's appearing by himself, or by his angels, to any of his prophets or saints, in a crowd: but frequently when they were alone.

Richard Baxter (1615–1691)—Although he was an Anglican chaplain during the English Civil War and chaplain to the king after the Restoration, Richard Baxter left the Church of England at the time of the Act of Uniformity and became a leader of the Nonconformists. Baxter published his views and preached to large audiences, for which he was arrested twice and spent a total of eighteen years in prison. C. S. Lewis took the term "mere Christianity" from Baxter's *The Saint's Everlasting Rest*.

BROTHER LAWRENCE

The Practice of the Presence of God

Since, by His mercy, He gives us still a little time, let us begin in earnest, let us redeem the time that is lost, let us return with a whole-hearted trust to this Father of Mercies, who is always ready to receive us into His loving arms. Let us renounce, and renounce generously, with single heart, for the love of Him, all that is not His; He deserves infinitely more. Let us think of Him unceasingly; in Him let us put all our confidence. I doubt not but that we shall soon experience the effects of it in receiving the abundance of His grace, with which we can do all things, and without which we can do naught but sin.

We cannot escape the dangers which abound in life, without the actual and continual help of God; let us then pray to Him for it continually. How can we pray to Him without being with Him? How can we be with Him, but in thinking of Him often? And how can we have Him often in our thoughts, unless by a holy habit of thought which we should form? You will tell me that I am always saying the same thing: it is true, for this is the best and easiest method that I know; and as I use no other, I advise the whole world to it. We must know before we can love. In order to know God, we must often think of Him; and when we come to love Him, we shall also think of Him often, for our heart will be with our treasure!

Brother Lawrence, or Nicholas Herman of Lorraine (1611–1691)—Low-born Frenchman and Carmelite monk, Brother Lawrence lived a saintly life, which is reflected in his writings.

Samuel Johnson

Dr. Johnson's Prayers

O God, the Creator and Preserver of all Mankind, Father of all mercies, I your unworthy servant do give You most humble thanks, for all your goodness and loving-kindness to me. I bless You for my Creation, Preservation, and Redemption, for the knowledge of your Son Jesus Christ, for the means of Grace and the Hope of Glory. In the days of Childhood and Youth, in the midst of weakness, blindness, and danger, you have protected me; amid Afflictions of Mind, Body, and Estate, You have supported me; and amid vanity and Wickedness You have spared me. Grant, O merciful Father, that I may have a lively sense of your mercies. Create in me a contrite Heart, that I may worthily lament my sins and acknowledge my wickedness, and obtain Remission and forgiveness, through the satisfaction of Jesus Christ. And, O Lord, enable me, by your Grace, to redeem the time which I have spent in Sloth, Vanity, and wickedness; to make use of your Gifts to the honor of your Name; to lead a new life in your Faith, Fear, and Love; and finally to obtain everlasting Life. Grant this, Almighty Lord, for the merits and through the mediation of our most holy and blessed Savior Jesus Christ; to whom, with You and the Holy Ghost, Three Persons and one God, be all honor and Glory, World without end. *Amen.*

Samuel Johnson (1709–1784)—A lexicographer and literary critic, Johnson is considered by some, including Malcolm Muggeridge, to be among the greatest Englishmen of letters. Nevill Coghill compared C. S. Lewis to Samuel Johnson in terms of his physical stature and his scholarship and wit.

WALTER HILTON

The Ladder of Perfection

You may through devout and continuous beholding of the meekness of his incarnate humanity, feel his goodness and the grace of his divinity. This may come when your desire is somewhat reshaped, aided and liberated from all carnal thoughts and appetites. Then, when your heart is mightily uplifted by the power of the Holy Spirit into a spiritual apprehension and delight in Him, and is held there continuously through the time of your prayer, you will have little concern for earthly things, and your mind will pay little attention to them.

If you pray in this spirit, then you pray well. For prayer is nothing if not an ascending desire of the heart unto God, with a corresponding withdrawal of the heart from all earthly thoughts. And so prayer is likened to a fire, which of its own nature leaves the earth and strives ever upward, ascending into the air. Just so, desire in prayer, when it is touched and lit by that spiritual fire which is God Himself, is ever ascending unto Him from whom it comes.

Not all those who talk about the "fire of love" well understand what it is. Indeed, *what* it is I cannot tell you myself, except this much: it is not of the body, nor is it experienced physically. A soul may feel it in prayer, or in devotion, and that soul will still be, of course, in the body. But it does not feel this fire by any physical sense. For even though it is possible that it will work so fervently in a soul that the body feels the heat and becomes, as it were, burning for a sympathetic travail within the spirit, nevertheless the fire of love is not itself a physical sensation. It lives only in the spiritual desires of the soul.

Walter Hilton (d. 1396)—Hilton was an English mystic and hermit and became the Augustinian Canon of Thurgarton in Nottinghamshire.

COVENTRY PATMORE

The Rod, the Root, and the Flower

The imagination has a mighty and most real and necessary function in the life of faith. "We are saved by hope," but we cannot hope for what we cannot or do not apprehend. It is written, "He shall fulfil all your desires," and "your heart" (*i.e.* your desire) "shall live for ever." Every felicity, however dimly divined by the imagination as to its form, shall be fulfilled beyond thought and in a form more perfect than we know how to picture to ourselves, where, for them that believe, good things are laid up, "beyond all that they know how to desire or imagine." We *cannot* desire any good which is not a reality and a destined part of our eternity if we attain, and our imaginations of felicity are both samples and promises. The great praise of a contemplative life is that it is the seed-time of the celestial harvest. A true contemplative will receive into his heart and apprehension in half an hour more of these inspired initiatory pledges, which are seeds as well as promises, than another will acquire in a whole lifetime; and the harvest will be in proportion to the sowing. The more extravagant and audacious your demands the more pleasing to God will be your prayer; for his joy is in giving; but He cannot give that for which you have not acquired a capacity; and desire is capacity. Take care, however, that you do not waste your strength and craze your brain by striving to acquire desires which are not human and natural; for heaven is but nature and humanity fulfilled, and God speaks His promises not in the active effort but the receptive silence of thought and endeavor.

Coventry Patmore (1823–1896)—The works of this Victorian poet, who is best known for *The Angel in the House*, *The Unknown Eros*, and *The Root and the Flower*, are a mixture of homeyness, erotic mysticism, and spirituality. C. S. Lewis expressed appreciation for Patmore in his letters.

Francis Bacon

The Moral and Historical Works

It had been hard for him that spoke it to have put more truth and untruth together in few words than in that speech, "Whoever is delighted in solitude, is either a wild beast or a god": for it is most true, that a natural and secret hatred and aversion towards society in any man has somewhat of the savage beast; but it is most untrue that it should have any character at all of the divine nature, except it proceed, not out of a pleasure in solitude, but out of a love and a desire to sequester a man's self for a higher conversation: such as is found to have been falsely and feignedly in some of the heathen...and truly and really in divers of the ancient hermits and holy fathers of the Church. But little do men perceive what solitude is, and how far it extends; for a crowd is not company, and faces are but a gallery of pictures, and talk but a tinkling cymbal, where there is no love...it is a mere and miserable solitude to want true friends, without which the world is but a wilderness; and even in this sense also of solitude, whoever in the frame of his nature and affections is unfit for friendship, he takes it out of the beast, and not from humanity.

Francis Bacon (1561–1626)—Cambridge-educated author, statesman, and philosopher, Sir Francis Bacon was knighted in 1603. His inductive method of experimentation made a profound impact on scientific methodology.

BROTHER LAWRENCE

The Practice of the Presence of God

My most usual method is this simple attention and this absorbing, passionate regard to God, to Whom I find myself often attached with greater sweetness and delight, than that of an infant at his mother's breast: so that, if I dare use the expression, I should choose to call this state the bosom of God, by reason of the inexpressible sweetness which I taste and experience there. If sometimes my thoughts wander from it by necessity or by infirmity, I am soon recalled by inward emotions, so charming and delightful that I am confused to mention them.

I beg you to reflect rather upon my great wretchedness, of which you are fully informed, than upon the great favors which God does me, all unworthy and ungrateful as I am.

As for my set hours of prayer, they are only a continuation of the same exercise. Sometimes I consider myself as a stone in the hands of a carver, whereof he wills to make a statue: presenting myself thus before God, I beseech Him to render me entirely like Himself, and to fashion in my soul His Perfect Image.

At other times so soon as I apply myself to prayer, I feel my whole spirit and my whole soul lift itself up without any trouble or effort of mine; and it remains as it were in elevation, fixed firm in God as in its center and its resting-place.

I know that some charge this state with inactivity, delusion, and self-love. I avow that it is a holy inactivity, and would be a happy self-love, were the soul in that state capable of such; because, in fact, while the soul is in this repose, it cannot be troubled by such acts, as it was formerly accustomed to, and which were then its support, but which would now rather injure than assist it.

Yet I cannot bear that this should be called delusion; because the soul which thus enjoys God, desires herein nothing but Him. If this be delusion in me, it is for God to remedy it. May He do with me what He pleases: I desire only Him, and want to be wholly devoted to Him. You will, however, oblige me in sending me your opinion, to which I always pay great deference, for I have a very special esteem for your Reverence, and, am, in our Lord, my Reverend Father,—Yours, etc.

Brother Lawrence, or Nicholas Herman of Lorraine (1611–1691)—Low-born Frenchman and Carmelite monk, Brother Lawrence lived a saintly life, which is reflected in his writings.

Richard Rolle

Selected Works

Every contemplative loves solitude, that he may be hindered by no man, that he may more fervently and more often be practiced in his desires. Whence it is known therefore that contemplative life is more worthy and more meritorious than active life; and all contemplatives, loving solitary life by the agency of God, and because of the sweetness of contemplation, are especially fervent in love.

A truly contemplative man is set towards the invisible light with such great desire that by men he is often deemed a fool or insane; and that is because his mind is deeply inflamed with the love of Christ, his bodily bearing changes outwardly, and his body also departing from all earthly works, it makes the child of God look like a man out of his mind.

A devout soul given to contemplative life, filled with everlasting love, despises all vainglory of this world and, rejoicing only in Jesus, desires to be freed; because it is despised by those who love and savor the world and not heaven, and it longs ardently for love and greatly desires to be given to joys that worldly adversity cannot hurt, in the lovely company of angels. There is nothing more profitable and nothing more wonderful than the grace of contemplation that lifts us from this lowness and offers us to God.

What is the grace of contemplation but the beginning of joy? What is the perfection of joy but grace confirmed? In which for us is kept a joyful happiness and happy joy, a glorious endlessness and everlasting glory, to live with saints and to dwell with angels.

And that which is above all things is to know God truly, to love him perfectly, to see Him in the brightness of His majesty, and to praise Him endlessly with wonderfully joyful song and melody. To Whom be worship and joy, with acts of thanksgiving, for ever and ever. Amen.

Richard Rolle of Hampole (ca. 1295–1349)—Rolle was born in Yorkshire and educated at Oxford, but he lived as a hermit and contemplative. He broke with the scholars of his day and wrote in the vernacular to reach those not formally trained in the gospel.

BARON FRIEDRICH VON HUGEL

Man of God

The religious sense exercises a *prodigious* influence. It is the religious sense, even at this stage, where it seems no more (on strict analysis) than a deep, delicate, obstinate sense of Other-ness, of Eternity, of Prevenience, of more than merely human Beauty, Truth and Goodness, which really keeps our poor little human world a-going. No great artist, no great philosopher or scientist, no great ethical striver will ever, fully consciously and deliberately, admit that what he strives to paint, to sculpt, to compose, or to discover or to understand, or to live and to be, is just human so-and-so-ness, very possibly without any further significance or truth about it whatsoever.

We have to be truthful, conscientious: why? Because these are the dispositions for putting us into fuller touch with realities of all sorts, especially with the reality of God.

The first and central act of religion is *adoration*, sense of God. His otherness though nearness, His distinctness from all finite beings, though not separateness—aloofness—from them. If I cannot completely know even a single daisy, still less can I ever completely know God. One of the councils of the Church launched the anathema against all who should declare that God is comprehensible. Yet God too, God in some real senses especially, we can most really know, since, as does even the rose, how much more He? since He deigns to reveal Himself to us. He does so in a twofold manner—vaguely, but most powerfully—in the various laws and exigencies of life and of our knowledge of it; and clearly, concretely, in and by the historic manifestations in and through the great geniuses and revealers of religion—the prophets and especially Jesus Christ.

Baron Friedrich von Hugel (1853–1925)—A Roman Catholic philosopher of religion, von Hugel was considered too Protestant for some Catholics and too Catholic for some Protestants. Beloved by many from both parties, he was a mystic with a wise and broad intellectual grasp.

Creation in Christ

"But if God is so good as you represent Him, and if He knows all that we need, and better far than we do ourselves, why should it be necessary to ask him for anything?"

I answer, What if He knows prayer to be the thing we need first and most? What if the main object in God's idea of prayer be the supplying of our great, our endless need—the need of Himself? What if the good of all our smaller and lower needs lies in this, that they help to drive us to God?

Hunger may drive the runaway child home, and he may or may not be fed at once, but he needs his mother more than his dinner. Communion with God is the one need of the soul beyond all other need; prayer is the beginning of that communion, and some need is the motive of that prayer. Our wants are for the sake of our coming into communion with God, our eternal need.

If gratitude and love immediately followed the supply of our needs, if God our Savior was the one thought of our hearts, then it might be unnecessary that we should ask for anything we need. But seeing we take our supplies as a matter of course, feeling as if they came out of nothing, or from the earth, or our own thoughts—instead of out of a heart of love and a will which alone is force—it is needful that we should be made to feel some at least of our wants, that we may seek Him who alone supplies all of them, and find His every gift a window to His heart of truth.

So begins a communion, a talking with God, a coming-to-one with Him, which is the sole end of prayer, yea, of existence itself in its infinite phases. We must ask that we may receive; but that we should receive what we ask in respect of our lower needs, is not God's end in making us pray, for He could give us everything without that. To bring His child to His knee, God withholds that man may ask.

George MacDonald (1824–1905)—Scottish Congregationalist pastor, novelist, myth maker, and poet, MacDonald had a profound influence on C. S. Lewis. Lewis said that MacDonald's *Phantastes* "baptized my imagination."

RICHARD BAXTER

The Saint's Everlasting Rest

It is not improper to illustrate a little the manner in which we have described this duty of meditation, or the considering and contemplating of spiritual things. It is *confessed to be a duty* by all, but practically denied by most. Many, that make conscience of other duties, easily neglect this. They are troubled if they omit a sermon, a fast, or a prayer, in public or private; yet were never troubled that they have omitted meditation perhaps all their lifetime to this very day; though it be that duty by which all other duties are improved, and by which the soul digests truth for its nourishment and comfort. It was God's command to Joshua, "This book of the law shall not depart out of your mouth, but you shall meditate therein day and night, that you may observe to do according to all that is written therein." Meditation turns the truths received and remembered into warm affection, firm resolution, and holy conversation.

This meditation is the acting of *all the powers of the soul*. It is the work of the living, and not of the dead. It is a work the most spiritual and sublime, and therefore not to be well performed by a heart that is merely carnal and earthly. Men must necessarily have some relation to heaven before they can familiarly converse there.

Richard Baxter (1615–1691)—Although he was an Anglican chaplain during the English Civil War and chaplain to the king after the Restoration, Richard Baxter left the Church of England at the time of the Act of Uniformity and became a leader of the Nonconformists. Baxter published his views and preached to large audiences, for which he was arrested twice and spent a total of eighteen years in prison. C. S. Lewis took the term "mere Christianity" from Baxter's *The Saint's Everlasting Rest*.

11

"THE EYES OF YOUR HEART"

Faith

Martin Luther

Table Talk

God alone, through his word, instructs the heart, so that it may come to the serious knowledge how wicked it is, and corrupt and hostile to God. Afterwards God brings man to the knowledge of God, and how he may be freed from sin, and how, after this miserable, evanescent world, he may obtain life everlasting. Human reason, with all its wisdom, can bring it no further than to instruct people how to live honestly and decently in the world, how to keep house, build, etc., things learned from philosophy and heathenish books. But how they should learn to know God and his dear Son, Christ Jesus, and to be saved, this the Holy Ghost alone teaches through God's word; for philosophy understands naught of divine matters. I don't say that men may not teach and learn philosophy; I approve thereof, so that it be within reason and moderation. Let philosophy remain within her bounds, as God has appointed, and let us make use of her as of a character in a comedy; but to mix her up with divinity may not be endured; nor is it tolerable to make faith an *accidens* or quality, happening by chance; for such words are merely philosophical,—used in schools and in temporal affairs, which human sense and reason may comprehend. But faith is a thing in the heart, having its being and substance by itself, given of God as his proper work, not a corporal thing, that may be seen, felt, or touched.

Martin Luther (1483–1546)—An Augustinian monk who became the father of the Protestant Reformation, Luther was an indefatigable theologian and pastor and champion of the doctrine of justification by "faith alone."

City of God

It is not permitted with a heart impure to see that which is seen only by the pure heart. You will be repelled, driven back from it, and will not see it. For "Blessed are the pure in heart, for they shall see God." How often already has he enumerated the blessed, and the causes of their blessedness, and their works and recompenses, their merits and rewards! But nowhere has it been said, "They shall see God." "Blessed are the poor in Spirit, for theirs is the kingdom of heaven." "Blessed are the meek, for they shall inherit the earth." "Blessed are they that mourn, for they shall be comforted." In none of these has it been said, "They shall see God." When we come to the "pure in heart," there is the vision of God promised. And not without good cause; for there, in the heart, are the eyes, by which God is seen. Speaking of these eyes, the Apostle Paul says, "The eyes of your heart being enlightened." At present then these eyes are enlightened, as is suitable to their infirmity, by faith; hereafter as shall be suited to their strength, they shall be enlightened by sight. "For as long as we are in the body we are absent from the Lord; For we walk by faith, not by sight." Now as long as we are in this state of faith, what is said of us? "We see now through a glass darkly; but then face to face."

Saint Augustine of Hippo (354–430)—Born in Numidia, a Roman province in North Africa, to a pagan father and Christian mother, Saint Augustine was consecrated bishop of Hippo and wrote numerous treatises on Christianity, including *The Confessions.*

ARTHUR JAMES BALFOUR

The Foundations of Belief

Everyone has a "right" to adopt any opinions he pleases. It is his "duty," before exercising this "right," critically to sift the reasons by which such opinions may be supported, and so to adjust the degree of his convictions that they shall accurately correspond with the evidences adduced in their favor. Authority, therefore, has no place among the legitimate causes of belief. If it appears among them, it is as an intruder to be jealously hunted down and mercilessly expelled. Reason, and reason only, can be safely permitted to mould the convictions of mankind. By its inward counsels alone should beings who boast that they are rational submit to be controlled.

Sentiments like these are among the commonplaces of political and social philosophy. Yet, looked at scientifically, they seem to me to be, not merely erroneous, but absurd. Suppose for a moment a community of which each member should deliberately set himself to the task of throwing off so far as possible all prejudices due to education; where each should consider it his duty critically to examine the grounds whereon rest every positive enactment and every moral precept which he has been accustomed to obey; to dissect all the great loyalties which make social life possible, and all the minor conventions which help to make it easy; and to weigh out with scrupulous precision the exact degree of assent which in each particular case the results of this process might seem to justify. To say that such a community, if it acted upon the opinions thus arrived at, would stand but a poor chance in the struggle for existence is to say far too little. It could never even begin to be; and if by a miracle it was created, it would without doubt immediately resolve itself into its constituent elements.

Arthur James Balfour (1848–1930)—This Scottish philosopher and statesman had his Gifford Lectures (1915) published as *Theism and Humanism,* a work enjoyed by C. S. Lewis. He was responsible for the famous Balfour Declaration, which promised Zionists a home in Palestine.

MARTIN LUTHER

Table Talk

Everything that is done in the world is done by hope. No husbandman would sow one grain of corn, if he hoped not it would grow up and become seed; no bachelor would marry a wife, if he hoped not to have children; no merchant or tradesman would set himself to work, if he did not hope to reap benefit thereby. How much more, then, does hope urge us on to everlasting life and salvation?

Faith's substance is our will; its manner is that we take hold on Christ by divine instinct; its final cause and fruit, that it purifies the heart, makes us children of God, and brings with it the remission of sin.

A Christian must be well armed, grounded, and furnished with sentences out of God's Word, that so he may stand and defend religion and himself against the devil, in case he should be asked to embrace another doctrine.

The article of our justification before God is as with a son who is born heir to all his father's goods, and comes not thereto by deserts, but naturally, of ordinary course. But yet, meantime, his father admonishes him to do such and such things, and promises him gifts to make him the more willing. As when he says to him: if you will be good, be obedient, study diligently, then I will buy you a fine coat; or, come here to me, and I will give you an apple. In such ways does he teach his son industry; though the whole inheritance belongs to him of course, yet will he make him, by promises, pliable and willing to do what he would have done.

Even so God deals with us; he is loving unto us with friendly and sweet words, promises us spiritual and temporal blessings, though everlasting life is presented to those who believe in Christ, by mere grace and mercy, gratis, without any merits, works, or worthiness.

Martin Luther (1483–1546)—An Augustinian monk who became the father of the Protestant Reformation, Luther was an indefatigable theologian and pastor and champion of the doctrine of justification by "faith alone."

RICHARD HOOKER

The Certainty and Perpetuity of Faith in the Elect

Blessed for ever and ever be that mother's child whose faith has made him the child of God. The earth may shake, the pillars of the world may tremble under us, the countenance of the heaven may be appalled, the sun may lose his light, the moon her beauty, the stars their glory; but concerning the man that trusts in God, if the fire has proclaimed itself unable as much as to singe a hair of his head, if lions, beasts ravenous by nature and keen with hunger, being set to devour, have as it were religiously adored the very flesh of the faithful man; what is there in the world that shall change his heart, overthrow his faith, alter his affection towards God, or the affection of God to him? If I be of this note, who shall make a separation between me and my God? "Shall tribulation, or anguish, or persecution, or famine, or nakedness, or peril, or sword?" No; "I am persuaded that neither tribulation, nor anguish, nor persecution, nor famine, nor nakedness, nor peril, nor sword, nor death, nor life, nor angels, nor principalities, nor powers, nor things present, nor things to come, nor height, nor depth, nor any other creature," shall ever prevail so far over me. "I know in whom I have believed"; I am not ignorant whose precious blood has been shed for me; I have a Shepherd full of kindness, full of care, and full of power: unto him I commit myself; his own finger has engraven this sentence in the tables of my heart, "Satan has desired to winnow you as wheat, but I have prayed that your faith fail not." Therefore the assurance of my hope I will labor to keep as a jewel unto the end; and by labor, through the gracious mediation of his prayer, I shall keep it.

Richard Hooker (ca. 1554–1600)—Theologian and defender of the Church of England during the reign of Queen Elizabeth, Hooker wrote *The Laws of Ecclesiastical Politie*. C. S. Lewis believed this book to be well written and full of wisdom and good sense.

Simone Weil

Waiting on God

The sympathy of the weak for the strong is natural, for the weak in putting himself into the place of the other acquires an imaginary strength. The sympathy of the strong for the weak, being in the opposite direction, is against nature.

That is why the sympathy of the weak for the strong is only pure if its sole object is the sympathy received from the other, when the other is truly generous. This is supernatural gratitude, which means gladness to be the recipient of supernatural compassion. It leaves self-respect absolutely intact. The preservation of true self-respect in affliction is also something supernatural. Gratitude which is pure, like pure compassion, is essentially the acceptance of affliction. The afflicted man and his benefactor, between whom diversity of fortune places an infinite distance, are united in this acceptance. There is friendship between them in the sense of the Pythagoreans, miraculous harmony and equality.

Both of them recognize at the same time, with all their soul, that it is better not to command wherever one has power to do so. If this thought fills the whole soul and controls the imagination, which is the source of our actions, it constitutes true faith. For it places the Good outside this world, where are all the sources of power; it recognizes it as the archetype of the secret point which lies at the center of human personality and which is the principle of renunciation.

Even in art and science, though second-class work, brilliant or mediocre, is an extension of the self, work of the very highest order, true creation, means self-loss. We do not perceive this truth, because fame confuses, and covers with its glory achievements of the highest order, often giving the advantage to the latter.

Love for our neighbors, being made of creative attention, is analogous to genius.

Simone Weil (1909–1943)—Weil was born into a Jewish intellectual family and became a philosopher, essayist, thinker, contemplative, and mystic who opposed institutional abuse and sought to identify with the oppressed.

J. B. Phillips

Ring of Truth

When I started translating some of Paul's shorter letters I was at first alter-
nately stimulated and annoyed by the outrageous certainty of his faith. It was
not until I realised afresh what the man had actually achieved, and suffered,
that I began to see that here was someone who was writing, not indeed at
God's dictation, but by the inspiration of God himself. Sometimes you can
see the conflicts between the pharisaic spirit of the former Saul (who could
say such grudging things about marriage and insist upon the perennial submission of women), and the Spirit of God who inspired Paul to write that in
Christ there is neither "Jew nor Greek...male nor female"!

Paul had, and still has, his detractors. There are those who say he is like
the man who says "I don't want to boast, but—," and then proceeds to do
that very thing! Very well then, but let us look at his list of "boasting." We
have only to turn up 2 Corinthians 11:23–27. Have any of us gone through
a tenth of that catalogue of suffering and humiliation? Yet this is the man
who can not only say that in all these things we are more than conquerors,
but can also "reckon that the sufferings of this present time are not worthy
to be compared with the glory which shall be revealed in us" (Rom. 8:18).
Here is no armchair philosopher, no ivory-tower scholar, but a man of almost
incredible drive and courage, living out in actual human dangers and agonies
the implications of his unswerving faith.

John Bertram Phillips (1906–1982)—This Bible translator, author, and broadcaster
was an acquaintance of C. S. Lewis and claimed to have had a visitation by Lewis's
apparition after his death. Lewis wrote the introduction to Phillips's *Letters to Young
Churches*.

12

"DIVINE INFLUENCE"

Living a Devout Life

BROTHER LAWRENCE

The Practice of the Presence of God

The first time I saw Brother Lawrence was upon the third of August 1666.
He told me...

That we should establish ourselves in a sense of God's Presence, by continually conversing with Him. That it was a shameful thing to quit His conversation to think of trifles and fooleries.

That we should feed and nourish our souls with high notions of God; which would yield us great joy in being devoted to Him.

That we ought to *quicken, i.e. to enliven our faith.* That it was lamentable that we had so little; and that instead of taking *faith* for the rule of their conduct, men amused themselves with trivial devotions, which changed daily. That the way of faith was the spirit of the Church, and that it was sufficient to bring us to a high degree of perfection.

That we ought to give ourselves up entirely to God, with regard both to things temporal and spiritual, and seek our satisfaction only in the fulfilling of His will, whether He lead us by suffering or by consolation; for all would be equal to a soul truly resigned. That there was need of fidelity in those times of dryness, or insensibility and irksomeness in prayer, by which God tries our love to Him: that *then* was the time for us to make good and effectual acts of resignation, whereof one alone would oftentimes very much promote our spiritual advancement.

That as for the miseries and sins he heard of daily in the world, he was so far from wondering at them, that, on the contrary, he was surprised that there were not more, considering the malice sinners were capable of: that for his part, he prayed for them; but knowing that God could remedy the mischiefs they did, when He pleased, he gave himself no farther trouble.

That to arrive at such resignation as God requires, we should watch attentively over all the passions, which mingle as well in spiritual things as those of a grosser nature; that God would give light concerning those passions to those who truly desire to serve Him. That if this was my design, viz., sincerely to serve God, I might come to him (B. Lawrence) as often as I pleased, without any fear of being troublesome; but, if not, that I ought no more to visit him.

Brother Lawrence, or Nicholas Herman of Lorraine (1611–1691)—Low-born Frenchman and Carmelite monk, Brother Lawrence lived a saintly life, which is reflected in his writings.

C. H. Dodd

The Authority of the Bible

To attempt to free His sayings from their relativity to the particular situation is often to blunt their edge rather than to bring out their universality.

To take an example: there is a saying reported several times in the Gospels, about "bearing the cross." Luke, intent on applying it directly to the situation of his readers, represents Jesus as saying that His follower must "take up his cross *daily* and follow me." That rendering of the saying has largely influenced its application. It has been taken to refer to habitual forms of self-sacrifice or self-denial. The ascetic voluntarily undergoing austerities felt himself to be bearing his daily cross. We shallower folk have often reduced it to a metaphor for casual unpleasantnesses which we have to bear. A neuralgia or a defaulting servant is our "cross," and we make a virtue of necessity. What Jesus actually said, according to our earliest evidence, was, quite bluntly, "Whoever wants to follow me must shoulder his gallows-beam"—for such is perhaps the most significant rendering of the word for "cross." It meant a beam which a condemned criminal carried to the place of execution, to which he was then nailed until he died. Jesus was not using the term metaphorically. Under Rome, crucifixion was the likeliest fate for those who defied the established powers. Nor did those who heard understand that He was asking for "daily" habits of austerity. He was enrolling volunteers for a desperate venture and He wished them to understand that in joining it they must hold their lives forfeit. To march behind Him on that journey was as good as to tie a halter around one's neck. It was a saying for an emergency. A similar emergency may arise for some Christians in any age. In such a situation it is immediately applicable, in its original form and meaning. For most of us, in normal situations, it is not so applicable. But it is surely good for us to go back and understand that this is what Christ stood for in His day. We shall then at least not suppose that we are meeting His demands in our day by bearing a toothache bravely or fasting during Lent.

Charles Harold Dodd (1884–1973)—Professor at Cambridge and lecturer at Oxford, Congregationalist pastor and biblical scholar, Dodd was the general director of the *New English Bible* translation.

GEORGE HERBERT

The Country Parson

The Country Parson preaches constantly, the pulpit is his joy and his throne: if he at any time intermit, it is either for want of health, or against some great Festival, that he may the better celebrate it, or for the variety of the hearers, that he may be heard at his return more attentively. When he intermits, he is ever very well supplied by some able man who treads in his steps, and will not throw down what he has built; whom also he entreats to press some point, that he himself has often urged with no great success, that so in the mouth of two or three witnesses the truth may be more established. When he preaches, he procures attention by all possible art, both by earnestness of speech, it being natural to men to think, that where is much earnestness, there is something worth hearing; and by a diligent, and busy cast of his eye on his auditors, with letting them know, that he observes who marks, and who not; and with particularizing of his speech now to the younger sort, then to the elder, now to the poor, and now to the rich. This is for you, and This is for you; for particulars ever touch, and awake more than generals. Herein also he serves himself of the judgments of God, as of those of ancient times, so especially of the late ones; and those most, which are nearest to his Parish; for people are very attentive at such discourses, and think it behooves them to be so, when God is so near them, and even over their heads. Sometimes he tells them stories, and sayings of others, according as his text invites him; for them also men heed, and remember better than exhortations; which though earnest, yet often die with the Sermon, especially with Country people; which are thick, and heavy, and hard to raise to a point of Zeal, and fervency, and need a mountain of fire to kindle them; but stories and sayings they will well remember. He often tells them, that Sermons are dangerous things, that none goes out of Church as he came in, but either better, or worse; that none is careless before his Judge, and that the word of God shall judge us. By these and other means the Parson procures attention; but the character of his Sermon is Holiness; he is not witty, or learned, or eloquent, but Holy.

George Herbert (1593–1633)—Anglican rector of the parish church of Bremerton, near Salisbury, Herbert was one of the seventeenth-century metaphysical poets.

MEISTER JOHANNES ECKHART

Miscellaneous Writings

The more his heart is trained to be sensitive to divine influences, the happier man is; the further he pushes his preparation, the higher he ascends in the scale of happiness.

But no man can be sensitive to divine influence except by conforming to God, and in proportion to his conformity he is sensitive to divine influence. Conformity comes of submission to God. The more subject to creatures a man is, the less he conforms to God, but the pure, disinterested heart, being void of creatures, is constantly worshiping God and conforming to him, and is therefore sensitive to his influence. That is what St. Paul means by saying: "Put on the Lord Jesus Christ"—that is, conform to Christ! Remember that when Christ became man, he was not one man but took all human nature on himself. If you get out, therefore, and clear of creatures, what Christ took on himself will be left to you and you will have to put on Christ.

If any man will see the excellence and use of perfect disinterest, let him take seriously what Christ said to his disciples about his humanity: "It is expedient for you that I go away: for if I go not away, the Comforter will not come unto you"—as if he said: "You take too much pleasure in my visible form and therefore the perfect pleasure of the Holy Spirit cannot be yours." Therefore discard the form and be joined to the formless essence, for the spiritual comfort of God is very subtle and is not extended except to those who despise physical comforts.

Johannes Eckhart (ca. 1260–1327)—Meister (Master) Eckhart was a German theologian, mystic, Dominican preacher, and professor of theology at Parisian University. He was arraigned for heresy late in life, and his writings were condemned by the Catholic Church after his death.

EVELYN UNDERHILL

The School of Charity

"My Lord!" says St. Thomas, seeing, touching, and measuring the Holiness so meekly shown to him in his own crude terms; and then, passing beyond that sacramental revelation to the unseen, untouched, unmeasured, uttering the word every awakened soul longs to utter—"My God!" The very heart of the Christian revelation is disclosed in that scene.

So it is that the real mark of spiritual triumph is not an abstraction from this world, but a return to it; a willing use of its conditions as material for the expression of love. There is nothing high-minded about Christian holiness. It is most at home in the slum, the street, the hospital ward: and the mysteries through which its gifts are distributed are themselves chosen from among the most homely realities of life. A little water, some fragments of bread, and a chalice of wine are enough to close the gap between two worlds; and give soul and senses a trembling contact with the Eternal Charity. By means of these its creatures, that touch still cleanses, and that hand still feeds. The serene, unhurried, self-imparting which began before Gethsemane continues still. Either secretly or sacramentally, every Christian is a link in the chain of perpetual penitents and perpetual communicants through which the rescuing Love reaches out to the world. Perhaps there is no more certain mark of a mature spirituality than the way in which those who possess it are able to enter a troubled situation and say, "Peace," or turn from the exercise of heroic love to meet the humblest needs of men.

Evelyn Underhill (1875–1941)—Anglican mystic and philosopher of religion, Underhill was the first woman granted lecture status at Oxford University; she was also a fellow of King's College, London. Underhill authored thirty-nine books on church history and Christian mysticism.

CHRISTINA ROSSETTI

The Poetical Works

Sorrow of saints is sorrow of a day,
    Gladness of saints is gladness evermore:
    Send on your hope, send on your will before,
To chant God's praise along the narrow way.
Stir up His praises if the flesh would sway,
Exalt His praises if the world press sore,
    Peal out His praises if black Satan roar
A hundred thousand lies to say them nay.
Devil and Death and Hades, three-fold cord
    Not quickly broken, front you to your face;
    Front thou them with a face of tenfold flint:
    Shout for the battle, David! never stint.
    Body or breath or blood, but, proof in grace,
Die for your Lord, as once for you your Lord.

Christina Rossetti (1830–1894)—Sister of the Pre-Raphaelite Dante Gabriel Rossetti, Christina Rossetti was a notable Victorian poet whose work, while often melancholy and erotic, is filled with rich spirituality.

The Writings

Chapter V. That no one should be proud, but rather glory in the Cross of the Lord
Be attentive, oh man, to how many excellent things the Lord God has placed in you, since He created and formed you "to the image" of His own Beloved Son according to the body "and to (His) likeness" according to the spirit (cf. Gen. 1:26). And all the creatures, which are under heaven, after you serve, know and obey their Creator better than you. And even the demons did not crucify Him, but you with them have crucified Him and even now you crucify (Him) by delighting in vices and sins. Whence therefore can you glory? For if you were so subtle and wise that you had "all knowledge" (cf. 1 Cor. 13:2) and knew how to interpret every "kind of tongue" (cf. 1 Cor. 12:28) and to search subtly after celestial things, in all these things you cannot glory; since one demon knew of celestial things and now knows of earthly things more than all men, (even) granted that there has been someone, who received from the Lord a special understanding of the highest wisdom. Similarly even if you were more handsome and wealthy than all and even if you were working miracles, as would put demons to flight, all those things are injurious to you and nothing (about them) pertains to you and you can glory in them not at all. But in this we can glory, "in" our "infirmities" (cf. 2 Cor. 12:5) and bearing each day the Holy Cross of our Lord Jesus Christ (Lk. 14:27).

Chapter VI. On the imitation of the Lord
Let us be attentive, all friars, to the Good Shepherd, who to save His own sheep endured the Passion of the Cross. The sheep of the Lord have followed Him in tribulation and persecution, shame and hunger, in infirmity and temptation and all other things; and because of these they have received from the Lord everlasting life. Whence it is a great shame to us servants of God,

that the saints did the works, but we, by reciting them, want to receive the glory and honor.

Francis of Assisi (1181–1226)—Roman Catholic saint, preacher, and founder of the Franciscan Order, Francis ministered throughout Europe and traveled as far as the Holy Land. His friars were required to take vows of poverty, chastity, and obedience.

J. B. Phillips

Your God Is Too Small

Many moralists, both Christian and non-Christian, have pointed out the decline in our moral sense, observed in recent years. It is at least arguable that this is almost wholly due to the decline in the first-hand absorption of Christian ideals. True Christianity has never had a serious rival in the training of the moral sense which exists in ordinary people.

Yet there are many, even among professing Christians, who are made miserable by a morbidly developed conscience, which they quite wrongly consider to be the voice of God. Many a housewife overdrives herself to please some inner voice that demands perfection. The voice may be her own demands or the relics of childhood training, but it certainly is not likely to be the voice of the Power behind the Universe.

On the other hand, the middle-aged business man who has long ago taught his conscience to come to heel may persuade himself that he is a good-living man. He may even say, with some pride, that he would never do anything against his conscience. But it is impossible to believe that the feeble voice of the half-blind thing which he calls a conscience is in any real sense the voice of God.

Surely neither the hectically over-developed nor the falsely-trained, nor the moribund conscience can ever be regarded as God, or even part of Him. For if it is, God can be made to appear to the sensitive an over-exacting tyrant, and to the insensitive a comfortable accommodating "Voice Within" which would never interfere with a man's pleasure.

John Bertram Phillips (1906–1982)—This Bible translator, author, and broadcaster was an acquaintance of C. S. Lewis and claimed to have had a visitation by Lewis's apparition after his death. Lewis wrote the introduction to Phillips's *Letters to Young Churches*.

RUDOLPH OTTO

Religious Essays

The holiness demanded by Isaiah, and thenceforth the holiness demanded by the scriptures as the ideal of man, and therefore also "the better righteousness" of the gospel, is rather in its essential nature a peculiar direction of the interest and will and feeling as a whole, which, indefinable in itself, we symbolize in the expressions: "not to be worldly," "not to be of this world," not to be fleshly but to be "spiritual," to be ruled by the "spirit." Such an ideal of "spirituality" is quite distinctly already perceptible in Isaiah, bearing just those traits which the opponents of this ideal, especially the pure moralists, have always resented in it. With Isaiah it makes itself felt characteristically in certain antipathies to things valued by "worldly" persons, which have at all times recurred as a mark of "spiritual" persons. The antipathies which we have in mind, and which reflect the nature of that ideal, take concrete form in Isaiah's remarkable invective against what we should call fashion and modernity. Fashionable clothing, modern luxury, the twanging of the new big Egyptian harps, the ivory bedsteads and the horses imported from Egypt are hateful to him. Isaiah detests politics, the diplomacy of the Court, his people's predilection for treaty-mongering, the running after the great ones of the earth. He detests these things because they lead men astray, causing them to trust in the might of men rather than in *ruach* and in the power of God. He hates them because all this is "flesh," because Israel seeks thereby to be "like other peoples" instead of being spiritual and holding aloof from such *worldly* business.

He demands "holiness," and holiness is to be shown primarily in fulfilling the injunctions of simple social morality. But that is not an end in itself, the aim is thereby to fulfil the "will of Jahveh" and to serve His honor. It is incorporated in the higher idea of being a people of Jahveh, appropriated to Jahveh, a sanctified group withdrawn from the world. Its ideal is to enter into a higher state, a state of consecration, an idealized order of Nazirites embracing the whole people, which is to be withdrawn from all profane contact in accordance with the words of Exodus 19:6: "And you shall be unto Me a kingdom of priests, and a holy nation."

Rudolph Otto (1869–1937)—German Protestant theologian, philosopher, and educator, Otto studied non-Christian religions, focusing particularly on religious experience.

WILLIAM LAW

A Serious Call to a Devout and Holy Life

How is it possible for a man who intends to please God financially to bury his money in finery? This is just as impossible as a person who intends to please God with his words, then meets other people with swearing and lying. All wasting and unreasonable spending are done deliberately.

I have chosen to explain the problem of unholy living by appealing to intention, for it makes the case so plain. It is easy for an employee to know whether he intends to please his employer in all his actions. Likewise, a Christian can certainly know if he intends to please God with his life.

Consider two people; one prays regularly and the other doesn't. The difference between them is not that the one has the physical strength required to pray and the other doesn't. The difference is simply that one intends to please God by praying, and the other one doesn't.

One person throws away his time and money on useless diversions. Another person is careful of every hour and uses his money for charity. The difference is not that one has power over his time and money and the other doesn't; it is that one desires to please God, and the other one doesn't.

The problem of unholy living does not stem from the fact that we desire to use money and time wisely, but fail due to the weaknesses of human nature. The problem is that we do not *intend* to be as responsible and devout as we can.

I do not mean to suggest that human intention can take the place of divine grace. Nor do I mean to say that through pure intention we can make ourselves perfect. I am simply saying that lack of desire to please God causes irregularities that by grace we should have the power to avoid.

William Law (1686–1761)—Law was educated at Cambridge and later became a fellow of the university. Law was ordained as an Anglican clergyman and is best known for his devotional classics, especially *A Serious Call to a Devout and Holy Life*, which influenced Samuel Johnson and the Wesleys as well as Lewis.

SAINT FRANCIS DE SALES

Introduction to the Devout Life

In God's name, would you forfeit the eternal glory that God will certainly give you? The worthless amusements on which you have hitherto wasted your time will again come to lure your heart away and ask it to return to them. Can you resolve to reject eternal happiness for such deceitful and trivial things? You may take my word, if you persevere it will not be long before you obtain consolations so delicious and pleasing that you will acknowledge that the world is mere gall compared to such honey and that a single day of devotion is better than a thousand years of worldly life.

You see that the mountain of Christian perfection is very lofty and you say "O God, how shall I be able to climb it!" Courage, Philothea! When young bees begin to take form they are called nymphs and they cannot yet fly out among the flowers, mountains, or nearby hills to gather honey. Little by little, by continuing to eat honey the older bees have prepared, the little nymphs take on wings and grow strong so that later they fly all over the country in search of food. It is true that in devotion we are still only little bees and cannot fly up high according to our plan, which is nothing less than to reach the peak of Christian perfection. But as our desires and resolutions begin to take form and our wings start to grow, we hope that some day we shall become spiritual bees and be able to fly aloft. In the meantime let us feed on honey found in works of instruction that devout persons of ancient days have left us. Let us pray to God to give us "wings like a dove" not only to fly upward during the time of our present life but also to find repose in the eternity that is to come.

Francis de Sales (1567–1622)—Roman Catholic saint, bishop, preacher, and author, Francis was born in Sales, France, and was elected bishop of Geneva in 1602.

Andrew Murray

Abide in Christ

Christian, fear not to claim God's promises to make you holy. Listen not to the suggestion that the corruption of your old nature would render holiness an impossibility. In your flesh dwells no good thing, and that flesh, though crucified with Christ, is not yet dead, but will continually seek to rise and lead you to evil. But the Father is the Husbandman. He has grafted the life of Christ on your life. That holy life is mightier than your evil life; under the watchful care of the Husbandman, that new life can keep down the workings of the evil life within you. The evil nature is there, with its unchanged tendency to rise up and show itself. But the new nature is there too,—the living Christ, your sanctification, is there,—and through Him all your powers can be sanctified as they rise into life, and be made to bear fruit to the glory of the Father.

And now, if you would live a holy life, abide in Christ your sanctification. Look upon Him as the Holy One of God, made man that He might communicate to us the holiness of God. Listen when Scripture teaches that there is within you a new nature, a new man, created in Christ Jesus in righteousness *and true holiness*. Remember that this holy nature which is in you is singularly fitted for living a holy life, and performing all holy duties, as much so as the old nature is for doing evil.

Andrew Murray (1828–1917)—Evangelical and leader in the South African Dutch Reformed Church, Murray was educated in Scotland and Holland. He served several pastorates and was six times the moderator of the Reformed Church.

JEREMY TAYLOR

Holy Living

God is especially present in the hearts of his people, by his Holy Spirit: and indeed the hearts of holy men are temples in the truth of things, and, in type and shadow, they are heaven itself. For God reigns in the hearts of his servants: there is his kingdom. The power of grace has subdued all his enemies: there is his power. They serve him night and day, and give him thanks and praise: that is his glory. This is the religion and worship of God in the temple. The temple itself is the heart of man; Christ is the High Priest, who from there sends up the incense of prayers, and joins them to his own intercession, and presents all together to his Father; and the Holy Ghost, by his dwelling there, has also consecrated it into a temple; and God dwells in our hearts by faith, and Christ by his Spirit, and the Spirit by his purities; so that we are also cabinets of the mysterious Trinity; and what is this short of heaven itself, but as infancy is short of manhood, and letters of words? The same state of life it is, but not the same age. It is heaven in a looking-glass, dark, but yet true, representing the beauties of the soul, and the graces of God, and the images of his eternal glory, by the reality of a special presence.

Jeremy Taylor (1613–1667)—After his education at Cambridge, Taylor became an Anglican bishop and a prolific writer and served in ministry during the turbulent years of the English Civil War. William Mason called him the "Shakespeare of English prose," and Samuel Taylor Coleridge spoke of him as the "Spenser of Prose."

WILLIAM LAW

A Serious Call to a Devout and Holy Life

It is not Christianity that makes life anxious or uncomfortable, but the lack of it.

Many people believe a moderate dose of Christianity—not an excessive amount—will fulfill our lives. They believe vaulting ambition to be bad, but moderate ambition good. One might as well say that excessive pain hurts, but moderate pain feels good.

Another possible objection to rules for holy living is that so many things in this world are good. Created by God, they should be used; but following strict guidelines limits our enjoyment of them.

In effect, Christianity teaches us how to properly use the world. It teaches us what is strictly right about food, drink, clothing, housing, employment, and other items. We learn to expect no more from them than they can properly provide.

The Scriptures tell us that although this world can satisfy physical needs, there is a much greater good prepared for mankind, reserved for us to enjoy when this short life is over. Christianity teaches that this state of glory awaits those who do not blind themselves with gold dust or eat gravel or load themselves with chains in their pain—in other words, those who use things rightly and reasonably.

If Christianity calls us to a life of prayer and watchfulness, it is only because we are surrounded by enemies and always in need of God's assistance. If we are to confess our sins, it is because such confessions relieve the mind and restore it to ease, just as weights taken off the shoulders relieve the body.

If prayer were not important, we would not be called to continue in it. When we consider that the other things we do are primarily or solely for the body, we should rejoice at prayer—it raises us above these poor concerns and opens our minds to heavenly things.

How ignorant people are to think that a life of strict devotion is dull and without comfort. It is plain that there is neither comfort nor joy to be found in anything else!

William Law (1686–1761)—Law was educated at Cambridge and later became a fellow of the university. Law was ordained as an Anglican clergyman and is best known for his devotional classics, especially *A Serious Call to a Devout and Holy Life*, which influenced Samuel Johnson and the Wesleys as well as Lewis.

13

"THE MOST PLEASING SACRIFICE TO GOD"

Obedience and Will

George MacDonald

Unspoken Sermons

To put off obeying him till we find a credible theory concerning him, is to set aside the potion we know it our duty to drink, for the study of the various schools of therapy. You know what Christ requires of you is right—much of it at least you believe to be right, and your duty to do, whether he said it or not: *do it.* If you do not do what you know of the truth, I do not wonder that you seek it intellectually, for that kind of search may well be, as Milton represents it, a solace even to the fallen angels. But do not call anything that may be so gained, *The Truth.* How can you, not caring to *be* true, judge concerning him whose life was to do for very love the things you confess your duty, yet do them not? Obey the truth, I say, and let theory wait. Theory may spring from life, but never life from theory.

George MacDonald (1824–1905)—Scottish Congregationalist pastor, novelist, myth maker, and poet, MacDonald had a profound influence on C. S. Lewis. Lewis said that MacDonald's *Phantastes* "baptized my imagination."

CHARLES GORE

The Sermon on the Mount

He asked the great question of the apostles; and Peter gave the great answer: "You are the Christ, the Son of the living God." Then, as it were with a sigh of relief, our Lord turns upon him, and greets him with His supreme benediction, and recognizes in him—if not yet something which is ready to His hand, yet something which is capable of being made ready.

Thus our Lord illustrated in His own practice what He teaches here. He would have men dig down to the rock, and build their spiritual fabrics there; and the rock is nothing else than His own person and His own word. To hear Him, and go away without imbibing His teaching and putting it into practice, to be nominally a Christian but in reality of the world, that is to build a house upon the sand.

And the test of all spiritual fabrics is their capacity to stand the strain of wild and rough experiences. That is a formidable lesson for an age of rapid workmanship; an age which resents the necessity for underground work and silent preparation.

It suggests a momentous question with regard to the spiritual fabric of our own personal lives, and also in regard to any spiritual enterprise in which we may be engaged: Have we dug deep enough and got down to the rock, or have we preferred quick results to solid foundations? Have we thought Christ's words impossible of application, and so been content with something short of Him? If so, our work is doomed. It will not last. It will not stand the rain and the wind and the storm.

Charles Gore (1853–1932)—Anglican theologian, author, and fellow of Trinity College, Oxford, Gore was, during his career, elected bishop of Worcester, Birmingham, and Oxford. He worked for social justice and was involved in the Christian Social Union.

George MacDonald

Donal Grant

"He is a well-meaning man," she said to herself, "but dreadfully mistaken: the Bible says *believe*, not *do!*"

The poor girl, though she read her Bible regularly, was so blinded by the dust and ashes of her teaching, that she knew very little of what was actually in it. The most significant things slipped from her as if they were merest words without shadow of meaning or intent: they did not support the doctrines she had been taught, and therefore said nothing to her. The story of Christ and the appeals of those who had handled the Word of Life had another end in view than making people understand how God arranged matters to save them. God would have us live: if we live we cannot but know; all the knowledge in the universe could not make us live. Obedience is the road to all things—the only way in which to grow able to trust him. Love and faith and obedience are sides of the same prism.

George MacDonald (1824–1905)—Scottish Congregationalist pastor, novelist, myth maker and poet, George MacDonald had a profound influence on C. S. Lewis. Lewis said that MacDonald's *Phantastes* "baptized my imagination."

C. H. DODD

The Authority of the Bible

As they [the Psalmists] began by accepting the doctrine, taught by the prophets and laid down with mechanical rigor in Deuteronomy, that good is rewarded and evil punished in this life, their ethics have a utilitarian and prudential cast. They are sure that to be good is the only sensible course in a world like this, and that the sinner is a fool. "Wisdom" is the all-inclusive virtue, and "the fear of the Lord is the beginning of Wisdom." We have seen that the prophets valued highly the intellectual qualities of insight and judgment, and here "the Wise" are their true followers. It was a great thing to state religion in terms of a reasonable morality, where clear common sense keeps fanaticism and superstition at a distance. If a good deal of their teaching has the air of moral commonplace, it is not necessarily the worse for that. The moralist can hardly dispense with the commonplace, since so much of the groundwork of his subject belongs to the unchanging qualities of human nature. It is for him to recommend such fundamental virtues as kindliness, honesty, diligence, sobriety, temperance, chastity, truthfulness, modesty, and to discourage their contrary vices, with such arguments and inducements as he has at his command. Such are the prevailing themes of the "Wisdom" writers. They handle them with the freshness and vigor which spring from conviction and wide experience. Their criticism of life is shrewd, based on a cool and humorous observation, pointed with wit and adorned with a pretty fancy. Their praises of Wisdom often rise to the level of great poetry. Their moral outlook has its limitations. They rarely reach out towards such heroic ideals as self-sacrifice and forgiveness. Yet in their pedestrian way these writers often get far on the road.

Charles Harold Dodd (1884–1973)—Professor at Cambridge and lecturer at Oxford, Congregationalist pastor and biblical scholar, Dodd was the general director of the *New English Bible* translation.

John Henry Newman

Parochial and Plain Sermons

Be not afraid,—it is but a pang now and then, and a struggle; a covenant with your eyes, and a fasting in the wilderness, some calm habitual watchfulness, and the hearty effort to obey, and all will be well. Be not afraid. He is most gracious, and will bring you on by little and little. He does not show you whither He is leading you; you might be frightened did you see the whole prospect at once. Sufficient for the day is its own evil. Follow His plan; look not on anxiously; look down at your present footing "lest it be turned out of the way," but speculate not about the future. I can well believe that you have hopes now, which you cannot give up, and even which support you in your present course. Be it so; whether they will be fulfilled, or not, is in his hand. He may be pleased to grant the desires of your heart; if so, thank Him for His mercy; only be sure, that all will be for your highest good, and "as your days, so shall your strength be. There is none like unto the God of Jeshurun, who rides upon the heaven in your help, and in His excellency on the sky. The Eternal God is your refuge, and underneath are the everlasting arms." He knows no variableness, neither shadow of turning; and when we outgrow our childhood, we but approach, however feebly, to His likeness, who has no youth nor age, who has no passions, no hopes, nor fears, but who loves truth, purity, and mercy, and who is supremely blessed, because He is supremely holy.

Lastly, while we thus think of Him, let us not forget to be up and doing. Let us beware of indulging a mere barren faith and love, which dreams instead of working, and is fastidious when it should be hardy. This is only spiritual childhood in another form; for the Holy Ghost is the Author of active good works, and leads us to the observance of all lowly deeds of ordinary obedience as the most pleasing sacrifice to God.

John Henry Newman (1801–1890)—Fellow of Oriel College, Oxford, ordained in the Anglican Church, and leader of the Tractarians (later known as the Oxford Movement), Newman converted to Roman Catholicism in 1845 and was made a cardinal in 1879. Newman published his essays, sermons, lectures, and a spiritual autobiography.

Thomas Traherne

Centuries

O the nobility of Divine Friendship! Are not all His treasures yours, and yours His? Is not your very Soul and Body His: is not His life and felicity yours: is not His desire yours? Is not His will yours? And if His will be yours, the accomplishment of it is yours, and the end of all is your perfection. You are infinitely rich as He is: being pleased in everything as He is. And if His will be yours, yours is His. For you will what He willeth, which is to be truly wise and good and holy. And when you delight in the same reasons that moved Him to will, you will know it. He willed the Creation not only that He might Appear but Be: wherein is seated the mystery of the Eternal Generation of His Son. Do you will it as He did, and you shall be glorious as He. He willed the happiness of men and angels not only that He might appear, but be good and wise and glorious. And He willed it with such infinite desire, that He is infinitely good: infinitely good in Himself, and infinitely blessed in them. Do you will the happiness of men and angels and He did, and you shall be good, and infinitely blessed as He is. All their happiness shall be your happiness as it is His. He willed the glory of all ages, and the government and welfare of all Kingdoms, and the felicity also of the highest Cherubims. Do you extend your Will like Him and you shall be great as He is, and concerned and happy in all these. He willed the redemption of mankind, and therefore is His Son Jesus Christ an infinite treasure.

Thomas Traherne (1637–1674)—Son of a poor shoemaker, educated at Oxford, and one of the metaphysical poets, Traherne became the Anglican rector of Credenhill in Herefordshire.

JOHN HENRY NEWMAN

Parochial and Plain Sermons

Let a man once set his heart upon learning to pray, and strive to learn, and no failures he may continue to make in his manner of praying are sufficient to cast him from God's favor. Let him but persevere, not discouraged at his wanderings, not frightened into a notion he is a hypocrite, not shrinking from the honorable titles which God puts on him. Doubtless he should be humbled at his own weakness, indolence, and carelessness; and he should feel (he cannot feel too much) the guilt, alas! which he is ever contracting in his prayers by the irreverence of his inattention. Still he must not leave off his prayers, but go on looking towards Christ his Savior. Let him but be in earnest, striving to master his thoughts, and to be serious, and all the guilt of his incidental failings will be washed away in his Lord's blood. Only let him not be contented with himself; only let him not neglect to *attempt* to obey. What a simple rule it is, to *try* to be attentive in order to be so! And yet it is continually overlooked; that is, we do not *systematically* try, we do not make a point of attempting and attempting over and over again in spite of bad success; we attempt only now and then, and our best devotion is merely when our hearts are excited by some accident which may or may not happen again.

John Henry Newman (1801–1890)—Fellow of Oriel College, Oxford, ordained in the Anglican Church, and leader of the Tractarians (later known as the Oxford Movement), Newman converted to Roman Catholicism in 1845 and was made a cardinal in 1879. Newman published his essays, sermons, lectures, and a spiritual autobiography.

GEORGE MACDONALD

Unspoken Sermons

I can well imagine an honest youth, educated in Christian forms, thus reasoning with himself:—..."the Lord said, 'If you would be perfect, go, sell that you have.' I cannot be perfect; it is hopeless; and he does not expect it." —It would be more honest if he said, "I do not want to be perfect; I am content to be saved." Such as he do not care for being perfect as their Father in heaven is perfect, but for being what they call *saved*. They little think that without perfection there is no salvation—that perfection is salvation: they are one.

I will suppose myself in immediate communication with such a youth. I should care little to set forth anything called truth, except in siege for surrender to the law of liberty. If I cannot persuade, I would be silent. Nor would I labor to instruct the keenest intellect; I would rather learn for myself. To persuade the heart, the will, the action, is alone worth the full energy of a man. His strength is first for his own, then for his neighbor's manhood. He must first pluck out the beam out of his own eye, then the mote out of his brother's—if indeed the mote in his brother's be more than the projection of the beam in his own. To make a man happy as a lark, *might be* to do him grievous wrong: to make a man wake, rise, look up, turn, is worth the life and death of the Son of the Eternal.

George MacDonald (1824–1905)—Scottish Congregationalist pastor, novelist, myth maker, and poet, MacDonald had a profound influence on C. S. Lewis. Lewis said that MacDonald's *Phantastes* "baptized my imagination."

A. C. HARWOOD

The Recovery of Man in Childhood

Never was it clearer than it is today that through his knowledge man has achieved a power which he is not morally mature enough to wield. This tragic fact lies behind all responsible utterances of our time. To give one example, the President of the British Association for the Advancement of Science in an inaugural address recently diagnosed the *malaise* of mankind in an interesting manner. What is wrong with man, he said in effect, is that his knowledge is heritable, each generation beginning with the stock left by its predecessor: but morality is not heritable, everybody has to begin again at the beginning. We know far more than our forefathers, but we are not better men.

Regrettable as it may seem, this state of affairs is a condition of human freedom. If we inherited a stock of virtue from our parents we should be virtuous by the very fact of that inheritance, without the exercise of our own free will. But we cannot shut our eyes to the fearful picture of almost illimitable power in the hands of almost irresponsible men.

Alfred Cecil Harwood (1898–1975)—Anthroposophist, friend of Owen Barfield, and, through him, a friend of C. S. Lewis, Harwood was, along with Barfield, a trustee of the C. S. Lewis estate. Lewis dedicated *Miracles* to Harwood and his wife, Daphne, and mentions him in *Surprised by Joy*.

John Henry Newman

Parochial and Plain Sermons

If a certain character of mind, a certain state of the heart and affections, be necessary for entering heaven, our *actions* will avail for our salvation, chiefly as they tend to produce or evidence this frame of mind. Good works (as they are called) are required, not as if they had any merit in them, not as if they could of themselves turn away God's anger for our sins, or purchase heaven for us, but because they are the means, under God's grace, of strengthening and showing forth that holy principle which God implants in the heart, and without which (as the text tells us) we cannot see Him. The more numerous are our acts of charity, self-denial, and forbearance, of course the more will our minds be schooled into a charitable, self-denying, and forbearing temper. The more frequent are our prayers, the more humble, patient, and religious are our daily deeds, this communion with God, these holy works, will be the means of making our hearts holy, and of preparing us for the future presence of God. Outward acts, done on principle, create inward habits. I repeat, the separate acts of obedience to the will of God, good works as they are called, are of service to us, as gradually severing us from this world of sense, and impressing our hearts with a heavenly character.

John Henry Newman (1801–1890)—Fellow of Oriel College, Oxford, ordained in the Anglican Church, and leader of the Tractarians (later known as the Oxford Movement), Newman converted to Roman Catholicism in 1845 and was made a cardinal in 1879. Newman published his essays, sermons, lectures, and a spiritual autobiography.

GEORGE MacDONALD

Unspoken Sermons

He gives us the will wherewith to will, and the power to use it, and the help needed to supplement the power, whatever in any case the need may be; but we ourselves must will the truth, and for that the Lord is waiting, for the victory of God his father in the heart of his child. In this alone can he see of the travail of his soul, in this alone be satisfied. The work is his, but we must take our willing share. When the blossom breaks forth in us, the more it is ours the more it is his, for the highest creation of the Father, and that pre-eminently through the Son, is the being that can, like the Father and the Son, of his own self will what is right. The groaning and travailing, the blossom and the joy, are the Father's and the Son's and ours. The will, the power of willing, may be created, but the willing is begotten. Because God wills first, man wills also.

When my being is consciously and willedly in the hands of him who called it to live and think and suffer and be glad—given back to him by a perfect obedience—I thenceforward breathe the breath, share the life of God himself. Then I am free, in that I am true—which means one with the Father. And freedom knows itself to be freedom. When a man is true, if he were in hell he could not be miserable.

George MacDonald (1824–1905)—Scottish Congregationalist pastor, novelist, myth maker, and poet, MacDonald had a profound influence on C. S. Lewis. Lewis said that MacDonald's *Phantastes* "baptized my imagination."

SAMUEL JOHNSON

The Works of Samuel Johnson

By those who have compared the military genius of the English with that of the French nation, it is remarked that the French officers will always lead, if the soldiers will follow; and that the English soldiers will always follow, if their officers will lead.

In all pointed sentences, some degree of accuracy must be sacrificed to conciseness; and, in this comparison, our officers seem to lose what our soldiers gain. I know not any reason for supposing that the *English* officers are less willing than the *French* to lead; but it is, I think, universally allowed, that the *English* soldiers are more willing to follow. Our nation may boast, beyond any other people in the world, of a kind of epidemic bravery, diffused equally through all its ranks. We can show a peasantry of heroes, and fill our armies with clowns, whose courage may vie with that of their general.

Samuel Johnson (1709–1784)—A lexicographer and literary critic, Johnson is considered by some, including Malcolm Muggeridge, to be among the greatest Englishmen of letters. Nevill Coghill compared C. S. Lewis to Samuel Johnson in terms of his physical stature and his scholarship and wit.

George MacDonald

Proving the Unseen

This is the thought that I want to impress upon you: The only true liberty lies in obedience. Can you comprehend that?

Do you think that Jesus Christ would have felt free one moment if He had not been absolutely devoted to the will of His Father in heaven? Suppose it had been possible for Jesus Christ to have been less devoted to His Father. Do you think that He would have felt that He was a free man?

Do you not think that that was what made the devil? He had a notion of being free: "Here I am. I will be the slave of no one—not even of the God that made me." And so evil enters the universe and all goes wrong, and he is the devil, not an archangel any longer, and a mean devil at that, a devil who tries to pull all down in the same abyss with himself, well knowing that he cannot even give them his pride to uphold them.

Well, then, we are the born slaves of Jesus Christ, but then He is liberty Himself, and all His desire is that we should be such noble, true, and right creatures that we never can possibly do or think a thing that shall bind even a thread round our spirits and make us feel as if we were tied anywhere. He wants us to be free—not as the winds—not to be free as the man who owns no law, but to be free by having God's law in our hearts and by being incarnations of God's truth. When you know that the law goes in one way, is it freedom to bring your will against that law, or to avoid it and to go another way, when the very essence of your existence means that you do not oppose but yield to the conditions of your being, those conditions that make your being divine, for God has made us after His own fashion?

When we do as God would do, when we act according to the divine mind and nature, we are acting according to our own deepest self, which is the will and law of God.

But let me show you a little more. I do not say that the moment you begin to obey the Lord Jesus Christ and to be His slave, that then you know what is meant by liberty.

Many things we know are right, but we are not inclined to do them. Other things we know are wrong, and we are inclined to do them. But when the law of liberty comes, the will of Jesus Christ, we begin to try to do the things we are not inclined to do and not to do the things that we are inclined to do.

George MacDonald (1824–1905)—Scottish Congregationalist pastor, novelist, myth maker, and poet, MacDonald had a profound influence on C. S. Lewis. Lewis said that MacDonald's *Phantastes* "baptized my imagination."

DOROTHY L. SAYERS

The Mind of the Maker

"Sacrifice" is another word liable to misunderstanding. It is generally held to be noble and loving in proportion as its sacrificial nature is consciously felt by the person who is sacrificing himself. The direct contrary is the truth. To feel sacrifice consciously as self-sacrifice argues a failure in love. When a job is undertaken from necessity, or from a grim sense of disagreeable duty, the worker is self-consciously aware of the toils and pains he undergoes, and will say: "I have made such and such sacrifices for this." But when the job is a labor of love, the sacrifices will present themselves to the worker—strange as it may seem—in the guise of enjoyment. Moralists, looking on at this, will always judge that the former kind of sacrifice is more admirable than the latter, because the moralist, whatever he may pretend, has far more respect for pride than for love. The Puritan assumption that all action disagreeable to the doer is *ipso facto* more meritorious than enjoyable action, is firmly rooted in this exaggerated valuation set on pride. I do not mean that there is no nobility in doing unpleasant things from a sense of duty, but only that there is more nobility in doing them gladly out of sheer love of the job. The Puritan thinks otherwise; he is inclined to say, "Of course, So-and-so works very hard and has given up a good deal for such-and-such a cause, but there's no merit in that—he enjoys it." The merit, of course, lies precisely in the enjoyment, and the nobility of So-and-so consists in the very fact that he is the kind of person to whom the doing of that piece of work is delightful.

Dorothy L. Sayers (1893–1957)—Translator of Dante's *The Divine Comedy*, literary critic, playwright, and detective novelist, Sayers was a friend and correspondent of C. S. Lewis.

Thomas à Kempis

The Imitation of Christ

Jesus has many lovers of His heavenly kingdom, but few cross-bearers. Many desire His consolation, but few His tribulation. Many will sit down with Him at table, but few will share His fast. All desire to rejoice with Him, but few will suffer for Him.

Many will follow Him to the breaking of the bread, but few will drink the bitter cup of His Passion. Many revere His miracles, but few follow the shame of His cross. Many love Jesus when all goes well with them, and praise Him when He does them a favor; but if Jesus conceals Himself and leaves them for a little while, they fall to complaining or become depressed.

They who love Jesus purely for Himself and not for their own sake bless Him in all trouble and anguish as well as in time of consolation. Even if He never sent them consolation, they would still praise Him and give thanks.

Oh how powerful is the pure love of Jesus, when not mixed with self-interest or self-love! They who think only of their own advantage, do they not show themselves to be lovers of self rather than of Christ? Where will a person be found ready to serve God without looking for a reward?

It is hard to find anyone so spiritual who is willing to be stripped of all things. Where will you find a person truly poor in spirit and free from all attachment to creatures? Such a one is a *rare treasure brought from distant shores* (cf. Proverbs 31:14).

Thomas à Kempis (ca. 1380–1471)—Born at Kempin (thus the surname à Kempis) near Cologne, Germany, Thomas Hämmerlien entered the Augustinian monastery at Mount Saint Agnes, where he worked as a copyist and spiritual director. He was a mystic, and his *Imitation of Christ* is thought by many to be second only to the Bible in its spiritual influence on readers. It was highly valued by C. S. Lewis.

14

"WORTHY TO
RECEIVE MORE"

Humility

SAINT AUGUSTINE

The City of God

There is, therefore, something in humility which, strangely enough, exalts the heart, and something in pride which debases it. This seems, indeed, to be contradictory, that loftiness should debase and lowliness exalt. But pious humility enables us to submit to what is above us; and nothing is more exalted above us than God; and therefore humility, by making us subject to God, exalts us. But pride, being a defect of nature, by the very act of refusing subjection and revolting from Him who is supreme, falls to a low condition; and then comes to pass what is written: "You casted them down when they lifted up themselves." For he does not say, "when they had been lifted up," as if first they were exalted, and then afterwards cast down; but "when they lifted up themselves" even then they were cast down,—that is to say, the very lifting up was already a fall.

And therefore it is that humility is specially recommended to the city of God as it sojourns in this world, and is specially exhibited in the city of God, and in the person of Christ its King; while the contrary vice of pride, according to the testimony of the sacred writings, specially rules his adversary the devil. And certainly this is the great difference which distinguishes the two cities of which we speak, the one being the society of the godly men, the other of the ungodly, each associated with the angels that adhere to their party, and the one guided and fashioned by love of self, the other by love of God.

The devil, then, would not have ensnared man in the open and manifest sin of doing what God had forbidden, had man not already begun to live for himself. It was this that made him listen with pleasure to the words, "You shall be as gods," which they would much more readily have accomplished by obediently adhering to their supreme and true end than by proudly living to themselves. For created gods are gods not by virtue of what is in themselves, but by a participation of the true God. By craving to be more, man becomes less; and by aspiring to be self-sufficing, he fell away from Him who truly suffices him.

Saint Augustine of Hippo (354–430)—Born in Numidia, a Roman province in North Africa, to a pagan father and Christian mother, Saint Augustine was consecrated bishop of Hippo and wrote numerous treatises on Christianity, including *The Confessions.*

Thomas à Kempis

The Imitation of Christ

Always set yourself in the lowest place and you will be given the highest; for the highest cannot exist without the lowest. The Saints who are highest in God's sight are the least in their own; and the more glorious they are, the more humble they are in heart, full of truth and heavenly joy and not desirous of vainglory.

Being grounded and confirmed in God, they can in no way be proud. They who ascribe to God whatever good they have received do not seek glory from one another, but only that glory which is from God; and the desire of their hearts is that God be praised in Himself and in all His Saints, and to this end they always tend.

Be grateful, therefore, for the least gift and you will be worthy to receive more.

Thomas à Kempis (ca. 1380–1471)—Born at Kempin (thus the surname à Kempis) near Cologne, Germany, Thomas Hämmerlien entered the Augustinian monastery at Mount Saint Agnes, where he worked as a copyist and spiritual director. He was a mystic, and his *Imitation of Christ* is thought by many to be second only to the Bible in its spiritual influence on readers. It was highly valued by C. S. Lewis.

CHARLES GORE

The Sermon on the Mount

We may have to assert ourselves for the sake of the moral order of the church and of the world. But no one gets true peace, or has really got to the foundation of things, until, as far as his own dignity is concerned, he is in a position to say, You can wrong God and you can wrong society; and it may be my duty to stand up for God and for society; but me, as far as I am concerned, you cannot provoke. That is the ideal to which we have to attain. That is the meekness which is appropriate to sinners like ourselves who know what we deserve, who *on a general review of life* can seldom feel that we are suffering unmerited wrong; but it is the meekness also of the sinless and righteous one.

And the result of this entire absence of self-assertion is that we can make no claim on the world which God will not at the last substantiate. "Blessed are the meek"—our Lord is here quoting the psalm—"for they shall *inherit* the earth." What is an heir? An heir is a person who enters into rightful possession. He is in no fear that any other can ever come and turn him out. He moves at ease among his possessions, because the things that he inherits are really his. No one with a better claim can come to oust him. Now, if we go about the world making claims on society which God does not authorize, refusing to bear what God will have us bear, the day will come when the true Master appears, and we shall be exposed to shame. We have made claims which He did not authorize; we have asserted ourselves where He gave us no right or title to assert ourselves; we shall be ousted. But the meek, who ever committed themselves to Him that judges righteously, have nothing to fear.

Charles Gore (1853–1932)—Anglican theologian, author, and fellow of Trinity College, Oxford, Gore was, during his career, elected bishop of Worcester, Birmingham, and Oxford. He worked for social justice and was involved in the Christian Social Union.

WILLIAM LAW

A Serious Call to a Devout and Holy Life

Humility does not mean having a lower opinion of ourselves than we deserve, but having a just sense of our weakness and sin. We are too weak of ourselves to do anything, even exist. It is solely the power of God which allows us to do anything, including moving toward him. Thus pride is like theft; the proud take God's glory to themselves.

To develop personal humility during your meditations, simply examine your life. Suppose that all of your thoughts would suddenly be transparent to the world. If everyone knew what secret motivations corrupt even your most noble actions, you would no longer expect to be respected for your goodness.

Think how shameful the nature of sin is, how great the atonement necessary to cleanse us of its guilt. Nothing less was required than the suffering and death of the Son of God. Is there any room for pride while we partake in such a nature as this?

All of us love humility and hate pride—in other people.

Turn your eyes toward heaven and consider how different you are from the angels. They do not contemplate their perfections, but they all have the same joy. Consider how unreasonable it is for human sinners to bask in their positions of respect while the magnificent seraphim give honor to God alone. Let a person who is pleased with himself contemplate our blessed Lord nailed and stretched out upon a cross, comparing himself to that meek and crucified Savior.

William Law (1686–1761)—Law was educated at Cambridge and later became a fellow of the university. Law was ordained as an Anglican clergyman and is best known for his devotional classics, especially *A Serious Call to a Devout and Holy Life,* which influenced Samuel Johnson and the Wesleys as well as Lewis.

G. K. Chesterton

St. Francis of Assisi

I have said that St. Francis deliberately did not see the wood for the trees. It is even more true that he deliberately did not see the mob for the men. What distinguishes this very genuine democrat from any mere demagogue is that he never either deceived or was deceived by the illusion of mass-suggestion. Whatever his taste in monsters, he never saw before him a many-headed beast. He only saw the image of God multiplied but never monotonous. To him a man was always a man and did not disappear in a dense crowd any more than in a desert. He honored all men; that is, he not only loved but respected them all. What gave him his extraordinary personal power was this; that from the Pope to the beggar, from the sultan of Syria in his pavilion to the ragged robbers crawling out of the wood, there was never a man who looked into those brown burning eyes without being certain that Francis Bernardone was really interested in *him;* in his own inner individual life from the cradle to the grave; that he himself was being valued and taken seriously, and not merely added to the spoils of some social policy or the names in some clerical document. Now for this particular moral and religious idea there is no external expression except courtesy. Exhortation does not express it, for it is not mere abstract enthusiasm; beneficence does not express it, for it is not mere pity. It can only be conveyed by a certain grand manner which may be called good manners. We may say if we like that St. Francis, in the bare and barren simplicity of his life, had clung to one rag of luxury; the manners of a court. But whereas in a court there is one king and a hundred courtiers, in this story there was one courtier moving among a hundred kings. For he treated the whole mob of men as a mob of kings. And this was really and truly the only attitude that will appeal to that part of man to which he wished to appeal.

Francis of Assisi (1181–1226)—Roman Catholic saint, preacher, and founder of the Franciscan Order, Francis ministered throughout Europe and traveled as far as the Holy Land. His friars were required to take vows of poverty, chastity, and obedience.

Gilbert Keith Chesterton (1874–1936)—Roman Catholic artist, poet, journalist, essayist, and author, Chesterton wrote over one hundred books. C. S. Lewis says, in *Surprised by Joy,* that Chesterton's Christian apologetics had a marked impact on him, and Lewis's own apologetic work owes a debt to Chesterton.

The Cloud of Unknowing

Humility is nothing else but a true knowledge and awareness of oneself as one really is. For surely whoever truly saw and felt himself as he is, would truly be humble. Two things cause humility. One is the degradation, wretchedness, and weakness of man to which by sin he has fallen: he ought to be aware of this, partially at any rate, all the time he lives, however holy he may be. The other is the superabundant love and worth of God in himself: gazing on which all nature trembles, all scholars are fools, all saints and angels blind.

This latter cause is the "perfect" one; it is eternal. The former is "imperfect": not only is it temporal, but often as not a soul in this mortal body, because the grace of God increases his longing (as often and for as long as God wishes), suddenly becomes completely oblivious of himself.

For though I call it "imperfect" humility, I would much rather have a real knowledge and awareness of myself as I am in this way than be without it. And I fancy it would bring me sooner to "perfect" humility itself, its cause and its virtue, than would be the case if the whole company of heaven, saints and angels, with Holy Church on earth, men and women, religious and secular, in their different states, were to band together for this one thing, to pray God that I might get perfect humility! Yes, it is impossible for a sinner to get or keep perfect humility without it.

Therefore strain every nerve in every possible way to know and experience yourself as you really are. It will not be long, I suspect, before you have a real knowledge and experience of God as he is. Not as he is in himself, of course, for that is impossible to any save God; and not as you will in Heaven, both in body and soul. But as much as is now possible for a humble soul in a mortal body to know and experience him...and as much as he will permit.

The Cloud of Unknowing is a late fourteenth-century mystical, contemplative work of Christian devotion. Though unknown, the author was probably a Dominican monk.

WALTER HILTON

The Scale of Perfection

This contemplative adoration and love of God brings the soul such comfort and elevates it so powerfully and so sweetly that it can take pleasure and rest in no earthly joy, and it has no wish to do so. The man who experiences it is indifferent to praise or blame, honor or contempt. He does not trouble to be pleased if men's contempt makes him humble, nor to be sorry for their honor and praise. He had rather forget both the one and the other, and to think only of God and get humility in that way. And that is much the safest way for whoever can attain it. My eyes are always turned to God, for he will preserve my feet from the snares of sin (Psalm 24:15). When a man acts in this way he forsakes himself entirely and casts himself wholly at the feet of God. Then he is in safe keeping, for the shield of truth which he holds protects him so well that no movement of pride will hurt him as long as he keeps behind it. Truth shall encompass you as a shield, if, leaving all other things, you regard it alone. For then you will not fear the terror of the night, that is, you will not be afraid of the spirit of pride, whether it comes in the night or in the day.

Walter Hilton (d. 1396)—Hilton was an English mystic and hermit and became the Augustinian Canon of Thurgarton in Nottinghamshire.

Richard Rolle

Selected Works

Let him seek without ceasing the saving virtue by which we are cleansed from the wretchedness of sin in this life, and in the next enjoy freedom from all pain, in blessed life for ever. And thus in this exile he shall be worthy to feel the joyful mirth of God's love.

Begin therefore by voluntary poverty, so that, desiring nothing in this world, you live soberly, chastely, and meekly before God and man.

To have nothing is sometimes a matter of necessity, but to wish to have nothing is a great virtue. We may, however, have many things and yet not wish to have them when those things which we have we do not keep from desire but from necessity; so in that sense he who has nothing may wish for many things. For it behooves the most perfect to accept necessaries, because he would not be perfect if he refused to take those things whereby he should live.

The way to perfect men is to despise all worldly things for God, yet to take meat and clothing; and if this be lacking at any time, to praise God, and to refuse superfluity as much as they can.

The warmer a man waxes with the heat of everlasting light the more meek shall he be in all adversities. He also that is truly meek, not feigning, holds himself worthy to be despised, and is not provoked to wrath either by injury or reproof. Wherefore humbling himself in busy meditation, it is given to him to rise to the beholding of heavenly things, and the vision of his mind being cleansed as he suffers sickness of the flesh, it is given to him to sing sweetly and ardently with inward joy. And when he goes to seek any outward thing he goes not with a proud foot, but only rejoicing in high delights, as it were ravished in a trance with the sweetness of the love of God, and being marvelously ravished he is glad.

Richard Rolle of Hampole (ca. 1295–1349)—Rolle was born in Yorkshire and educated at Oxford, but he lived as a hermit and contemplative. He broke with the scholars of his day and wrote in the vernacular to reach those not formally trained in the gospel.

Saint Francis of Assisi

Little Flowers of St. Francis

But if we endure not tribulation well, we shall never attain to consolation eternal. It is a meritorious thing and far more blessed to endure injuries and reproaches patiently, without murmuring, for the love of God, than to feed a hundred poor men, or to keep a perpetual fast. But what profits it a man, or how does it benefit him, to afflict his body with many fasts, vigils and disciplines, if he cannot endure a little injury from his neighbor? And yet from this might he derive greater reward and higher merit than from all the sufferings he could inflict upon himself of his own will; for to endure reproaches and injuries from our neighbor with humble and uncomplaining patience, will purge away our sins more speedily than they could be by a fountain of many tears.

Blessed is the man who has ever before the eyes of his mind the remembrance of his sins and of the favors of God; for he will endure with patience all tribulations and adversities for which he expects so great consolation. The man who is truly humble looks for no reward from God, but endeavors only to satisfy him in all things, knowing himself to be his debtor; every good thing which he has he acknowledges to come from the free bounty of God, while every evil that befalls him proceeds from his sins alone.

Francis of Assisi (1181–1226)—Roman Catholic saint, preacher, and founder of the Franciscan Order, Francis ministered throughout Europe and traveled as far as the Holy Land. His friars were required to take vows of poverty, chastity, and obedience.

15

"A Peculiar Joy"

Truth, Apologetics, and Christianity

G. K. Chesterton

St. Thomas Aquinas

There is the abstraction of the contemplative, whether he is the true sort of Christian contemplative, who is contemplating Something, or the wrong sort of Oriental contemplative, who is contemplating Nothing. Obviously St. Thomas was not a Buddhist mystic; but I do not think his fits of abstraction were even those of a Christian mystic. If he had trances of true Christian mysticism, he took jolly good care that *they* should not occur at other people's dinner-tables. I think he had the sort of bemused fit, which really belongs to the practical man rather than the entirely mystical man. He uses the recognized distinction between the active life and the contemplative life, but in the cases concerned here, I think even his contemplative life was an active life. It had nothing to do with his higher life, in the sense of ultimate sanctity. It rather reminds us that Napoleon would fall into a fit of apparent boredom at the Opera, and afterwards confess that he was thinking how he could get three army corps at Frankfurt to combine with two army corps at Cologne. So, in the case of Aquinas, if his daydreams were dreams, they were dreams of day; and dreams of the day of battle. If he talked to himself, it was because he was arguing with somebody else.

Thomas Aquinas (1225–1274)—Roman Catholic saint, theologian, mystic, and scholar, Aquinas was educated by Benedictine monks at Monte Cassino and at the University of Naples. He became a Dominican friar at age seventeen. He is perhaps best known for his major work, the *Summa Theologiae*.

Gilbert Keith Chesterton (1874–1936)—Roman Catholic artist, poet, journalist, essayist, and author, Chesterton wrote over one hundred books. C. S. Lewis says, in *Surprised by Joy*, that Chesterton's Christian apologetics had a marked impact on him, and Lewis's own apologetic work owes a debt to Chesterton.

C. W. FORMBY

The Unveiling of the Fall

If we would test...that a disbelief in the Fall is really such an insidious source of spiritual weakness, we need only confine our attention to individuals, and in them study the difficulties and standpoint of the intelligent modern mind. If conversation is not hampered by restraint their outlook upon Christianity will usually be found to be mistaken from the beginning. They are not thinking of humanity as fallen, or in any sense as being really in serious need of redemption and an uplifting Grace. Their idea of mankind is a picture showing all the natural facts of life, but with the Fall entirely painted out. Their views are summed up in such expressions as these: "What you call sin cannot be very wrong, it's quite natural after all." "I cannot see why any redemption should have been necessary. The tendency to do wrong is only a matter of being undeveloped." Thus the fatal deficiency becomes apparent at once. The great fundamental facts of the Fall have been practically wiped out of their mental horizon. With the loss of these facts, the truth of Christianity must become unintelligible, or at lest extremely visionary.

Charles Wykeham Formby—An early twentieth-century writer, the Reverend Formby was the author of *Education and Modern Secularism, Re-creation,* and *The Soul of England.*

G. K. Chesterton

Orthodoxy

To the Buddhist or the eastern fatalist existence is a science or a plan, which must end up in a certain way. But to a Christian existence is a *story*, which may end up in any way. In a thrilling novel (that purely Christian product) the hero is not eaten by cannibals; but it is essential to the existence of the thrill that he *might* be eaten by cannibals. The hero must (so to speak) be an eatable hero. So Christian morals have always said to the man, not that he would lose his soul, but that he must take care that he didn't. In Christian morals, in short, it is wicked to call a man "damned": but it is strictly religious and philosophic to call him damnable.

All Christianity concentrates on the man at the cross-roads. The vast and shallow philosophies, the huge syntheses of humbug, all talk about ages and evolution and ultimate developments. The true philosophy is concerned with the instant. Will a man take this road or that?—that is the only thing to think about, if you enjoy thinking. The aeons are easy enough to think about, any one can think about them. The instant is really awful: and it is because our religion has intensely felt the instant, that it has in literature dealt much with battle and in theology dealt much with hell. It is full of *danger*, like a boy's book: it is at an immortal crisis. There is a great deal of real similarity between popular fiction and the religion of the western people. If you say that popular fiction is vulgar and tawdry, you only say what the dreary and well-informed say also about the images in the Catholic churches. Life (according to the faith) is very like a serial story in a magazine: life ends with the promise (or menace) "to be continued in our next." Also, with a noble vulgarity, life imitates the serial and leaves off at the exciting moment. For death is distinctly an exciting moment.

Gilbert Keith Chesterton (1874–1936)—Roman Catholic artist, poet, journalist, essayist, and author, Chesterton wrote over one hundred books. C. S. Lewis says, in *Surprised by Joy*, that Chesterton's Christian apologetics had a marked impact on him, and Lewis's own apologetic work owes a debt to Chesterton.

AUSTIN FARRER

Lord, I Believe

Our creed shows us the truth of things, but when shall we attend to the truth it shows? The life of the world is a strong conspiracy not of silence only but of blindness concerning the side of things which faith reveals. We were born into the conspiracy and reared in it, it is our second nature, and the Christianity into which we are baptized makes little headway against it during the most part of our waking hours. But if we go into our room and shut the door, by main force stop the wheel of worldly care from turning in our head, and simply recollect; without either vision or love barely recall the creed, and redescribe a corner of our world in the light of it; then we have done something towards using and possessing a truth which Jesus died to tell, and rose to be.... Prayer is the active use or exercise of faith; and the creed defines the contours of that world on which faith trains her eyes. These statements are, or ought to be, platitudes. No dogma deserves its place unless it is prayable, and no Christian deserves his dogmas who does not pray them.

———————————————

Austin Farrer (1904–1968)—Doctor of Divinity and fellow of Trinity College, Oxford, and later warden of Keble College, Oxford, Austin Farrer was a member of the Inklings, a literary discussion group that included C. S. Lewis and J. R. R. Tolkien. Farrer was one of the witnesses at the civil marriage ceremony of C. S. Lewis and Joy Davidman, and he preached the sermon at Joy's funeral.

G. K. CHESTERTON

The Everlasting Man

Polytheism fades away at its fringes into fairy-tales or barbaric memories; it is not a thing like monotheism as held by serious monotheists. Again it does satisfy the need to cry out on some uplifted name or some noble memory in moments that are themselves noble and uplifted; such as the birth of a child or the saving of a city. But the name was so used by many to whom it was only a name. Finally it did satisfy, or rather it partially satisfied, a thing very deep in humanity indeed; the idea of surrendering something as the portion of the unknown powers; of pouring out wine upon the ground, of throwing a ring into the sea; in a word, of sacrifice. It is the wise and worthy idea of not taking our advantage to the full; of putting something in the other balance to ballast our dubious pride, of paying tithes to nature for our land. This deep truth of the danger of insolence, or being too big for our boots, runs through all the great Greek tragedies and makes them great. But it runs side by side with an almost cryptic agnosticism about the real nature of the gods to be propitiated. Where that gesture of surrender is most magnificent, as among the great Greeks, there is really much more idea that the man will be the better for losing the ox than that the god will be the better for getting it. It is said that in its grosser forms there are often actions grotesquely suggestive of the god really eating the sacrifice. But this fact is falsified by the error that I put first in this note on mythology. It is misunderstanding the psychology of day-dreams. A child pretending there is a goblin in a hollow tree will do a crude and material thing, like leaving a piece of cake for him. A poet might do a more dignified and elegant thing, like bringing to the god fruits as well as flowers. But the degree of *seriousness* in both acts may be the same or it may vary in almost any degree. The crude fancy is no more a creed than the ideal fancy is a creed. Certainly the pagan does not disbelieve like an atheist, any more than he believes like a Christian. He feels the presence of powers about which he guesses and invents. St. Paul said that the Greeks had one altar to an unknown god. But in truth all their gods were unknown gods. And the real break in history did come when St. Paul declared to them whom they had ignorantly worshipped.

Gilbert Keith Chesterton (1874–1936)—Roman Catholic artist, poet, journalist, essayist, and author, Chesterton wrote over one hundred books. C. S. Lewis says, in *Surprised by Joy,* that Chesterton's Christian apologetics had a marked impact on him, and Lewis's own apologetic work owes a debt to Chesterton.

To William Drummond

Sir

I did not expect to hear that it could be, in an assembly convened for the propagation of Christian knowledge, a question whether any nation uninstructed in religion should receive instruction; or whether that instruction should be imparted to them by a translation of the holy books in to their own language. If obedience to the will of God be necessary to happiness, and knowledge of his will be necessary to obedience, I know not how he that withholds this knowledge, or delays it, can be said to love his neighbor as himself. He that voluntarily continues ignorance, is guilty of all the crimes which ignorance produces; as to him that should extinguish the tapers of a light-house, might justly be imputed the calamities of shipwrecks. Christianity is the highest perfection of humanity; and as no man is good but as he wishes the good of others, no man can be good in the highest degree who wishes not to others the largest measures of the greatest good. To omit for a year, or for a day, the most efficacious method of advancing Christianity, in compliance with any purposes that terminate on this side of the grave, is a crime of which I know not that the world has yet had an example, except in the practice of the planters of America, a race of mortals whom, I suppose, no other man wishes to resemble.

The Papists have, indeed, denied to the laity the use of the Bible; but this prohibition, in few places now very rigorously enforced, is defended by arguments, which have for their foundation the care of souls. To obscure, upon motives merely political, the light of revelation, is a practice reserved for the reformed; and, surely, the blackest midnight of popery is meridian sunshine to such a reformation.

Samuel Johnson (1709–1784)—A lexicographer and literary critic, Johnson is considered by some, including Malcolm Muggeridge, to be among the greatest Englishmen of letters. Nevill Coghill compared C. S. Lewis to Samuel Johnson in terms of his physical stature and his scholarship and wit.

G. K. Chesterton

Orthodoxy

Paganism declared that virtue was in a balance; Christianity declared it was in a conflict: the collision of two passions apparently opposite. Of course they were not really inconsistent; but they were such that it was hard to hold simultaneously. Let us follow for a moment the clue of the martyr and the suicide; and take the case of courage. No quality has ever so much addled the brains and tangled the definitions of merely rational sages. Courage is almost a contradiction in terms. It means a strong desire to live taking the form of a readiness to die. "He that will lose his life, the same shall save it," is not a piece of mysticism for saints and heroes. It is a piece of everyday advice for sailors or mountaineers. It might be printed in an Alpine guide or a drill book. This paradox is the whole principle of courage; even of quite earthly or quite brutal courage. A man cut off by the sea may save his life if he will risk it on the precipice.

He can only get away from death by continually stepping within an inch of it. A soldier surrounded by enemies, if he is to cut his way out, needs to combine a strong desire for living with a strange carelessness about dying. He must not merely cling to life, for then he will be a coward, and will not escape. He must not merely wait for death, for then he will be a suicide, and will not escape. He must seek his life in a spirit of furious indifference to it; he must desire life like water and yet drink death like wine. No philosopher, I fancy, has ever expressed this romantic riddle with adequate lucidity, and I certainly have not done so. But Christianity has done more: it has marked the limits of it in the awful graves of the suicide and the hero, showing the distance between him who dies for the sake of living and him who dies for the sake of dying. And it has held up ever since above the European lances the banner of the mystery of chivalry: the Christian courage, which is a disdain of death; not the Chinese courage, which is a disdain of life.

Gilbert Keith Chesterton (1874–1936)—Roman Catholic artist, poet, journalist, essayist, and author, Chesterton wrote over one hundred books. C. S. Lewis says, in *Surprised by Joy,* that Chesterton's Christian apologetics had a marked impact on him, and Lewis's own apologetic work owes a debt to Chesterton.

PLOTINUS

Selected Works

With respect to eternity and time, we say that each of these is different from the other, and that one of them indeed is conversant with a perpetual nature, but the other about that which is generated. We also think that we have a certain clear perception of these in our souls spontaneously, and, as it were, from the more collected projections of intellectual conception; always and everywhere calling these by the same appellations. When, however, we endeavor to accede to the inspection of these, and to approach as it were nearer to them, again we are involved in doubt, admitting some of the decisions of the ancients about these, and rejecting others, and perhaps receiving differently the same decisions. Resting also in these, and thinking it sufficient if when interrogated we are able to relate the opinion of the ancients concerning time and eternity, we are liberated from any farther investigation about them. It is necessary, therefore, to think that some of the ancient and blessed philosophers have discovered the truth; but it is fit to consider who those are that have obtained it, and after what manner we also may acquire the same knowledge on these subjects.

Plotinus (ca. 203–262)—Greek philosopher Plotinus influenced early Christian thought with his Neoplatonism.

G. K. Chesterton

St. Thomas Aquinas

In so far as there was ever a bad break in philosophical history, it was not before St. Thomas, or at the beginning of medieval history; it was after St. Thomas and at the beginning of modern history. The great intellectual tradition that comes down to us from Pythagoras and Plato was never interrupted or lost through such trifles as the sack of Rome, the triumph of Attila or all the barbarian invasions of the Dark Ages. It was only lost after the introduction of printing, the discovery of America, the founding of the Royal Society and all the enlightenment of the Renaissance and the modern world. It was there, if anywhere, that there was lost or impatiently snapped the long thin delicate thread that had descended from distant antiquity; the thread of that unusual human hobby, the habit of thinking. This is proved by the fact that the printed books of this later period largely had to wait for the eighteenth century, or the end of the seventeenth century, to find even the names of the new philosophers. But the decline of the Empire, the Dark Ages and the early Middle Ages, though too much tempted to neglect what was opposed to Platonic philosophy, had never neglected philosophy. In that sense St. Thomas, like most other very original men, has a long and clear pedigree. He himself is constantly referring back to the authorities from St. Augustine to St. Anselm, and from St. Anselm to St. Albert; and even when he differs, he also defers.

Gilbert Keith Chesterton (1874–1936)—Roman Catholic artist, poet, journalist, essayist, and author, Chesterton wrote over one hundred books. C. S. Lewis says, in *Surprised by Joy,* that Chesterton's Christian apologetics had a marked impact on him, and Lewis's own apologetic work owes a debt to Chesterton.

Evelyn Underhill

Collected Papers

The gap between those spiritual realities and our apparent situation—between the great vision of the Principle and the teacher's everyday task—generally seems so great that only a steady feeling of the spirit of worship, a habit of delighted and humble adoration of the Perfect, a sturdy spiritual realism, can maintain our contact with the invisible Reality.

A traveler, who lately paid her first visit to Iona, was asked by the old Scottish gardener on her return to the mainland where she had been. When she told him, he said, "Ah! Iona is a very thin place!" She asked him what he meant by a thin place, and he answered, "There's very little between Iona and the Lord!"

I am far from denying that from our human point of view, some places are a great deal thinner than others: but to the eyes of worship, the whole of the visible world, even its most unlikely patches, is rather thin.

To see the world in that sort of way is an essential part of the Christian outlook; for the Christian is committed to an equal belief in the reality of eternity and the reality of time. In the days that are coming, I am sure that Christianity will have to move out from the churches and chapels—or rather, spread out, far beyond the devotional focus of its life—and justify itself as a complete philosophy of existence; beautifying and enriching all levels of being, physical, social and mental as well as spiritual, telling the truth about God and man, and casting its transfiguring radiance on the whole of that world in which man has to live.

Evelyn Underhill (1875–1941)—Anglican mystic and philosopher of religion, Underhill was the first woman granted lecture status at Oxford University; she was also a fellow of King's College, London. Underhill authored thirty-nine books on church history and Christian mysticism.

SIR THOMAS MORE

Selections from His English Works

Yet they say further that it is hard to translate the Scripture out of one tongue into another, and specially they say into ours, which they call a tongue vulgar and barbarous.... I never yet heard any reason laid, why it were not convenient to have the Bible translated into the English tongue; but all those reasons, seemed they never so gay and glorious at the first sight, yet when they were well examined, they might in effect, for aught that I can see, as well be laid against the holy writers that wrote the Scripture in the Hebrew tongue, and against the blessed Evangelists that wrote the Scripture in Greek, and against all those in likewise that translated it out of every of those tongues in to Latin, as to their charge that would well and faithfully translate it out of Latin into our English tongue. For as for that our tongue is called barbarous, is but a fantasy. For so is, as every learned man knows, every strange language to others. And if they would call it barren of words, there is no doubt but it is plenteous enough to express our minds in anything whereof one man has used to speak with another. Now as touching the difficulty which a translator finds in expressing well and so surely, but that he shall sometime diminish either of the sentence or of the grace that it bears in the former tongue: that point has lain in their light that have translated the Scripture already either out of Greek into Latin, or out of Hebrew into any of them both, as by many translations which we read already, to them that be learned appears.

Sir Thomas More (1478–1535)—An Oxford scholar, humanist, lawyer, author, and statesman, More resigned from his post as lord chancellor to protest King Henry VIII's break with the Roman Catholic Church. More was beheaded for his refusal to recognize Henry as the head of the Church of England and was canonized as a Roman Catholic saint in 1935.

Hilaire Belloc

On the Place of Gilbert Chesterton in English Letters

Now here we come to the thing of chief value and of chief effect in Gilbert Chesterton's life and work: his religion. In this department I have a task quite different from the common appreciation of literary style and matter. From a man's religion (or accepted and certain philosophy) all his actions spring, whether he be conscious of that connection or no. In the case of Gilbert Chesterton, the whole of whose expression and action were the story of a life's religion, the connection was not only evident to himself but to all around, and even to the general public. That public of modern England has been taught universally that religion is at once a private personal affair and of little external effect. Our public is more agreed upon religion, and less acquainted with its diverse and multitudinous actions, than any other in the modern world; but even so all those who know anything of him, even if it be but his name, are aware of that great accident (or design) whereby he advanced towards the Faith over many years and was ultimately in full communion with it.

He approached the Catholic Church gradually but by a direct road. He first saw the city from afar off, then approached it with interest and at last entered. Few of the great conversions in our history have been so deliberate or so mature. It will be for posterity to judge the magnitude of the event. We are too near it to see it in scale. It may be that England will soon lose what fragment it retains of the Creed which made Europe, and by the survival of which may Europe survive. It may be just the other way: England may be passing through a crisis and turning point in this matter and may be destined to recover by some unexpected return of fate the influence which brought the nation into being and against which the nation has come to stand in so extreme opposition.

These things are of the future and the future is veiled from man.

Hilaire Belloc (1870–1953)—Belloc was born in Paris, studied at Balliol College, Oxford, and became a British subject in 1906. He served in Parliament and then retired to full-time journalism and writing, during which time he edited several publications and wrote over one hundred works, many devoted to Catholic thought. He was a great friend of G. K. Chesterton's.

Gilbert Keith Chesterton (1874–1936)—Roman Catholic artist, poet, journalist, essayist, and author, Chesterton wrote over one hundred books. C. S. Lewis says, in *Surprised by Joy,* that Chesterton's Christian apologetics had a marked impact on him, and Lewis's own apologetic work owes a debt to Chesterton.

Thomas Aquinas

Summa Theologiae

It should be urged that human well-being has called for schooling in what God has revealed, in addition to the philosophical researches pursued by human reasoning.

Above all because God destines us for an end beyond the grasp of reason; according to Isaiah, *Eye has not seen, O God, without you what you have prepared for them that love you.* Now we have to recognize an end before we can stretch out and exert ourselves for it. Hence the necessity for our welfare that divine truths surpassing reason should be signified to us through divine revelation.

We also stand in need of being instructed by divine revelation even in religious matters the human reason is able to investigate. For the rational truth about God would be reached only by few, and even so after a long time and mixed with many mistakes; whereas on knowing this depends our whole welfare, which is in God. In these circumstances, then, it was to prosper the salvation of human beings, and the more widely and less anxiously, that they were provided for by divine revelation about divine things.

These then are the grounds of holding the sacred doctrine which has come to us through revelation beyond the discoveries of the rational sciences.

Hence: 1. Admittedly the reason should not pry into things too high for human knowledge, nevertheless when they are revealed by God they should be welcomed by faith: indeed the passage goes on to say, *Many things are shown you above the understanding of men.* And on them Christian teaching rests.

Thomas Aquinas (1225–1274)—Roman Catholic saint, theologian, mystic, and scholar, Aquinas was educated by Benedictine monks at Monte Cassino and at the University of Naples. He became a Dominican friar at age seventeen. He is perhaps best known for his major work, the *Summa Theologiae*.

G. K. Chesterton

Orthodoxy

All the towering materialism which dominates the modern mind rests ulti-mately upon one assumption; a false assumption. It is supposed that if a thing goes on repeating itself it is probably dead; a piece of clockwork. People feel that if the universe was personal it would vary; if the sun were alive it would dance. This is a fallacy even in relation to known fact. For the variation in human affairs is generally brought into them, not by life, but by death; by the dying down or breaking off of their strength or desire. A man varies his movements because of some slight element of failure or fatigue. He gets into an omnibus because he is tired of walking; or he walks because he is tired of sitting still. But if his life and joy were so gigantic that he never tired of going to Islington, he might go to Islington as regularly as the Thames goes to Sheerness. The very speed and ecstasy of his life would have the stillness of death. The sun rises every morning. I do not rise every morning; but the vari-ation is due not to my activity, but to my inaction. Now, to put the matter in a popular phrase, it might be true that the sun rises regularly because he never gets tired of rising. His routine might be due, not to a lifelessness, but to a rush of life. The thing I mean can be seen, for instance, in children, when they find some game or joke that they specially enjoy. A child kicks his legs rhythmically through excess, not absence, of life. Because children have abounding vitality, because they are in spirit fierce and free, therefore they want things repeated and unchanged. They always say, "Do it again"; and the grown-up person does it again until he is nearly dead. For grown-up people are not strong enough to exult in monotony. But perhaps God is strong enough to exult in monotony. It is possible that God says every morning, "Do it again" to the sun; and every evening, "Do it again" to the moon. It may not be automatic necessity that makes all daisies alike; it may be that

God makes every daisy separately, but has never got tired of making them. It may be that He has the eternal appetite of infancy; for we have sinned and grown old, and our Father is younger than we. The repetition in Nature may not be a mere recurrence; it may be a theatrical *encore*.

Gilbert Keith Chesterton (1874–1936)—Roman Catholic artist, poet, journalist, essayist, and author, Chesterton wrote over one hundred books. C. S. Lewis says, in *Surprised by Joy,* that Chesterton's Christian apologetics had a marked impact on him, and Lewis's own apologetic work owes a debt to Chesterton.

RICHARD BAXTER

The Truth of Christianity

What hope or consolation have we, but what depends upon the truth of the gospel? If these glad tidings should fail us, all fails us. What else gives us assurance of a future felicity? And without that, how wretched and despicable a creature is man; and how low and base are all the transactions and passages of his life, if they be not ennobled by their respects unto that end! Even the blindest infidel that denies the truth of the gospel should easily confess the goodness of its promised happiness; and therefore see cause to wish that it were true, unless as he has brought himself under its terrors.

You see, then, it is the best news that ever came to the ears of man, that is attested to you by the witness within you: it is that which may cause you to live in hope, and peace, and joy; and to die in hope, and peace, and joy while you believingly look to a blessed immortality, and upon your resurrection, as secured in the resurrection of Christ, and his promise of yours. Other men may confess that the truth of this is desirable; but you have the truth of it witnessed in your own hearts: to carry about with you such a witness, is to carry about the matter of continual joy. The same Spirit which is your sanctifier is your comforter, at least, by maintaining in you the grounds and fit matter of consolation. How happy is such a soul that has not only the voice behind him, saying, This is the way, walk in it; but also the witness within him, that this voice is divine, and telling him of the end, which by that way he may attain! No wonder if the life of such a man be as a continual feast, and if he has a peculiar joy, as he has a peculiar testimony, even such as the stranger meddles not with.

Richard Baxter (1615–1691)—Although he was an Anglican chaplain during the English Civil War and chaplain to the king after the Restoration, Richard Baxter left the

Church of England at the time of the Act of Uniformity and became a leader of the Nonconformists. Baxter published his views and preached to large audiences, for which he was arrested twice and spent a total of eighteen years in prison. C. S. Lewis took the term "mere Christianity" from Baxter's *The Saint's Everlasting Rest.*

G. K. CHESTERTON

The Everlasting Man

Indeed the Church from its beginnings, and perhaps especially in its beginnings, was not so much a principality as a revolution against the prince of the world. This sense that the world had been conquered by the great usurper, and was in his possession, has been much deplored or derided by those optimists who identify enlightenment with ease. But it was responsible for all that thrill of defiance and a beautiful danger that made the good news seem to be really both good and new. It was in truth against a huge unconscious usurpation that it raised a revolt, and originally so obscure a revolt. Olympus still occupied the sky like a motionless cloud molded into many mighty forms; philosophy still sat in the high places and even on the thrones of the kings, when Christ was born in the cave and Christianity in the catacombs.

In both cases we may remark the same paradox of revolution; the sense of something despised and of something feared. The cave in one aspect is only a hole or corner into which the outcasts are swept like rubbish; yet in the other aspect it is a hiding-place of something valuable which the tyrants are seeking like treasure. In one sense they are there because the inn-keeper would not even remember them, and in another because the king can never forget them. We have already noted that this paradox appeared also in the treatment of the early Church. It was important while it was still insignificant, and certainly while it was still impotent. It was important solely because it was intolerable; and in that sense it is true to say that it was intolerable because it was intolerant. It was resented, because, in its own still and almost secret way, it had declared war. It had risen out of the ground to wreck the heaven and earth of heathenism. It did not try to destroy all that creation of gold and marble; but it contemplated a world without it. It dared to look right through it as though the gold and marble had been glass. Those who charged the Christians with burning down Rome with firebrands were slanderers; but they were at least far nearer to the nature of Christianity than those among the moderns who tell us that the Christians were a sort of ethical society, being martyred in a languid fashion for telling men they had a duty to their neighbors, and only mildly disliked because they were meek and mild.

Gilbert Keith Chesterton (1874–1936)—Roman Catholic artist, poet, journalist, essayist, and author, Chesterton wrote over one hundred books. C. S. Lewis says, in *Surprised by Joy,* that Chesterton's Christian apologetics had a marked impact on him, and Lewis's own apologetic work owes a debt to Chesterton.

T. S. Eliot

The Idea of a Christian Society

Our preoccupation with foreign politics during the last few years has induced a surface complacency rather than a consistent attempt at self-examination of conscience. Sometimes we are almost persuaded that we are getting on very nicely, with a reform here and a reform there, and would have been getting on still better, if only foreign governments did not insist upon breaking all the rules and playing what is really a different game. What is more depressing still is the thought that only fear or jealousy of foreign success can alarm us about the health of our own nation; that only through this anxiety can we see such things as depopulation, malnutrition, moral deterioration, the decay of agriculture, as evils at all. And what is worst of all is to advocate Christianity, not because it is true, but because it might be beneficial. Towards the end of 1938 we experienced a wave of revivalism which should teach us that folly is not the prerogative of any one political party or any one religious communion, and that hysteria is not the privilege of the uneducated. The Christianity expressed has been vague, the religious fervor has been a fervor for democracy. It may engender nothing better than a disguised and peculiarly sanctimonious nationalism, accelerating our progress towards the paganism which we say we abhor. To justify Christianity because it provides a foundation of morality, instead of showing the necessity of Christian morality from the truth of Christianity, is a very dangerous inversion; and we may reflect, that a good deal of the attention of totalitarian states has been devoted, with a steadiness of purpose not always found in democracies, to providing their national life with a foundation of morality—the wrong kind perhaps, but a good deal more of it. It is not enthusiasm, but dogma, that differentiates a Christian from a pagan society.

Thomas Stearns Eliot (1888–1965)—Nobel Prize–winning poet and literary critic, Eliot wrote *The Waste Land*, which challenged and changed the conventions of poetry, much to the dismay of C. S. Lewis. Mutual respect developed between Lewis and Eliot when they later worked together on the *Revised Psalter*.

Joy Davidman

Smoke on the Mountain

The religion of Society has in our time become a well-organized worship, with its sociologist priests and its psychiatrist prophets. In that religion, "antisocial behavior" has been substituted for sin, and the "antisocial" man (i.e., the rebellious or merely unconventional man) is at once accused of "mental disturbance"—that is, of wrong thinking or what used to be called heresy. We lock up the heretic and torture him in ingenious ways with electric shocks and psychiatric third degrees, until he abjures his error and consents to serve the common good as *we* conceive it. And in all this we have the best intentions, as did the Spanish Inquisition. The "common good" may become a moloch to which countless individuals are sacrificed, if we forget that all good is in the love of God, and that God comes first.

There are other beast gods—as many as there are men to invent them. They wrangle in the temple, turning it into a den of thieves, deafening us with their conflicting counsel until we become incapable of acting effectively in any direction. In the end we cannot stay here; we shall choose one master or the other, and be saved or lost. But for the moment the choice is still before us. Let us remember that the complete backslider is always worse off than the man who never started to climb. The ancient polytheist was only a primitive, with a bright future of growth ahead of him. But the modern who whores after strange gods is a decadent, and there is nothing ahead of him but the dust and ashes of a burned-out world. Yet it was not to a primitive age that Christ came, but to one rotten with decay even beyond our own. Perhaps it is only the decadent—the man who has failed to live by the law, and who admits the measure of his failure—for whom the law will really prove a schoolmaster to bring him to Christ. Perhaps it is only the twentieth century self-worshiper who can learn the full meaning of the First Commandment.

Hold to this, and the beast in the heart has no power. The present loses its confusions, the future its terrors, and death itself is but the opening of a door.

"You shall have no other gods before me."

That is the law of life and happiness and courage. Courage himself, God the Lion, stands beside us to help us live by it. Whatever we desire, whatever we love, whatever we find worth suffering for, will be Dead Sea fruit in our mouths unless we remember that God comes first.

Joy Davidman (1915–1960)—Poet, author, and the wife of C. S. Lewis, Davidman is the mother of David and Douglas Gresham. C. S. Lewis dedicated his novel *Till We Have Faces* to her and wrote *A Grief Observed* upon her death.

16

"FINE FABLING"

Fantasy and Imagination

A. C. HARWOOD

The Recovery of Man in Childhood

It is the intellectual who tires of repetition; it was the intellectual age which abolished the old ritual forms of religion and substituted the sermon and the impromptu prayer. Today every drama must have a new plot, every detective novel display some fresh tricks of ingenuity. But something of former ages still lives in children, when the seasons brought round their customary festivals, songs and plays. They look forward to the return of the same events as the year comes round, the same carols and the same play at Christmas, in which the story of the Birth in the stable is always the same and yet ever new. Until childhood lost its own traditions there were always seasonal games, a season for marbles, a season for tops, a season for hoops or kites. In the marble season no one would look at a top, nor at a hoop when kites were in.

Alfred Cecil Harwood (1898–1975)—Anthroposophist, friend of Owen Barfield, and, through him, a friend of C. S. Lewis, Harwood was, along with Barfield, a trustee of the C. S. Lewis estate. Lewis dedicated *Miracles* to Harwood and his wife, Daphne, and mentions him in *Surprised by Joy*.

William Wordsworth

I Wandered Lonely as a Cloud

I wandered lonely as a cloud
That floats on high o'er vales and hills,
When all at once I saw a crowd,
A host of golden daffodils;
Beside the lake, beneath the trees,
Fluttering and dancing in the breeze.

Continuous as the stars that shine
And twinkle on the milky way,
They stretched in never-ending line
Along the margin of a bay:
Ten thousand saw I at a glance,
Tossing their heads in sprightly dance.

The waves beside them danced; but they
Out-did the sparkling waves in glee:
A poet could not but be gay,
In such a jocund company:
I gazed—and gazed—but little thought
What wealth the show to me had brought:

For oft, when on my couch I lie
In vacant or in pensive mood,
They flash upon that inward eye
Which is the bliss of solitude;

And then my heart with pleasure fills,
And dances with the daffodils.

William Wordsworth (1770–1850)—A major English Romantic poet, Wordsworth wrote *The Prelude*. Wordsworth's poetry was favored by C. S. Lewis, who drew the title of his autobiography, *Surprised by Joy*, from Wordsworth's poem of the same name.

DAVID LINDSAY

A Voyage to Arcturus

He witnessed an astonishing sight. A large and fully developed plant-animal appeared suddenly in front of him, out of empty space. He could not believe his eyes, but stared at the creature for a long time in amazement. It went on calmly moving and burrowing before him, as though it had been there all its life. Giving up the puzzle, Maskull resumed his striding from rock to rock up the gorge, and then, quietly and without warning, the same phenomenon occurred again. No longer could he doubt than he was seeing miracles—that Nature was precipitating its shapes into the world, without making use of the medium of parentage.... No solution of the problem presented itself.

The brook too had altered in character. A trembling radiance came up from its green water, like some imprisoned force escaping into the air. He had not walked in it for some time; now he did so, to test its quality. He felt new life entering his body, from his feet upward; it resembled a slowly moving cordial, rather than mere heat. The sensation was quite new in his experience, yet he knew by instinct what it was. The energy emitted by the brook was ascending his body neither as friend nor foe but simply because it happened to be the direct road to its objective elsewhere. But, although it had no hostile intentions, it was likely to prove a rough traveler—he was clearly conscious that its passage through his body threatened to bring about some physical transformation, unless he could do something to prevent it. Leaping quickly out of the water, he leaned against a rock, tightened his muscles, and braced himself against the impending charge. At that very moment the blurring again attacked his sight, and, while he was guarding against that, his forehead sprouted out into a galaxy of new eyes. He put his hand up and counted six, in addition to his old ones.

David Lindsay (1876–1945)—This Scottish novelist was influenced by the writings of George MacDonald. In turn, Lindsay's *Voyage to Arcturus* deeply affected C. S. Lewis and was a major influence on the latter's science fiction and fantasy works.

GEOFFREY CHAUCER

Canterbury Tales

In old Armorica, now Brittany,
There was a knight that loved and strove, did he
To serve a lady in the highest wise;
And many a labor, many a great emprise
He wrought for her, or ever she was won.
For she was of the fairest under sun,
And therewithal come of so high kindred
That scarcely could this noble knight, for dread,
Tell her his woe, his pain, and his distress.
But at the last she, for his worthiness,
And specially for his meek obedience,
Had so much pity that, in consequence,
She secretly was come to his accord
To take him for her husband and her lord,
Of such lordship as men have over wives;
And that they might be happier in their lives,
Of his free will he swore to her, as knight,
That never in his life, by day or night,
Would he assume a right of mastery
Against her will, nor show her jealousy,
But would obey and do her will in all
As any lover of his lady shall.

Geoffrey Chaucer (ca. 1343–1400)—Chaucer was one of C. S. Lewis's favorite authors. Lewis celebrated Chaucer's work in *The Allegory of Love* and in his essay "What Chaucer Really Did to *Il Filostrato*," published in *Selected Literary Essays*.

John Dryden

Miscellaneous Works

The sunny hills from far were seen to glow
With glittering beams, and in the meads below
The burnish'd brooks appear'd with liquid gold to flow.
At last they heard the foolish Cuckow sing,
Whose note proclaim'd the holy-day of spring.
       No longer doubting, all prepare to fly
And repossess their patrimonial sky.

       Who but the Swallow now triumphs alone?
The canopy of heaven is all her own:
Her youthful offspring to their haunts repair,
And glide along in glades, and skim in air,
And dip for insects in the purling springs,
And stoop on rivers to refresh their wings.

John Dryden (1631–1700)—English poet and literary critic, John Dryden is referred to in C. S. Lewis's essay "Shelley, Dryden, and Mr. Eliot," published in *Rehabilitations* and *Selected Literary Essays*.

SAMUEL TAYLOR COLERIDGE

Table Talk

Hamlet's character is the prevalence of the abstracting and generalizing habit over the practical. He does not want courage, skill, will, or opportunity; but every incident sets him thinking; and it is curious, and, at the same time, strictly natural, that Hamlet, who all the play seems reason itself, should be impelled, at last, by mere accident to effect his object. I have a smack of Hamlet myself, if I may say so.

Samuel Taylor Coleridge (1772–1834)—Poet, literary critic, and philosopher, Coleridge was best known for his *The Rime of the Ancient Mariner* and *Biographia Literaria*. Lewis, in *The Abolition of Man*, recounts the story of Coleridge at the Falls of the Clyde in Scotland.

G. K. Chesterton

Tremendous Trifles

I am sitting under tall trees, with a great wind boiling like surf about the tops of them, so that their living load of leaves rocks and roars in something that is at once exultation and agony. I feel, in fact, as if I were actually sitting at the bottom of the sea among mere anchors and ropes, while over my head and over the green twilight of water sounded the everlasting rush of waves and the toil and crash and shipwreck of tremendous ships. The wind tugs at the trees as if it might pluck them root and all out of the earth like tufts of grass. Or, to try yet another desperate figure of speech for this unspeakable energy, the trees are straining and tearing and lashing as if they were a tribe of dragons each tied by the tail.

As I look at these top-heavy giants tortured by an invisible and violent witchcraft, a phrase comes back into my mind. I remember a little boy of my acquaintance who was once walking in Battersea Park under just such torn skies and tossing trees. He did not like the wind at all; it blew in his face too much; it made him shut his eyes; and it blew off his hat, of which he was very proud. He was, as far as I remember, about four. After complaining repeatedly of the atmospheric unrest, he said at last to his mother, "Well, why don't you take away the trees, and then it wouldn't wind."

Nothing could be more intelligent or natural than this mistake. Any one looking for the first time at the trees might fancy that they were indeed vast and titanic fans, which by their mere waving agitated the air around them for miles. Nothing, I say, could be more human and excusable than the belief that it is the trees which make the wind. Indeed, the belief is so human and excusable that it is, as a matter of fact, the belief of about ninety-nine out of a hundred of the philosophers, reformers, sociologists, and politicians of the great age in which we live. My small friend was, in fact, very like the princi-ple modern thinkers; only much nicer.

Gilbert Keith Chesterton (1874–1936)—Roman Catholic artist, poet, journalist, essayist, and author, Chesterton wrote over one hundred books. C. S. Lewis says, in *Surprised by Joy,* that Chesterton's Christian apologetics had a marked impact on him, and Lewis's own apologetic work owes a debt to Chesterton.

W. R. INGE

More Lay Thoughts of a Dean

The pleasures of reading have been celebrated by a thousand pens, for writers are generally great readers, and are professionally interested in encouraging the habit of reading. For my own part, I confess that books are for me the most indispensable of all the pleasures of life. I agree with the Old English Song:

> Oh, for a booke and a shadie nooke,
>> Eyther in doore or out;
> With the grene leaves whispering overhead
>> Or the street cryes all about;
> Where I maie reade all at my ease,
>> Both of the newe and olde;
> For a jollie goode booke whereon to looke
>> Is better to me than golde.

I can find pleasure in almost all books, except trashy novels, obsolete theology, law books, field sports (except when the hunter is properly mauled by a wild beast), and mathematics, which I cannot understand.

History may no doubt be divided into events which do not matter and events which probably never occurred; but it is a fascinating subject. It tells us, at least, a good deal about the historian; and historians are agreeable people. Of poetry I do not read much, and when I do I choose the dead lion in preference to the live dog.

William Ralph Inge (1860–1954)—Fellow of King's College, Cambridge, and of Hertford College, Oxford, dean of Saint Paul's Cathedral, and theologian, Inge was notable for the pessimism of his sermons and writings.

SAMUEL TAYLOR COLERIDGE

Kubla Khan

In Xanadu did Kubla Khan
A stately pleasure-dome decree:
Where Alph, the sacred river, ran
Through caverns measureless to man
    Down to a sunless sea.
So twice five miles of fertile ground
With walls and towers were girdled round:
And here were gardens bright with sinuous rills,
Where blossomed many an incense-bearing tree;
And here were forests ancient as the hills,
Enfolding sunny spots of greenery.
But oh! that deep romantic chasm which slanted
Down the green hill athwart a cedarn cover!
A savage place! as holy and enchanted
As e'er beneath a waning moon was haunted
By woman wailing for her demon-lover!
And from this chasm, with ceaseless turmoil
      seething,
As if this earth in fast thick pants were breathing,
A mighty fountain momently was forced;
Amid whose swift half-intermitted burst
Huge fragments vaulted like rebounding hail,
Or chaffy grain beneath the thresher's flail:
And 'mid these dancing rocks at once and ever
It flung up momently the sacred river.
Five miles meandering with a mazy motion

Through wood and dale the sacred river ran,
Then reached the caverns measureless to man,
And sank in tumult to a lifeless ocean:
And 'mid this tumult Kubla heard from far
Ancestral voices prophesying war!

The shadow of the dome of pleasure
Floated midway on the waves;
Where was heard the mingled measure
From the fountain and the caves.
It was a miracle of rare device,
A sunny pleasure-dome with caves of ice!
A damsel with a dulcimer
In a vision once I saw:
It was an Abyssinian maid,
And on her dulcimer she played,
Singing of Mount Abora.
Could I revive within me,
Her symphony and song,
To such a deep delight 'twould win me,
That with music loud and long,
I would build that dome in air,
That sunny dome! those caves of ice!
And all who heard should see them there,
And all should cry, Beware! Beware!
His flashing eyes, his floating hair!
Weave a circle round him thrice,
And close your eyes with holy dread,
For he on honey-dew has fed,
And drunk the milk of Paradise.

Samuel Taylor Coleridge (1772–1834)—Poet, literary critic, and philosopher, Coleridge was best known for his *The Rime of the Ancient Mariner* and *Biographia Literaria*. Lewis, in *The Abolition of Man,* recounts the story of Coleridge at the Falls of the Clyde in Scotland.

WILLIAM WORDSWORTH

The Prelude

Imagination—here the Power so called
Through sad incompetence of human speech,
That awful Power rose from the mind's abyss
Like an unfathered vapor that enwraps,
At once, some lonely traveler. I was lost;
Halted without an effort to break through;
But to my conscious soul I now can say—
"I recognize your glory": in such strength
Of usurpation, when the light of sense
Goes out, but with a flash that has revealed
The invisible world, does greatness make abode,
There harbors; whether we be young or old,
Our destiny, our being's heart and home,
Is with infinitude, and only there;
With hope it is, hope that can never die,
Effort, and expectation, and desire,
And something evermore about to be.
Under such banners militant, the soul
Seeks for no trophies, struggles for no spoils
That may attest her prowess, blest in thoughts
That are their own perfection and reward.

William Wordsworth (1770–1850)—A major English Romantic poet, Wordsworth wrote *The Prelude*. Wordsworth's poetry was favored by C. S. Lewis, who drew the title of his autobiography, *Surprised by Joy*, from Wordsworth's poem of the same name.

EDITH NESBIT

The Phoenix and the Carpet

"Farewell, farewell, farewell, farewell!" said the Phoenix, in a far-away voice.

"Oh, *goodbye,*" said every one, and now all were in tears.

The bright bird fluttered seven times round the room and settled in the hot heart of the fire. The sweet gums and spices and woods flared and flickered around it, but its golden feathers did not burn. It seemed to grow red-hot to the very inside heart of it—and then before the eight eyes of its friends it fell together, a heap of white ashes, and the flames of the cedar pencils and the sandal-wood box met and joined above it.

"Whatever have you done with the carpet?" asked mother next day.

"We gave it to some one who wanted it very much. The name began with a P," said Jane. The others instantly hushed her.

"Oh, well, it wasn't worth twopence," said mother.

"The person who began with P said we shouldn't lose by it," Jane went on before she could be stopped.

"I daresay!" said mother, laughing.

But that very night a great box came, addressed to the children by all their names. Eliza never could remember the name of the carrier who brought it. It wasn't Carter Paterson or the Parcels Delivery.

It was instantly opened. It was a big wooden box, and it had to be opened with a hammer and the kitchen poker; the long nails came squeaking out, and boards scrunched as they were wrenched off. Inside the box was soft paper, with beautiful Chinese patterns on it—blue and green and red and violet. And under the paper—well, almost everything lovely that you can think of. Everything of reasonable size, I mean; for, of course, there were no motors or flying machines or thoroughbred chargers. But there really was almost everything else. Everything that the children had always wanted—toys and games and books, and chocolate and candied cherries and paint-boxes and photographic cameras, and all the presents they had always wanted to give to father and mother and the Lamb, only they had never had the money for them. At the very bottom of the box was a tiny golden feather. No one saw it but Robert, and he picked it up and hid it in the breast of his jacket, which had been so often the nesting-place of the golden bird. When he went to bed the feather was gone. It was the last he ever saw of the Phoenix.

Pinned to the lovely fur cloak that mother had always wanted was a paper, and it said—

"In return for the carpet. With gratitude.—P."

You may guess how father and mother talked it over. They decided at last the person who had had the carpet, and whom, curiously enough, the children were quite unable to describe, must be an insane millionaire who amused himself by playing at being a rag-and-bone man. But the children knew better.

They knew that this was the fulfillment, by the powerful Psammead, of the last wish of the Phoenix, and that this glorious and delightful boxful of treasures was really the very, very, very end of the Phoenix and the Carpet.

Edith Nesbit (1858–1924)—A poet and an author of children's books, Nesbit is perhaps best remembered for writing *The Railway Children*. C. S. Lewis admired Nesbit's work.

WILLIAM MORRIS

The Glittering Plain

Fair is the world, now autumn's wearing,
And the sluggard sun lies long abed;
Sweet are the days, now winter's nearing,
And all winds feign that the wind is dead.

Dumb is the hedge where the crabs hang yellow,
Bright as the blossoms of the spring;
Dumb is the close where the pears grow mellow,
And none but the dauntless redbreasts sing.

Fair was the spring, but amidst his greening
Grey were the days of the hidden sun;
Fair was the summer, but overweening,
So soon his o'er-sweet days were done.

Come then, love, for peace is upon us,
Far off is failing, and far is fear,
Here where the rest in the end has won us,
In the garnering tide of the happy year.

William Morris (1834–1896)—An artist and poet who was educated at Exeter College, Oxford, Morris was a member of the Pre-Raphaelite Brotherhood. C. S. Lewis's piece on Morris in his *Selected Literary Essays* reveals his deep appreciation of Morris's writing, especially his fantasy.

John Wain

Sprightly Running

For, of course, I shall give a quite false picture of Lewis and his friends if I represent them as merely reactionary, putting all their energies into being *against* things. Far from it; this was a circle of instigators, almost of incendiaries, meeting to urge one another on in the task of redirecting the whole current of contemporary art and life. Now that Williams was dead, the two most active members were Lewis and J. R. R. Tolkien. While Lewis attacked on a wide front, with broadcasts, popular theological books, children's stories, romances, and controversial literary criticism, Tolkien concentrated on the writing of his colossal *Lord of the Rings* trilogy. His readings of each successive installment were eagerly received, for "romance" was a pillar of this whole structure. The literary household gods were George MacDonald, William Morris (selectively), and an almost forgotten writer named E. R. Eddison, whose work seemed to me to consist of a meaningless proliferation of fantastic incident. All these writers had one thing in common: they *invented*. Lewis considered "fine fabling" an essential part of literature, and never lost a chance to push any author, from Spenser to Rider Haggard, who could be called a romancer. Once, unable to keep silence at what seemed to me a monstrous partiality, I attacked the whole basis of this view; a writer's task, I maintained, was to lay bare the human heart, and this could not be done if he were continually taking refuge in the spinning of fanciful webs. Lewis retorted with a theory that, since the Creator had seen fit to build a universe and set it in motion, it was the duty of the human artist to create as lavishly as possible in his turn. The romancer, who invents a whole world, is worshipping God more effectively than the mere realist who analyses that which lies about him. Looking back across fourteen years, I can hardly believe that Lewis said anything so manifestly absurd as this, and perhaps I misunderstood him; but that, at any rate, is how my memory reports the incident.

John Wain (1925–1994)—Wain was one of C. S. Lewis's students, a member of the Oxford Socratic Club, which was founded by Lewis, and a member of the Inklings, a literary discussion group that included Lewis and J. R. R. Tolkien.

17

"BORNE ON THE GUSTS OF GENIUS"

Creation, Poetry, and Writers

WILLIAM COWPER

The Poetical Works

Suppose (when thought is warm, and fancy flows,
What will not argument sometimes suppose?)
An isle possess'd by creatures of our kind,
Endued with reason, yet by nature blind.
Let Supposition lend her aid once more,
And land some grave optician on the shore:
He claps his lens, if haply they may see,
Close to the part where vision ought to be;
But finds that, though his tubes assist the sight,
They cannot give it, or make darkness light.
He reads wise lectures, and describes aloud
A sense they know not, to the wondering crowd;
He talks of light, and the prismatic hues,
As men of depth in erudition use;
But all he gains for his harangue is—Well—
What monstrous lies some travelers will tell!

William Cowper (1731–1800)—Poet laureate of England and presage of the English Romantic movement, Cowper was an evangelical and was influenced by John Newton, the former slave trader who wrote the hymn *Amazing Grace*. Cowper struggled with severe bouts of depression, which perhaps contributed to the honesty and humility in his writings.

LORD DAVID CECIL

Jane Austen

This considered intellectual foundation means that the interest of Jane
Austen's books is far more serious than their surface appearance would lead
us to expect. These spinsters and curates have the universal significance of the
scheme of values in whose light they are presented to us: these quiet come-
dies of country life propound fundamental problems of human conduct. In
every age, every country, people must decide whether they will direct their
lives by feeling or reason, decide how much importance they should attach
to considerations of prudence or worldly advantage; in every age and country, people are misled by first impressions, deceived by over-confidence in
their own powers. The issues between Elinor and Marianne are the issues
between Rousseau and Dr. Johnson: the errors that are the undoing of Emma
have undone many statesmen and social reformers; though the setting and
costumes of *Mansfield Park* may be those of *Cranford*, its drama expresses a
criticism of life as comprehensive as that of *Madame Bovary*.

Nor does the limited theatre of its presentation impair the power of this
criticism. On the contrary, it increases it. It gives it charm. The unique irresistible flavor of her work, its gay astringent buoyancy, its silvery common-
sense arises from the unexpected combination of her realistic moralism with
the polished serenity of its setting. Moreover the fact that she kept so care-
fully to the only world she knew thoroughly well, meant that she was not distracted by superficial idiosyncrasies, but could penetrate beneath them to
perceive its more general significance. *Emma* is universal just because it is
narrow; because it confines itself to the range of Jane Austen's profoundest
vision.

For it is a profound vision. There are other views of life both higher and
wider; concerned as it is exclusively with personal relationships, it leaves out

several of the most important aspects of experience. But on her own ground Jane Austen gets to the heart of the matter; her graceful unpretentious philosophy, founded as it is on an unwavering recognition of fact, directed by an unerring perception of moral quality, is as impressive as those of the most majestic novelists. Myself I find it more impressive. If I were in doubt as to the wisdom of one of my actions I should not consult Flaubert or Dostoievski. The opinion of Balzac or Dickens would carry little weight with me: were Stendhal to rebuke me, it would only convince me that I had done right: even in the judgement of Tolstoy I should not put complete confidence. But I should be seriously upset, I should worry for weeks and weeks, if I incurred the disapproval of Jane Austen.

Lord David Cecil (1902–1986)—A fellow of Wadham College, Oxford, Cecil was, along with C. S. Lewis, one of the most popular lecturers at Oxford. Cecil was a member of the Inklings, a literary discussion group that included Lewis and J. R. R. Tolkien.

William Hazlitt

Lectures on English Poets & the Spirit of the Age

Poetry is only the highest eloquence of passion, the most vivid form of expression that can be given to our conception of any thing, whether pleasurable or painful, mean or dignified, delightful or distressing. It is the perfect coincidence of the image and the words with the feeling we have, and of which we cannot get rid in any other way, that gives an instant "satisfaction to the thought." This is equally the origin of wit and fancy, of comedy and tragedy, of the sublime and the pathetic.... We see the thing ourselves, and show it to others as we feel it to exist, and as, in spite of ourselves, we are compelled to think of it. The imagination, by thus embodying and turning them to shape, gives an obvious relief to the indistinct and importunate cravings of the will. We do not wish the thing to be so; but we wish it to appear such as it is. For knowledge is conscious power; and the mind is no longer, in this case, the dupe, though it may be the victim of vice or folly. Poetry is in all its shapes the language of the imagination and the passions, of fancy and will.

William Hazlitt (1778–1830)—Lecturer, literary critic, and biographer, Hazlitt was an English liberal who supported both the French Revolution and Napoleon's government.

OWEN BARFIELD

Poetic Diction: A Study in Meaning

The part of poetry with which the actual *pleasure* of appreciation—the old, authentic thrill, which is so strong that it binds some men to their libraries for a lifetime, and actually hinders them from increasing knowledge—is most closely connected. This is that "element of strangeness in all beauty" which has been remarked in one way or another by so many critics. Alike in the greatest poetry and in the least, if pleasure is to arise, it must be there. And conversely, where it is, there will be some aesthetic pleasure. Thus, in Example 1 we saw how even the laughable semantic struggles of Pidgin English have their aesthetic value; nor is this simpler kind of strangeness by any means only to be found in the Southern Hemisphere. Aristotle in his *Poetics* showed that he knew the aesthetic value of "unfamiliar words," among which he included "foreign expressions"; in keeping diction above the "ordinary" level; and anyone who has been to the trouble of learning a foreign language after the age at which he had reached a certain degree of aesthetic maturity, will know that aesthetic pleasure arises from the contemplation of quite ordinary expressions couched in a foreign idiom. It is important, then, to note that this is not, in so far as it is aesthetic, the pleasure of comparing different ways of saying the same thing, but the pleasure of realizing the *slightly different thing that is said*. For, outside the purest abstractions and technicalities, no two languages can ever say quite the same thing.

Owen Barfield, *Poetic Diction: A Study in Meaning* (New York: McGraw-Hill, 1964).
Reprinted with permission of The McGraw-Hill Companies.

Owen Barfield (1898–1997)—Author, anthroposophist, and C. S. Lewis's solicitor, Owen Barfield became friends with Lewis while they were students at Oxford. Lewis dedicated *The Allegory of Love* to Barfield and lauded him as an unofficial teacher. Barfield was a member of the Inklings, a literary discussion group that included Lewis and J. R. R. Tolkien.

NEVILL COGHILL

The Poet Chaucer

In this brief romantic-epic [*The Knight's Tale*], leading from love to battle and back, Chaucer took one touch of humanity from Boccaccio unusual in this type of love-tangle. Emilia, the heroine, has no wish for either lover, having a temperament fully feminine and fully virginal, such as was more often manifest in times when convents were more plentiful than now. Such temperaments still exist, no doubt, but are seldom seen in the heroines of romances. Chaucer, who could understand the Wife of Bath, could also understand one who "could well endure the livery of a nun."

———————————————

Geoffrey Chaucer (ca. 1343–1400)—Chaucer was one of C. S. Lewis's favorite authors. Lewis celebrated Chaucer's work in *The Allegory of Love* and in his essay "What Chaucer Really Did to *Il Filostrato*," published in *Selected Literary Essays*.

Nevill Coghill (1899–1980)—Fellow of Exeter College, Oxford, and professor of English Literature, Coghill was a Chaucer scholar and taught drama at the university, numbering Richard Burton among his students. Coghill was a member of the Inklings, a literary discussion group that included C. S. Lewis and J. R. R. Tolkien.

SAMUEL JOHNSON

The Works of Samuel Johnson

Antiquity, like every other quality that attracts the notice of mankind, has undoubtedly votaries that reverence it, not from reason, but from prejudice. Some seem to admire indiscriminately whatever has been long preserved, without considering that time has sometimes cooperated with chance; all perhaps are more willing to honor past than present excellence; and the mind contemplates genius through the shades of age, as the eye surveys the sun through artificial opacity. The great contention of criticism is to find the faults of the moderns, and the beauties of the ancients. While an author is yet living we estimate his powers by his worst performance, and when he is dead, we rate them by his best.

Samuel Johnson (1709–1784)—A lexicographer and literary critic, Johnson is considered by some, including Malcolm Muggeridge, to be among the greatest Englishmen of letters. Nevill Coghill compared C. S. Lewis to Samuel Johnson in terms of his physical stature and his scholarship and wit.

An Essay on the Life and Genius of Dr. Johnson

"I find," said Mr. Boswell, "that I am come to London at a bad time, when great popular prejudice has gone forth against us North Britons; but when I am talking to you, I am talking to a large and liberal mind, and you know that I cannot *help coming from Scotland*." "Sir," said Johnson, "no more can the rest of your countrymen."

He had other reasons that helped to alienate him from the natives of Scotland. Being a cordial well-wisher to the constitution in Church and State, he did not think that Calvin and John Knox were proper founders of a national religion. He made, however, a wide distinction between the Dissenters of Scotland and the Separatists of England. To the former he imputed no disaffection, no want of loyalty. Their soldiers and their officers had shed their blood with zeal and courage in the service of Great Britain; and the people, he used to say, were content with their own established modes of worship, without wishing, in the present age, to give any disturbance to the Church of England. This he was at all times ready to admit; and therefore declared, that whenever he found a Scotchman, that Scotchman should be as an Englishman to him. In this, surely there was no rancor, no malevolence. The Dissenters on this side the Tweed appeared to him in a different light. Their religion, he frequently said, was too worldly, too political, too restless and ambitious. The doctrine of *cashiering* kings, and erecting on the ruins of the constitution a new form of government, which lately issued from their pulpits, he always thought was, under a calm disguise, the principle that lay lurking in their hearts. He knew that a wild democracy had overturned Kings, Lords, and Commons; and that a set of Republican Fanatics, who would not bow at the name of Jesus, had taken possession of all the livings and all the parishes in the kingdom. That those scenes of horror might never be renewed, was the ardent wish of Dr. Johnson; and though he apprehended no danger from Scotland, it is probable that his dislike of Calvinism mingled sometimes with his reflections on the natives of that country. The association of ideas could not be easily broken; but it is well known that the loved and respected many gentlemen from that part of the island.

Samuel Johnson (1709–1784)—A lexicographer and literary critic, Johnson is considered by some, including Malcolm Muggeridge, to be among the greatest Englishmen of letters. Nevill Coghill compared C. S. Lewis to Samuel Johnson in terms of his physical stature and his scholarship and wit.

Arthur Murphy (1727–1805)—Actor, translator, barrister, and playwright, Arthur Murphy wrote nineteen plays. He was the Commissioner of Bankruptcy under King George III.

ARISTOTLE

The Art of Rhetoric

It is pleasant to do the same things often; for that which is familiar is, as we said, pleasant. Change also is pleasant, since change is in the order of nature; for perpetual sameness creates an excess of the normal condition; whence it was said: Change in all things is sweet. This is why what we only see at intervals, whether men or things, is pleasant; for there is a change from the present, and at the same time it is rare. And learning and admiring are as a rule pleasant; for admiring implies the desire to learn, so that what causes admiration is to be desired, and learning implies a return to the normal. It is pleasant to bestow and to receive benefits; the latter is the attainment of what we desire, the former the possession of more than sufficient means, both of them things that men desire. Since it is pleasant to do good, it must also be pleasant for men to set their neighbors on their feet, and to supply their deficiencies. And since learning and admiring are pleasant, all things connected with them must also be pleasant; for instance, a work of imitation, such as painting, sculpture, poetry, and all that is well imitated, even if the object of imitation is not pleasant; for it is not this that causes pleasure or the reverse, but the inference that the imitation and the object imitated are identical, so that the result is that we learn something. The same may be said of sudden changes and narrow escapes from danger; for all these things excite wonder. And since that which is in accordance with nature is pleasant, and things which are akin are akin in accordance with nature, all things akin and like are for the most part pleasant to each other, as man to man, horse to horse, youth to youth. This is the origin of the proverbs:

> The old have charms for the old, the young for the young,
> Like to like,

Beast knows beast,
Birds of a feather flock together,
and all similar sayings.

Aristotle (384–322 BC)—After being a student of Plato for twenty years at the academy in Athens, Greece, Aristotle started his own school at the Lyceum, and Alexander the Great was one of his students. Much of Aristotle's thought made its way into Christianity through the writings of Thomas Aquinas.

William Hazlitt

Lectures on English Poets & the Spirit of the Age

But I may say of [Samuel Taylor Coleridge] here that he is the only person I ever knew who answered to the idea of a man of genius. He is the only person from whom I ever learnt any thing.... He was the first poet I ever knew. His genius at that time had angelic wings, and fed on manna. He talked on for ever; and you wished him to talk on for ever. His thoughts did not seem to come with labor and effort; but as if borne on the gusts of genius, and as if the wings of his imagination lifted him from off his feet. His voice rolled on the ear like the pealing organ, and its sound alone was the music of thought. His mind was clothed with wings; and raised on them, he lifted philosophy to heaven. In his descriptions, you then saw the progress of human happiness, and liberty in bright and never-ending succession, like the steps of Jacob's ladder, with airy shapes ascending and descending, and with the voice of God at the top of the ladder. And shall I, who heard him then, listen to him now? Not I! That spell is broke; that time is gone for ever; that voice is heard no more: but still the recollection comes rushing by with thoughts of long-past years, and rings in my ears with never-dying sound.

William Hazlitt (1778–1830)—Lecturer, literary critic, and biographer, Hazlitt was an English liberal who supported both the French Revolution and Napoleon's government.

SIR THOMAS MALORY

The Death of King Arthur

Now more of the death of King Arthur could I never find, but that these ladies brought him to his grave, and such one was interred there which the hermit bare witness that sometime was Bishop of Canterbury. But yet the hermit knew not in certain that he was truly the body of King Arthur; for this tale Sir Bedwere, a knight of the Table Round, made it to be written.

Yet some men say in many parts of England that King Arthur is not dead, but had by the will of our Lord Jesus into another place; and men say that he shall come again, and he shall win the Holy Cross. Yet I will not say that it shall be so, but rather I would say: here in this world he changed his life. And many men say that there is written upon the tomb this:

HIC IACET ARTHURUS REX QUONDAM REXQUE FUTURUS.

Sir Thomas Malory (ca. 1405–1471)—Malory may have produced *Le Morte D'Arthur* by translating an earlier French composition. Nevertheless, much of the Arthurian material comes to its maturity in Malory.

Thomas Malory, *The Works of Malory*, ed. Eugène Vinaver (Oxford: Oxford University Press, 1971). Reprinted by permission of Oxford University Press.

JAMES GEORGE FRAZER

The Golden Bough

Tree-spirits.—In the religious history of the Aryan race in Europe the worship of trees has played an important part. Nothing could be more natural. For at the dawn of history Europe was covered with immense primeval forests, in which the scattered clearings must have appeared like islets in an ocean of green. Down to the first century before our era the Hercynian forest stretched eastward from the Rhine for a distance at once vast and unknown; Germans whom Caesar questioned had traveled for two months through it without reaching the end. Four centuries later it was visited by the Emperor Julian and the solitude, the gloom, the silence of the forest appear to have made a deep impression on his sensitive nature. He declared that he knew nothing like it in the Roman Empire. In our own country the wealds of Kent, Surrey, and Sussex are remnants of the great forest of Anderida, which once clothed the whole of the south-eastern portion of the island. Westward it seems to have stretched till it joined another forest that extended from Hampshire to Devon. In the reign of Henry II the citizens of London still hunted the wild bull and the boar in the woods of Hampstead. Even under the later Plantagenets the royal forests were sixty-eight in number. In the forest of Arden it was said that down to modern times a squirrel might leap from tree to tree for nearly the whole length of Warwickshire.

Sir James George Frazer (1854–1941)—This Scottish author was educated at Glasgow and Cambridge and was a fellow of Trinity College, Cambridge. He was a professor of social anthropology, and his major work was *The Golden Bough*. C. S. Lewis noted "Mirkwood" (the forest in *The Hobbit*) beside this passage in his copy of *The Golden Bough*.

JAMES STEPHENS

The Crock of Gold

"The only trouble the body can know is disease. All other miseries come from the brain, and, as these belong to thought, they can be driven out by their master as unruly and unpleasant vagabonds; for a mental trouble should be spoken to, confronted, reprimanded and so dismissed. The brain cannot afford to harbor any but pleasant and eager citizens who will do their part in making laughter and holiness for the world, for that is the duty of thought."

While the Philosopher spoke [these words] the girl had been regarding him steadfastly.

"Sir," said she, "we tell our hearts to a young man and our heads to an old man, and when the heart is a fool the head is bound to be a liar. I can tell you the things I know, but how will I tell you the things I feel when I myself do not understand them? If I say these words to you 'I love a man' I do not say anything at all, and you do not hear one of the words which my heart is repeating over and over to itself in the silence of my body. Young people are fools in their heads and old people are fools in their hearts, and they can only look at each other and pass by in wonder."

"You are wrong," said the Philosopher. "An old person can take your hand like this and say, 'May every good thing come to you my daughter.' For all trouble there is sympathy, and for love there is memory, and these are the head and the heart talking to each other in quiet friendship. What the heart knows to-day the head will understand to-morrow, and as the head must be the scholar of the heart it is necessary that our hearts be purified and free from every false thing, else we are tainted beyond personal redemption."

James Stephens (1882–1950)—Irish-born poet, storyteller, and leader of the Irish literary renaissance, Stephens incorporated Irish folk tales and legends into his fanciful prose works. A talented orator, Stephens gave recitations of his writings and became a popular radio lecturer.

BRUNO S. JAMES

Saint Bernard of Clairvaux

The king swore a public oath that so long as he lived Peter would never have possession of his see; Peter took refuge with Count Theobald of Champagne; and the Pope laid the King under an interdict. It was a dangerous situation and Bernard viewed it with grave anxiety. Believing the interdict to be a mistake and only likely to make the King more stubborn, which is precisely what it did, he wrote to his friends in curia asking them to use their influence to have it raised. "For two things I cannot excuse the King," he wrote, "he took an unlawful oath and kept in unjustly. He did the last not willingly but because he is ashamed to do otherwise. As you well know, it is considered a disgrace among the French to break an oath however ill-advisedly it may have been taken, although no wise man can doubt that unlawful oaths ought not to be kept. Yet even so I cannot admit that he is to be excused in the matter. But I have undertaken to obtain pardon for him not to excuse him. It is for you to consider, whether, on the grounds of his youth, anger, or position, he can be excused. He could be without doubt if you let mercy triumph over justice, taking into account that he is a mere youth, albeit a king, and thus deserving of leniency on the understanding that he will not presume on it in future. I would say: let him be spared if he can be without prejudice to the liberties of the Church, or to the reverence due to the archbishop who was consecrated by the Apostolic hands. This is what the King himself humbly begs for, and what our afflicted Church on this side of the Alps implores. Otherwise we join hands with death, pining and withering away for dread of what we fear will come upon the world."

Saint Bernard of Clairvaux (1090–1153)—Mystic, monastic reformer, and influential figure in the twelfth-century church, Saint Bernard founded the Cistercian Monastery at Clairvaux.

Bruno Scott James (1906–)—Roman Catholic priest, educator, author, and translator, James specializes in mysticism and Greek and Roman classical literature.

OWEN BARFIELD

Poetic Diction: A Study in Meaning

Thus, an introspective analysis of my experience obliges me to say that appreciation of poetry involves a "felt change of consciousness." The phrase must be taken with some exactness. Appreciation takes place at the actual moment of change. It is not simply that the poet enables me to see with his eyes, and so to apprehend a larger and fuller world. He may indeed do this, as we shall see later; but the actual moment of the pleasure of appreciation depends upon something rarer and more transitory. It depends on the change itself. If I pass a coil of wire between the poles of a magnet, I generate in it an electric current—but I only do so while the coil is positively moving across the lines of force. I may leave the coil at rest between the two poles and in such a position that it is thoroughly permeated by the magnetic field; but in that case no current will flow along the conductor. Current only flows when I am actually bringing the coil in or taking it away again. So it is with the poetic mood, which, like the dreams to which it has so often been compared, is kindled by the passage from one plane of consciousness to another. It lives during that moment of transition and then dies, and if it is to be repeated, some means must be found of renewing the transition itself.

Poetry, as a possession, as our own souls enriched, is another matter. But when it has entered as deeply as that into our being, we no longer concern ourselves with its *diction*. At this stage the diction has served its end and may be forgotten. For, if ever we go back to linger lovingly over the exquisite phrasing of some fragment of poesy whose essence has long been our own, and of which the spirit has become a part of our every waking moment, if we do this, is it not *for the very reason* that we want to renew the thrill which accompanied the first acquisition of the treasure? As our lips murmur the well-known—or it may be the long-forgotten words, we are trying, whether deliberately or no, to cast ourselves back, into the frame of mind which was ours before we had learnt the lesson. Why? Because we know instinctively that, if we are to feel pleasure, we must have change. Everlasting day can no more freshen the earth with dew than everlasting night, but the change from night to day and from day back again to night.

Owen Barfield (1898–1997)—Author, anthroposophist, and C. S. Lewis's solicitor, Owen Barfield became friends with Lewis while they were students at Oxford. Lewis dedicated *The Allegory of Love* to Barfield and lauded him as an unofficial teacher. Barfield was a member of the Inklings, a literary discussion group that included Lewis and J. R. R. Tolkien.

Owen Barfield, *Poetic Diction: A Study in Meaning* (New York: McGraw-Hill, 1964). Reprinted with permission of The McGraw-Hill Companies.

David Nichol Smith

Wordsworth: Poetry and Prose

Nature was to Wordsworth a living soul that reveals herself alike in the movements of the stars, the yearnings of the heart, the sleep of a great city, or the decay of a flower.

> To every Form of being is assigned
> An *active* Principle: howe'er removed
> From sense and observation it subsists
> In all things, in all natures; in the stars
> Of azure heaven, the unenduring clouds,
> In flower and tree, in every pebbly stone
> That paves the brooks, the stationary rocks,
> The moving waters, and the invisible air.
> Whate'er exists has properties that spread
> Beyond itself, communicating good,
> A simple blessing, or with evil mixed;
> Spirit that knows no insulated spot,
> No chasm, no solitude; from link to link
> It circulates, the Soul of all the worlds.
> *The Excursion IX.*

His poetry makes no division between man and the world in which he lives. He thinks of all created things, human or inanimate, as parts of one great whole, filling their appointed place, moving in their established order. He is our greatest nature poet because he is the poet of more than external nature; he is, in a higher degree, the poet of man. No other poet is more consistently original and faithful in his pictures of what the eye can see, more luminous in his interpretation of it. But he could never dissociate it from the human heart.

One purpose runs throughout all his poems. He never stated it more simply than in a casual sentence in a letter which he wrote when his long career was drawing to its close. "What I should myself most value in my attempts" he there defined as being "the spirituality with which I have endeavored to invest the material universe, and the moral relations under which I have wished to exhibit its most ordinary appearances."

David Nichol Smith (1875–1962)—Educated at Edinburgh and the Sorbonne and Merton Professor of English Literature, Oxford, Smith wrote widely on English and French literature, particularly that of the eighteenth century and Shakespeare.

William Wordsworth (1770–1850)—A major English Romantic poet, Wordsworth wrote *The Prelude.* Wordsworth's poetry was favored by C. S. Lewis, who drew the title of his autobiography, *Surprised by Joy,* from Wordsworth's poem of the same name.

JOHN WAIN

Sprightly Running

Universities provide meeting-places for young talent and, if they did nothing more, that would justify their existence. But, of course, there is always the wistful hope, deep down in the heart of everyone who would like to see civilization continue, that these young will not merely benefit from meeting each other, but will, somewhere along the line, actually be *taught* something. Every serious writer I have ever met has acknowledged that the problem of keeping literature alive is just as much a problem of reception as of production; a dearth of appreciators can be just as fatal as a dearth of creators. One sees this particularly in poetry. The last thirty years have been the hey-day of the poetic charlatan; any young man (or, I suppose, woman) who wanted, for any kind of reason, to acquire a literary reputation which could then be exploited, has been able to do it via "poetry," usually without being challenged at any point. It's so easy: announce, as loudly and as often as possible, "I AM A POET!" and begin immediately to make personal claims which imply that you can't be expected to live under the same restraints as ordinary, non-poetic humanity. For some time, this alone will suffice; ultimately, the day will come when you will be asked to produce some poems to go along with the act, but this is nothing to worry about. Scribble down anything that comes into your head, produce the poetic output of three years in one evening at a café table—nobody will notice that it's worthless; this is the age of the ad man, when anything at all can be sold by advertising.

John Wain (1925–1994)—Wain was one of C. S. Lewis's students, a member of the Oxford Socratic Club, which was founded by Lewis, and a member of the Inklings, a literary discussion group that included Lewis and J. R. R. Tolkien.

Sir Walter Scott

Essays

Dr. Johnson has defined romance, in its primary sense, to be "a military fable of the middle ages; a tale of wild adventures in love and chivalry." But although this definition expresses correctly the ordinary idea of the word, it is not sufficiently comprehensive to answer our present purpose. A composition may be a legitimate romance, yet neither refer to love nor chivalry—to war nor to the Middle Ages. The "wild adventures" are almost the only absolutely essential ingredient in Johnson's definition. We would be rather inclined to describe a *Romance* as "a fictitious narrative in prose or verse; the interest of which turns upon marvelous and uncommon incidents"; being thus opposed to the kindred term *Novel*, which Johnson has described as a "smooth tale, generally of love"; but which we would rather define as "a fictitious narrative, differing from the romance, because the events are accommodated to the ordinary train of human events, and the modern state of society." Assuming these definitions, it is evident, from the nature of the distinction adopted, that there may exist compositions which it is difficult to assign precisely or exclusively to the one class or the other; and which, in fact, partake of the nature of both. But the distinction will be found broad enough to answer all general and useful purposes.

Sir Walter Scott (1771–1832)—Educated at Edinburgh University, Scott is best known for his Waverly novels. C. S. Lewis was a great admirer of Scott; his appreciation is evident in his *Selected Literary Essays* piece which bears Scott's name as its title.

William Cowper

Selected Letters

He that would write, should read, not that he may retail the observations of other men, but that, being thus refreshed and replenished, he may find himself in a condition to make and to produce his own. I reckon it among my principle advantages, as a composer of verses, that I have not read an English poet these thirteen years, and but one these twenty years. Imitation, even of the best models, is my aversion; it is servile and mechanical, a trick that has enabled many to usurp the name of author, who could not have written at all, if they had not written upon the pattern of somebody indeed original. But when the ear and the taste have been much accustomed to the manner of others, it is almost impossible to avoid it; and we imitate in spite of ourselves, just in proportion as we admire.

William Cowper (1731–1800)—Poet Laureate of England and presage of the English Romantic movement, Cowper was an evangelical and was influenced by John Newton, the former slave trader who wrote the hymn *Amazing Grace*. Cowper struggled with severe bouts of depression, which perhaps contributed to the honesty and humility in his writings.

JAMES BOSWELL

The Journal of a Tour to the Hebrides, with Samuel Johnson, L.L.D.

The English chapel, to which we went this morning, was but mean. The altar was a bare fir table, with a coarse stool for kneeling on, covered with a piece of thick sailcloth doubled, by way of cushion. The congregation was small. Mr. Tait, the clergyman, read prayers very well, though with much of the Scotch accent. He preached on "Love your Enemies." It was remarkable that, when talking of the connections among men, he said, that some connected themselves with men of distinguished talents, and since they could not equal them, tried to deck themselves with their merit, by being their companions. The sentence was to this purpose. It had an odd coincidence with what might be said of my connecting myself with Dr. Johnson.

After church, we walked down to the Quay. We then went to MacBeth's castle. I had a romantic satisfaction in seeing Dr. Johnson actually in it. It perfectly corresponds with Shakespeare's description.... Just as we came out of it, a raven perched on one of the chimney-tops, and croaked. Then I repeated

> The raven himself is hoarse,
> That croaks the fatal entrance of Duncan
> Under my battlements.

James Boswell (1740–1795)—A Scottish man of letters and friend of Samuel Johnson, Boswell achieved a high standard for biography with his *Life of Johnson*. Some consider this work the fifth greatest biography ever written, after *Matthew, Mark, Luke,* and *John.*

WILLIAM HAZLITT

Lectures on English Poets & the Spirit of the Age

Chaucer's characters are narrative, Shakespeare's dramatic, Milton's epic. That is, Chaucer told only as much of his story as he pleased, as was required for a particular purpose. He answered for his characters himself. In Shakespeare they are introduced upon the stage, are liable to be asked all sorts of questions, and are forced to answer for themselves. In Chaucer we perceive a fixed essence of character. In Shakespeare there is a continual composition and decomposition of its elements, a fermentation of every particle in the whole mass, by its alternate affinity or antipathy to other principles which are brought in contact with it. Till the experiment is tried, we do not know the result, the turn which the character will take in its new circumstances. Milton took only a few simple principles of character, and raised them to the utmost conceivable grandeur, and refined them from every base alloy. His imagination "nigh sphered in Heaven," claimed kindred only with what he saw from that height, and could raise to the same elevation with itself. He sat retired and kept his state alone, "playing with wisdom"; while Shakespeare mingled with the crowd, and played the host, "to make society the sweeter welcome."

William Hazlitt (1778–1830)—Lecturer, literary critic, and biographer, Hazlitt was an English liberal who supported both the French Revolution and Napoleon's government.

GEOFFREY ASHE

King Arthur's Avalon

St. Bridget was an Irishwoman of boundless vigor and charity, born illegitimately in 453. Bridget took the veil at sixteen and persuaded other girls to join her. She spent the rest of a long life in semi-political activity and the foundation of convents, Kildare being the chief. Her tact and humor seem to have been extraordinarily endearing, and her special ministry to lepers, whom she washed with her own hands, helped to canonize her at once in public esteem. There is no trustworthy evidence that Bridget ever left Ireland, but when her cult penetrated Britain, a story grew up that she came to Somerset, died there, and was buried at Glastonbury. The monks doughtily exhibited relics—and attracted Irish pilgrims, who tested the relics' efficacy in curing their ailments, and did not always retire disappointed.

Geoffrey Ashe (1923–)—Educated at Trinity College, Cambridge, Ashe is a lecturer and historian. He specializes in British mythology and has written over twenty books. He is a founder of the Camelot Research Committee, which excavated Cadbury Castle, considered by some to be a possible site of King Arthur's Camelot.

Samuel Pepys

The Diary

To my Lord's in the morning, where I met with Captain Cuttance. But my Lord not being up, I went out to Charing-cross to see Major-General Harrison hanged, drawn, and quartered—which was done there—he looking as cheerfully as any man could do in that condition. He was presently cut down and his head and his heart shown to the people, at which there was great shouts of joy. It is said that he said that he was sure to come shortly at the right hand of Christ to judge them that now have judged him. And that his wife expects his coming again.

Thus it was my chance to see the King beheaded at White-hall and to see the first blood shed in revenge for the blood of the King at Charing-cross. From there to my Lord's and took Captain Cuttance and Mr. Shebly to the Sun tavern and did give them some oysters. After that I went by water home, where I was angry with my wife for her things lying about, and in my passion kicked the little fine Basket which I bought her in Holland and broke it, which troubled me after I had done it.

Within all the afternoon, setting up shelves in my study. At night to bed.

Samuel Pepys (1633–1703)—Educated at Magdalen College, Oxford, and Secretary of the Admiralty, Pepys is best known for the diary he kept from 1660 to 1669. His record of life in London, particularly his account of the Great London Fire of 1666, is invaluable to historians. His library is housed at Magdalen College, where C. S. Lewis studied and taught.

SAMUEL JOHNSON

The Works of Samuel Johnson

Shakespeare is, above all writers, at least above all modern writers, the poet of nature; the poet that holds up to his readers a faithful mirror of manners and of life. His characters are not modified by the customs of particular places, unpracticed by the rest of the world; by the peculiarities of studies or professions, which can operate but upon small numbers, or by the accidents of transient fashions or temporary opinions: they are the genuine progeny of common humanity, such as the world will always supply, and observation will always find. His persons act and speak by the influence of those general passions and principles by which all minds are agitated, and the whole system of life is continued in motion. In the writings of other poets a character is too often an individual: in those of *Shakespeare* it is commonly a species.

Samuel Johnson (1709–1784)—A lexicographer and literary critic, Johnson is considered by some, including Malcolm Muggeridge, to be among the greatest Englishmen of letters. Nevill Coghill compared C. S. Lewis to Samuel Johnson in terms of his physical stature and his scholarship and wit.

George MacDonald

A Dish of Orts

No artist can have such a claim to the high title of *creator*, as that he invents for himself the forms, by means of which he produces his new result; and all the forms of man and nature which he modifies and combines to make a new region in his world of art, have their own original life and meaning. The laws likewise of their various combinations are natural laws, harmonious with each other. While, therefore, the artist employs many or few of their original aspects for his immediate purpose, he does not and cannot thereby deprive them of the many more which are essential to their vitality, and the vitality likewise of his presentation of them, although they form only the background from which his peculiar use of them stands out. The objects presented must therefore fall, to the eye of the observant reader, into many different combinations and harmonies of operation and result, which are indubitably there, whether the writer saw them or not. These latent combinations and relations will be numerous and true, in proportion to the scope and the truth of the representation; and the greater the number of meanings, harmonious with each other, which any work of art presents, the greater claim it has to be considered a work of genius.

George MacDonald (1824–1905)—Scottish Congregationalist pastor, novelist, myth maker, and poet, MacDonald had a profound influence on C. S. Lewis. Lewis said that MacDonald's *Phantastes* "baptized my imagination."

WILLIAM HAZLITT

Lectures on English Poets & the Spirit of the Age

[Robert] Burns was not like Shakespeare in the range of his genius; but there is something of the same magnanimity, directness, and unaffected character about him. He was not a sickly sentimentalist, a namby-pamby poet, a mincing meter ballad-monger, any more than Shakespeare. He would as soon hear "a brazen candlestick tuned, or a dry wheel grate on the axletree." He was as much of a man—not a twentieth part as much of a poet as Shakespeare. With but little of his imagination or inventive power, he had the same life of mind: within the narrow circle of personal feeling or domestic incidents, the pulse of his poetry flows as healthily and vigorously. He had an eye to see; a heart to feel:—no more. His pictures of good fellowship, of social glee, of quaint humor, are equal to any thing: they come up to nature, and they cannot go beyond it. The sly jest collected in his laughing eye at the sight of the grotesque and ludicrous in manners—the large tear rolled down his manly cheek at the sight of another's distress. He has made us as well acquainted with himself as it is possible to be; has let out the honest impulses of his native disposition, the unequal conflict of the passions in his breast, with the same frankness and truth of description. His strength is not greater than his weakness: his virtues were greater than his vices. His virtues belonged to his genius: his vices to his situation, which did not correspond to his genius.

William Hazlitt (1778–1830)—Lecturer, literary critic, and biographer, Hazlitt was an English liberal who supported both the French Revolution and Napoleon's government.

ROBERT MARTIN ADAMS

Ikon: John Milton and the Modern Critics

It is, of course, futile to quarrel fundamentally with the taste of one's times. For reasons too elaborate and unwieldy to be explored, contemporary taste seems permanently impatient with the heroic mode. Our poetry, when it ventures beyond the mechanical grating of texture on texture, image on image, and tension on tension, tends either to hug the elemental facts of physical existence or to seek an ecstatic unification of experience in mystical contemplation of the godhead. There is nothing to be said against these modes of poetic thought and feeling except that as exclusive alternatives they radically limit the poet's power to deal with human experience. If one accepts these limitations without question, it is futile to pretend that Milton is anything but a peripheral figure; though something may perhaps be learned even from peripheral figures whom one takes the trouble to understand. But if one feels that modern writers of verse, with rare exceptions, exist within narrow bounds of style and convention, bounds which sometimes exclude the whole middle ground of human experience at its most distinctive, one may be impelled to feel not only respect for Milton, and sympathy, but also an emotion no less intimate and genuine than envy.

Robert Martin Adams (1915–1996)—Writer, educator, and translator, Adams was one of the founding editors of the *Norton Anthology of English Literature* and a member of the Department of English at Cornell University.

John Milton (1608–1674)—English Puritan and poet, Milton is perhaps best known for his *Paradise Lost*. C. S. Lewis wrote a literary critical work entitled *A Preface to Paradise Lost* and numbered Milton among his favorite authors.

Andrew Marvell

Poems

See how the flowers, as at parade,
Under their colors stand displayed;
Each regiment in order grows,
That of the tulip, pink, and rose.
But when the vigilant patrol
Of stars walks round about the pole,
Their leaves that to the stalks are curled
Seem to their staves the ensigns furled.
Then in some flower's beloved hut,
Each bee, as sentinel, is shut,
And sleeps so too, but, if once stirred,
She runs you through, nor asks the word.

Andrew Marvell (1621–1678)—Cambridge graduate, patriot, politician, poet, and satirist, Marvell was not recognized for his poetry until the twentieth century, when an essay by T. S. Eliot created interest in his work. Marvell is considered one of the seventeenth-century metaphysical poets.

18

"THE GLEAMING OF DIVINE BRIGHTNESS"

Heaven, Death, and Immortality

John Calvin

Golden Booklet of the True Christian Life

Our constant efforts to lower our estimate of the present world should not lead us to hate life, or to be ungrateful towards God. For this life, though it is full of countless miseries, deserves to be reckoned among the divine blessings which should not be despised. Therefore, if we discover nothing of God's goodness in it, we are already guilty of no small ingratitude toward him. But to believers especially this life should be a witness of God's kindness, since all of it is destined to advance their salvation.

For, before he fully reveals to us the inheritance of eternal glory, he intends to show himself as our Father in matters of minor importance; and those are the blessings which he daily showers upon us. Since this life, then, serves to teach us the divine kindness, should we dare to scorn it as if there were no particle of good in it? We must, therefore, have enough sense and appreciation to class it among the bounties of the divine love which should not be cast away. For, if Scriptural evidences were wanting, which are very numerous and clear, even nature itself urges us to give thanks to the Lord for having given us the light of life, and its many usages, and the means necessary to preserve it.

Moreover, we have far more reason to be thankful, if we consider that this life helps to prepare us for the glory of the heavenly kingdom. For the Lord has ordained that those who are to be crowned in heaven, should first fight the good fight on earth, that they may not celebrate their triumph without actually having overcome the difficulties of warfare, and having gained the victory. Another reason is that here on earth we may have a foretaste of the divine kindness, so that our hope and longing may be kindled for the full revelation of it.

John Calvin (1509–1564)—French Reformer and political leader in Geneva, Switzerland, Calvin published *The Institutes of the Christian Religion* when he was twenty-seven years old. Apart from Luther, Calvin is considered the most notable of the Protestant Reformers.

RICHARD BAXTER

The Saint's Everlasting Rest

What is the devil's daily business? Is it not to keep our souls from God? And shall we be content with this? Is it not the one half of hell which we wish to ourselves, while we desire to be absent from heaven? What sport is this to Satan, that his desires and yours, Christian, should so concur; that, when he sees he cannot get you to hell, he can so long keep you out of heaven, and make you the earnest petitioner for it yourself. O gratify not the devil so much to your own injury. Do not our daily fears of death make our lives a continual torment? Those lives, which might be full of joy in the daily contemplation of the life to come, and the sweet, delightful thoughts of bliss, how do we fill them up with causeless terrors. Thus we consume our own comforts, and prey upon our truest pleasures. When we might lie down, and rise up, and walk abroad with our hearts full of the joys of God, we continually fill them with perplexing fears; for he that fears dying must be always fearing, because he has always reason to expect it. And how can that man's life be comfortable who lives in continual fear of losing his comforts? Are not these fears of death self-created sufferings, as if God had not inflicted enough upon us, but we must inflict more upon ourselves? Is not death bitter enough to the flesh of itself, but we must double and treble its bitterness? The sufferings laid upon us by God do all lead to happy issues; the progress is from tribulation to patience, from there to experience, and so to hope, and at last to glory.

Richard Baxter (1615–1691)—Although he was an Anglican chaplain during the English Civil War and chaplain to the king after the Restoration, Richard Baxter left the Church of England at the time of the Act of Uniformity and became a leader of the Nonconformists. Baxter published his views and preached to large audiences, for which he was arrested twice and spent a total of eighteen years in prison. C. S. Lewis took the term "mere Christianity" from Baxter's *The Saint's Everlasting Rest.*

Samuel Johnson

The Intellectual World

Let us then according to the Gospel consider this visible world chiefly in this view, as an emblem of things invisible, and a means to lead us by reason and faith to the sight of God our great, our chief good. For according to the Apostle's philosophy in the 17th of Acts, v. 24, etc., God has to that end made the world and all things in it, and has made of one blood all nations of men to dwell on all the face of the earth, that they should seek the Lord, and that they might feel after Him, and find Him whose offspring they are, and in whom they all live, move and have their being. For, says he, Romans 1:20, the invisible things of Him from the creation of the world are clearly seen, being understood from the things that are made, even his eternal power and Godhead. Let me then from the visible things before our eyes, direct you to look to the invisible things of Him who is the Father and Lord of all things. Let us consider the objects of our sight as leading us directly to Him who is invisible. We know they are effects produced in our minds of which we are not the cause and yet nothing that is an effect can exist without a cause. The Father of Lights, therefore must be the cause of all that light that is let into our minds, and consequently of all the objects of our sight. We certainly find that light and all these visible objects serve to guide and direct us in every thing that it concerns us to do for avoiding things hurtful and procuring things advantageous to us; we must therefore conclude that the great and good author of them designs by them to guide and direct us in every thing that concerns us, and consequently is ever present with us in them, and ever watching over us and speaking to us and directing us in everything that concerns us, enlightening our eyes from without us, while He enlightens our minds within us.

Samuel Johnson (1709–1784)—A lexicographer and literary critic, Johnson is considered by some, including Malcolm Muggeridge, to be among the greatest Englishmen of letters. Nevill Coghill compared C. S. Lewis to Samuel Johnson in terms of his physical stature and his scholarship and wit.

Samuel Taylor Coleridge

Table Talk

I am dying, but without expectation of a speedy release. Is it not strange that very recently by-gone images, and scenes of early life, have stolen into my mind, like breezes blown from the spice-islands of Youth and Hope—those two realities of this phantom world! I do not add Love,—for what is Love but Youth and Hope embracing, and so seen as *one?* I say *realities;* for reality is a thing of degrees, from the Iliad to a dream.... Yet, in a strict sense, reality is not predicable at all of aught below Heaven.... Hooker wished to live to finish his Ecclesiastical Polity;—so I own I wish life and strength had been spared to me to complete my Philosophy. For, as God hears me, the originating, continuing, and sustaining wish and design in my heart was to exalt the glory of his name; and, which is the same thing in other words, to promote the improvement of mankind. But *visum aliter Deo,* and his will be done.

Samuel Taylor Coleridge (1772–1834)—Poet, literary critic, and philosopher, Coleridge was best known for his *The Rime of the Ancient Mariner* and *Biographia Literaria.* Lewis, in *The Abolition of Man,* recounts the story of Coleridge at the Falls of the Clyde in Scotland.

Thomas Aquinas

Summa Theologiae

It is impossible to see God by the power of sight or by any other sense or sensitive power. Any power of this kind is, as we shall be seeing later, the proper activity of some corporeal organ. Such activity must belong to the same order as that of which it is the activity, hence no such power could extend beyond corporeal things. God, however, is not corporeal, as has been shown, hence he cannot be seen by sense or imagination but only by the mind.

Hence: 1. *In my flesh I shall see God* does not mean that I shall see God by means of the bodily eye, but that I shall see him when I am in the flesh, i.e., after the resurrection. *Now my eye sees you* refers to the eye of the mind, as when St. Paul says, *May he grant you a spirit of wisdom in knowing him, may he enlighten the eyes of your mind.*

2. Augustine here is merely making a suggestion and not committing himself to a definite position. This is clear from what he says immediately afterwards; *They* (the eyes of the glorified body) *would have to have an altogether different power if they were to see incorporeal things.* Later he finds his own solution; *It is extremely likely that we shall then see the bodies that make up the new heaven and the new earth in such a way as to see God present everywhere in them, governing everything, even material things. We shall not merely see him as we now do when "the invisible things of God are made known to us by the things he has made" but rather as we now see the life of the living breathing people we meet. The fact that they are alive is not something we come to believe in but something we see.* Hence it is evident that our glorified eyes will see God as now they see the life of another. For life is not seen by bodily eyesight as though it were visible in itself as a proper object of sight; it is an indirect sense-object, not itself perceived by sense, yet straightway known in sensation by some other cognitive power. That divine presence is instantly perceived by

the mind on the sight of and through bodily things comes from two causes, from its own penetrating clearness and from the gleaming of divine brightness in our renewed bodies.

Thomas Aquinas (1225–1274)—Roman Catholic saint, theologian, mystic, and scholar, Aquinas was educated by Benedictine monks at Monte Cassino and at the University of Naples. He became a Dominican friar at age seventeen. He is perhaps best known for his major work, the *Summa Theologiae*.

Charles Williams

Descent into Hell

So there entered into him a small, steady, meaningless flow of sound, which stung and tormented him with the same lost knowledge of meaning; small burning flames flickered down on his soul. His eyes opened again in mere despair. A little hopeless voice came from his throat. He said, and rather gasped than spoke: "Ah! ah!" Then everything at which he was looking rushed together and became a point, very far off, and he also was a point opposite it; and both points were rushing together, because in this place they drew towards each other from the more awful repulsion of the void. But fast as they went they never reached one another, far out of the point that was not he there expanded an anarchy of unintelligible shapes and hid it, and he knew it had gone out, expiring in the emptiness before it reached him. The shapes turned themselves into alternate panels of black and white. He had forgotten the name of them, but somewhere at some time he had thought he knew similar forms and they had had names. These had no names, and whether they were or were not anything, and whether that anything was desirable or hateful he did not know. He had now no consciousness of himself as such, for the magical mirrors of Gomorrah had been broken, and the city itself had been blasted, and he was out beyond it in the blankness of a living oblivion, tormented by oblivion. The shapes stretched out beyond him, and half turned away, all rigid and silent. He was sitting at the end, looking up an avenue of nothingness, and the little flames licked his soul, but they did not now come from without, for they were the power, and the only power, his dead past had on him; the life, and the only life, of his soul. There was, at the end of the grand avenue, a bobbing shape of black and white that hovered there and closed it. As he saw it there came on him a suspense; he waited for something to happen. The silence lasted; nothing happened. In that pause expectancy faded. Presently then the shape went out and he was drawn, steadily, everlastingly, inward and down through the bottomless circles of the void.

Charles Williams (1886–1945)—Author, poet, and editor for the Oxford University Press, Williams was a member of the Inklings, a literary discussion group that included C. S. Lewis and J. R. R. Tolkien. Lewis published *The Arthurian Torso*, a critical look at Williams's Arthurian poetry, and dedicated his *A Preface to Paradise Lost* to Williams.

A. E. TAYLOR

The Christian Hope of Immortality

We are expected to believe that the heroic dead derive their happiness from the consumption of spectral whiskies-and-sodas and the smoking of ghostly cigars, things which no intelligent man would reckon as more than very minor "conveniences" even of this earthly life. Eternity, we are asked to believe, is concerned with "fun and frolic," as though any man of character and intelligence would be content, even here, to give up a year of his life to "fun and frolic." This—and how much there is of it all round us—is worse than childishness; it is vulgar-minded worldliness. Its condemnation from the Christian point of view is already pronounced in the apostolic dictum that flesh and blood cannot inherit the kingdom of God. When Christ told the Sadducees that in the resurrection they neither marry nor are given in marriage, He was not saying, as He has sometimes been understood to say, that the deepest and tenderest affections of human life are extinguished at death, but He was saying that even in the truest and noblest of them as we know it in this life, there is bound up *something* which is of the earth earthy, and therefore is but for a time; they cannot be transferred, just as they stand, into the "eternal realm"; the best of them, in the continuance into eternity, must take on a touch of the "unearthly." If the pronouncement sounds austere, its austerity is of a kind that belongs to the whole Christian conception of the life to come. In the genuinely Christian life, even as it is lived by the Christian who is still in the flesh, there is always something unfamiliar and unaccountable, "wholly other," from the point of view of a contented secularism; how much more must it be so when that life is continued into a state where the homely terrestrial environment so familiar to us here has finally fallen away. To forget this essential "otherness" of the "resurrection" life is intellectual vulgarity, though it is a vulgarity to which all of us are only too prone. But we are certainly thinking of eternal life unworthily, if it does not affect us with awe as well as with hope.

Alfred Edward Taylor (1869–1945)—Fellow of Merton College, Oxford, philosopher, translator, author, and professor at St. Andrews University and Edinburgh University, Taylor wrote nineteen works on metaphysics and philosophy.

Selected Letters

To Mrs. Thrale

Dear Madam

This letter will not, I hope, reach you many days before me; in a distress which can be so little relieved, nothing remains for a friend but to come and partake it.

Poor dear sweet little boy! When I read the letter this day to Mrs. Aston, she said, "Such a death is the next to translation." Yet however I may convince myself of this, the tears are in my eyes, and yet I could not love him as you loved him, nor reckon upon him for a future comfort, as you and his father reckoned upon him.

He is gone, and we are going. We could not have enjoyed him long, and shall not long be separated from him. He has probably escaped many such pangs as you are now feeling.

Nothing remains, but that with humble confidence we resign ourselves to Almighty Goodness, and fall down, without irreverent murmurs, before the Sovereign Distributor of good and evil, with hope that though sorrow endures for a night yet joy may come in the morning.

I have known you, Madam, too long to think that you want any arguments for submission to the Supreme Will; nor can my consolations have any effect but that of showing that I wish to comfort you. What can be done you must do for yourself. Remember first, that your child is happy; and then, that he is safe, not only from the ills of this world, but from those more formidable dangers which extend their mischief to eternity. You have brought into the world a rational being; have seen him happy during the little life that has been granted him; and can have no doubt but that his happiness is now permanent and immutable.

When you have obtained by prayer such tranquility as nature will admit, force your attention, as you can, upon your accustomed duties and accustomed entertainments. You can do no more for our dear boy, but you must not therefore think less on those whom our attention may make fitter for the place to which he is gone.

> I am, dearest, dearest Madam,
> Your most affectionate humble servant,
> Sam Johnson

Samuel Johnson (1709–1784)—A lexicographer and literary critic, Johnson is considered by some, including Malcolm Muggeridge, to be among the greatest Englishmen of letters. Nevill Coghill compared C. S. Lewis to Samuel Johnson in terms of his physical stature and his scholarship and wit.

EDMUND SPENSER

The Faerie Queene

And is there care in heaven? and is there love
In heavenly spirits to these creatures base,
That may compassion of their evils move?
There is: else much more wretched were the case
Of men, than beasts. But O! th'exceeding grace
Of highest God, that loves his creatures so,
And all his works with mercy doth embrace,
That blessed angels, he sends to and fro,
To serve to wicked man, to serve his wicked foe.

How oft do they, their silver bowers leave,
To come to succor us, that succor want?
How oft do they with golden pinions, cleave
The flitting skies, like flying Pursuivant,
Against foul fiends to aide us militant?
They for us fight, they watch and duly ward,
And their bright squadrons round about us plant,
And all for love, and nothing for reward:
O why should heavenly God to man have such regard?

Edmund Spenser (1552–1599)—Best known for his *Faerie Queen,* Spenser is re-garded as one of the greatest English poets of the sixteenth century. C. S. Lewis, in his *English Literature of the Sixteenth Century Excluding Drama,* describes Spenser as the central poet of the "Golden" period.

HENRY VAUGHAN

Sacred Poems

Peace

My Soul, there is a country
    Afar beyond the stars,
Where stands a winged Sentry
    All skillful in the wars.
There, above noise and danger,
    Sweet peace sits, crown'd with smiles,
And One born in a manger
    Commands the beauteous files.
He is your gracious friend
    And (O my Soul awake!)
Did in pure love descend,
    To die here for your sake.
If you can get but thither,
    There grows the flower of peace,
The rose that cannot wither,
    Your fortress, and your ease.
Leave then your foolish ranges;
    For none can you secure,
But One, who never changes,
    Your God, your Life, your Cure.

Henry Vaughan (1622–1695)—Soldier, physician, poet, and brother of the alchemist Thomas Vaughan, Henry Vaughan is considered one of the metaphysical poets of the seventeenth century.

Christina Rossetti

The Poetical Works

When sick of life and all the world—
How sick of all desire but Thee!—
I lift mine eyes up to the hills,
    Eyes of my heart that see,
I see beyond all death and ills
Refreshing green for heart and eyes,
The golden streets and gateways pearled,
The trees of Paradise.

"There is a time for all things," saith
The Word of Truth, Thyself the Word:
And many things Thou reasonest of:
    A time of hope deferred,
But time is now for grief and fears;
A time for life, but now is death;
Oh when shall be the time of love
    When Thou shalt wipe our tears?

Then the new Heavens and Earth shall be
Where righteousness shall dwell indeed;
There shall be no more blight, nor need,
    Nor barrier of the sea;
No sun and moon alternating,
For God shall be the Light thereof;
No sorrow more, no death, no sting,
    For God Who reigns is Love.

Christina Rossetti (1830–1894)—Sister of the Pre-Raphaelite Dante Gabriel Rossetti, Christina Rossetti was a notable Victorian poet whose work, while often melancholy and erotic, is filled with rich spirituality.

D. E. HARDING

The Hierarchy of Heaven and Earth

The fact is that the Absolute which only absorbs, which demands the surrender of every self to itself, is the Devil. For God Himself, more than any creature, subjects Himself to the rule that it is not enough to find oneself in others: the others must be free and in no way coerced, must be independent Centers and not radii extending from one's own Center. He is the guarantor of our distinctness from Himself and from one another; each of us is eternally unique and inviolable, for He needs every member of His Hierarchy of Heaven and Earth to be itself and no other. Evil is the price of this freedom. Creatures incapable of sin, sustained in every perfection, would be mere projections of Himself, and His love for them would be the self-love which is of the essence of evil. Of necessity love individuates its object. So far from the crowning level of the hierarchy threatening the independence of the others, it stands guard over it as a thing most precious

The timeless realm of absolute unity is the realm where no distinction made apparent in time is lost. And here alone are fulfilled the conditions of love. Love demands that the loved one shall be himself and free; and love demands union. In the world of time these requirements are incompatible, and love is always working its own undoing. But in the timeless world they are realized together—the perfection of independence and of oneness do not cancel out, but reinforce each other. In Hell I am bent on finding myself in myself, but time destroys me; in Heaven I am bent on losing myself in Another, but eternity preserves me.

Douglas E. Harding (1909–)—A contemporary English philosopher, D. E. Harding is devoted to the promotion of self-examination and awareness. C. S. Lewis wrote the introduction to Harding's *The Hierarchy of Heaven and Earth.*

WALTER DE LA MARE

The Burning Glass and Other Poems

The Rapids

Grieve must my heart. Age hastens by.
No longing can stay Time's torrent now.
Once would the sun in eastern sky
Pause on the solemn mountain's brow.
Rare flowers he still to bloom may bring,
But day approaches evening;
And ah, how swift their withering!

The birds, that used to sing, sang then
As if in an eternal day;
Ev'n sweeter yet their grace notes, when
Farewell...farewell is theirs to say.
Yet, as a thorn its drop of dew
Treasures in shadow, crystal clear,
All that I loved I love anew,
    Now parting draweth near.

Walter de la Mare (1873–1956)—A graduate of St. Paul's Cathedral Choir School, London, and a clerk in the statistics department of the Anglo-American Standard Oil Company, de la Mare published stories and poetry. A government pension and the success of his works enabled him to focus on literary pursuits after 1908.

DANTE

Paradise

But through the sight, that fortified itself
In me by looking, one appearance only
To me was ever changing as I changed.
Within the deep and luminous subsistence
Of the High Light appeared to me three circles,
Of threefold color and of one dimension,
And by the second seemed the first reflected
As Iris is by Iris, and the third
Seemed fire that equally from both is breathed.
O how all speech is feeble and falls short
Of my conceit, and this to what I saw
Is such, tis not enough to call it little!
O Light Eterne, sole in thyself that dwellest,
Sole knowest thyself, and, known unto thyself
And knowing, lovest and smilest on thyself!
That circulation, which being thus conceived
Appeared in thee as a reflected light,
When somewhat contemplated by mine eyes,
Within itself, of its own very color
Seemed to me painted with our effigy,
Wherefore my sight was all absorbed therein.
As the geometrician, who endeavors
To square the circle, and discovers not,
By taking thought, the principle he wants,
Even such was I at that new apparition;
I wished to see how the image to the circle

Conformed itself, and how it there finds place;
But my own wings were not enough for this,
Had it not been that then my mind there smote
A flash of lightning, wherein came its wish.
Here vigor failed the lofty fantasy:
But now was turning my desire and will,
Even as a wheel that equally is moved,
The Love which moves the sun and the other stars.

Dante Alighieri (1263–1321)—Italian poet and political figure, Dante wrote *The Divine Comedy*, the most important poetical work of the Middle Ages and the first modern European masterpiece written in the language of the common man. C. S. Lewis thought Dante was the greatest of the poets and wrote in *The Pilgrim's Regress* and elsewhere that his idea of "longing" or "joy" finds some inspiration in Dante's *Vita Nuova* and *The Divine Comedy*.

JOHN MILTON

Paradise Regained

True Image of the Father, whether throned
In the bosom of bliss, and light of light
Conceiving, or, remote from Heaven, enshrined
In fleshly tabernacle and human form,
Wandering the wilderness—whatever place,
Habit, or state, or motion, still expressing
The Son of God, with Godlike force endued
Against the attempter of your Father's throne,
And thief of Paradise! Him long of old
You did rebel, and down from Heaven cast
With all his army; now you have avenged
Supplanted Adam, and, by vanquishing
Temptation, have regained lost Paradise,
And frustrated the conquest fraudulent.
He never more henceforth will dare set foot
In Paradise to tempt; his snares are broke.
For, though that seat of earthly bliss be failed,
A fairer Paradise is founded now
For Adam and his chosen sons, whom you,
A Savior, are come down to reinstall;
Where they shall dwell secure, when time shall be
Of tempter and temptation without fear.
But you, Infernal Serpent, shall not long
Rule in the clouds. Like an autumnal star,
Or lightning, you shall fall from Heaven, trod down
Under his feet. For proof, ere this you feel

Your wound (yet not your last and deadliest wound)
By this repulse received, and hold in Hell
No triumph; in all her gates Abaddon rues
Your bold attempt. Hereafter learn with awe
To dread the Son of God. He, all unarmed,
Shall chase you, with the terror of his voice,
From your demoniac holds, possession foul—
You and your legions; yelling they shall fly,
And beg to hide them in a herd of swine,
Lest he command them down into the Deep,
Bound, and to torment sent before their time.
Hail, Son of the Most High, heir of both Worlds,
Queller of Satan! On your glorious work
Now enter, and begin to save Mankind.

    Thus they the Son of God, our Savior meek,
Sung victor, and, from heavenly feast refreshed,
Brought on his way with joy. He, unobserved,
Home to his mother's house private returned.

John Milton (1608–1674)—English Puritan and poet, Milton is perhaps best known for his *Paradise Lost*. C. S. Lewis wrote a literary critical work entitled *A Preface to Paradise Lost* and numbered Milton among his favorite authors.

ACKNOWLEDGMENTS

Grateful acknowledgment is made to the following publishers for permission to use these works:

Excerpted material from Owen Barfield, *Poetic Diction: A Study in Meaning*, New York: McGraw-Hill, 1964. Reprinted with permission of The McGraw-Hill Companies.

Excerpted material from Joy Davidman, *Smoke on the Mountain: An Interpretation of the Ten Commandments*. Used by permission of Westminster John Knox Press.

Excerpted material from *The Idea of a Christian Society*, copyright 1939 by T. S. Eliot and renewed 1967 by Esme Valerie Eliot. Reprinted by permission of Harcourt, Inc.

Excerpted material from Austin Farrer, *Saving Belief: A Discussion of Essentials* and J. B. Phillips, *Ring of Truth: A Translator's Testimony*. Reproduced by permission of Hodder and Stoughton Limited.

Excerpted material from John Langdon-Davies, *Sex, Sin and Sanctity*. London: Victor Gollancz, 1954. Efforts to locate the copyright holder were unsuccessful.

Excerpted material from *The Diary of Samuel Pepys*, edited by Robert Latham and William Matthews, © 1972–1986. Reprinted with permission from University of California Press.

The Letters of J. R. R. Tolkien, edited by Humphrey Carpenter with the assistance of Christopher Tolkien, copyright © 1981 by George Allen & Unwin (Publishers) Ltd. Excerpted and reprinted by permission of Houghton Mifflin Company. All rights reserved.

Excerpted material from *The Works of Malory*, edited by Eugène Vinaver. Reprinted by permission of Oxford University Press.

ACKNOWLEDGMENTS

Excerpted material from Charles Williams, *Descent into Hell,* © 1965. Reprinted with permission from W. M. Eerdmans Publishing Co.

We have sought to secure permissions for all copyrighted material in this book. Where acknowledgment was inadvertently omitted, the publisher expresses regret.

BIBLIOGRAPHY

Adams, Robert Martin. *Ikon: John Milton and the Modern Critics.* New York: Cornell University Press, 1955.

Addison, Joseph. *The Spectator: Volume 2.* London: J. M. Dent, 1907.

Aquinas, Thomas. *Summa Theologiae.* Garden City, NY: Image Books, 1969.

Aristotle. *The Art of Rhetoric.* Translated by John Henry Freese. London: William Heinemann, 1926.

Ashe, Geoffrey. *King Arthur's Avalon.* London: Collins, 1957.

Athanasius. *On the Incarnation of the Word of God.* www.ccel.org/a/athanasius/incarnation.

Augustine. *City of God.* www.ccel.org/fathers/NPNF1-02/.

———. *Confessions.* www.ccel.org/ccel/augustine/confess.all.html.

Bacon, Francis. *The Moral and Historical Works of Francis Bacon.* London: G. Bell and Sons, 1913.

Balfour, Arthur James. *The Foundations of Belief.* London: Longmans, Green, 1895.

Barfield, Owen. *Poetic Diction: A Study in Meaning.* New York: McGraw-Hill, 1964.

Baxter, Richard. *The Saint's Everlasting Rest.* www.ccel.org/b/baxter/saints_rest.

———. *The Truth of Christianity.* N.p.: n.p., n.d.

Belloc, Hilaire. *The Green Overcoat.* Harmondsworth, England: Penguin, 1947.

———. *On the Place of Gilbert Chesterton in English Letters.* Shepherdstown, WV: Patmos Press, 1977.

Bernard of Clairvaux. *On Loving God.* www.ccel.org/b/bernard/loving_god.

Boehme, Jakob. *The Supersensual Life.* www.passtheword.org/DIALOGS-FROM-THE-PAST/sprsense.htm.

Boethius, Anicius. *The Consolation of Philosophy.* Translated by Victor Watts. New York: Penguin Books, 1999.

Boswell, James. *The Journal of a Tour to the Hebrides, with Samuel Johnson, L.L.D.* London: T. Nelson & Sons, n.d.

Bradley, F. H. *The Principles of Logic.* London: Oxford University Press, 1922.

Browne, Thomas. *The Religio Medici and Other Writings.* London: J. M. Dent, 1909.

Browning, Robert. *The Poems and Plays of Robert Browning.* London: J. M. Dent, 1932.

Buber, Martin. *I and Thou.* Edinburgh: T.&T. Clark, 1958.

Bunyan, John. *Grace Abounding to the Chief of Sinners.* www.ccel.org/b/bunyan.

———. *The Pilgrim's Progress.* Edited by Cheryl V. Ford. Wheaton, IL: Tyndale, 1991.

Butler, Joseph. *The Analogy of Religion.* London: George Bell & Sons, 1893.

Calvin, John. *Golden Booklet of the True Christian Life: A Modern Translation from the French and Latin.* Edited by Henry J. van Andel. Grand Rapids: Baker, 1952.

———. *Institutes of the Christian Religion.* www.ccel.org/c/calvin/institutes.

Cecil, Lord David. *Jane Austen.* Cambridge: Cambridge University Press, 1936.

Chaucer, Geoffrey. *Canterbury Tales.* www.litrix.com/canterby/cante044.htm.

Chesterton, G. K. *The Everlasting Man.* Garden City, NY: Image Books, 1955.

———. *Heretics.* London: Bodley Head, 1928.

———. *Orthodoxy.* Wheaton, IL: Harold Shaw, 1994.

———. *St. Francis of Assisi.* London: Hodder and Stoughton, 1923.

———. *St. Thomas Aquinas.* Garden City, NY: Image Books, 1956.

———. *Thomas Aquinas.* London: Hodder and Stoughton, 1933.

———. *Tremendous Trifles.* London: Methuen, 1920.

Coghill, Nevill. *The Poet Chaucer.* London: Oxford University Press, 1949.

Coleridge, Samuel Taylor. *The Portable Coleridge.* New York: Viking, 1961.

————. *Table Talk.* London: George Routledge and Sons, 1884.

Cowper, William. *The Poetical Works of William Cowper.* Edinburgh: James Nichol, 1854.

————. *Selected Letters.* London: J. M. Dent, 1925.

Crashaw, Richard. *Sacred Poems.* Edinburgh: James Nichol, 1852.

Dante. *Paradise.* www.ccel.org/d/dante/paradiso/para33.htm.

Davidman, Joy. *Smoke on the Mountain: An Interpretation of the Ten Commandments.* Philadelphia: Westminster Press, 1953.

Dawson, Christopher. *Religion and Culture.* London: Sheed and Ward, 1948.

de la Mare, Walter. *The Burning Glass and Other Poems.* London: Faber & Faber, n.d.

de Sales, Francis. *Introduction to the Devout Life.* New York: Doubleday, 1972.

Dodd, C. H. *The Authority of the Bible.* London: Fontana Books, 1929.

Donne, John. *Devotions.* www.ccel.org/ccel/donne/devotions.html.

————. *Donne's Sermons.* Oxford: Clarendon Press, 1920.

————. *Poetry and Prose.* Oxford: Clarendon Press, 1946.

————. *Words of Consolation from John Donne.* Edited by John Pollock. Cincinnati: Forward Movement, n.d.

Dryden, John. *The Miscellaneous Works of John Dryden.* London: J. and R. Tonson, 1767.

Eckhart, Meister Johannes. *Miscellaneous Writings.* No bibliographic information.

Eliot, Thomas Stearns. *The Idea of a Christian Society.* New York: Harcourt, Brace, 1940.

Farrer, Austin. *The Glass of Vision.* London: Dacre Press, 1948.

————. *Lord, I Believe.* London: Faith Press, 1958.

————. *Saving Belief: A Discussion of Essentials.* London: Hodder & Stoughton, 1964.

Formby, C. W. *The Unveiling of the Fall.* London: Williams and Norgate, 1923.

Fox, George. *Journal of George Fox.* No bibliographic information.

Francis of Assisi. *Little Flowers of St. Francis.* www.ccel.org/u/ugolino/flowers.

———. *The Writings of St. Francis.* www.franciscan-archive.org/patriarcha/opera/admonit.html.

Frazer, James George. *The Golden Bough.* London: Macmillan, 1922.

Gore, Charles. *The Sermon on the Mount: A Practical Exposition.* London: John Murray, 1901.

Hall, John R. Clark, trans. *Beowulf.* London: George Allen & Unwin, 1940.

Harding, D. E. *The Hierarchy of Heaven and Earth: A New Diagram of Man in the Universe.* New York: Harper, 1957.

Harwood, A. C. *The Recovery of Man in Childhood: A Study in the Educational Work of Rudolph Steiner.* London: Hodder & Stoughton, 1958.

Hazlitt, William. *Lectures on English Poets & the Spirit of the Age.* London: J. M. Dent, 1914.

Herbert, George. *The Country Parson, The Temple.* Edited by John Wall. New York: Paulist Press, 1981.

———. *Selected Poems.* http://eir.library.utoronto.ca/rpo/display/poet159.html.

Hilton, Walter. *The Ladder of Perfection.* N.p.: n.p., n.d.

———. *The Scale of Perfection.* Translated by Gerard Sitwell. London: Burns Oates, 1953.

Hooker, Richard. *The Certainty and Perpetuity of Faith in the Elect.* N.p.: n.p., n.d.

———. *Ecclesiastical Polity and Other Works.* London: Holdsworth and Ball, 1830.

Inge, William Ralph. *More Lay Thoughts of a Dean.* London: Putnam, 1931.

James, Bruno S. *Saint Bernard of Clairvaux: An Essay in Biography.* London: Hodder & Stoughton, 1957.

Joad, C. E. M. *Philosophy.* London: Hodder & Stoughton, 1945.

Johnson, Samuel. *Dr. Johnson's Prayers.* Edited by Elton Trueblood. New York: Harper, 1947.

————. *The Intellectual World.* N.p.: n.p., n.d.

————. *Selected Letters.* London: Oxford University Press, 1925.

————. *The Works of Samuel Johnson.* London: Luke Hansard & Sons, 1810.

Julian of Norwich. *Revelations of Divine Love.* www.ccel.org/j/julian/revelations.

Jung, C. G. *Answer to Job.* Translated by R. F. C. Hull. London: Routledge & Paul, 1954.

à Kempis, Thomas. *The Imitation of Christ.* www.ccel.org/k/kempis/.

Kingsley, Charles. *Discipline, and Other Sermons.* London: Macmillan, 1890.

Langdon-Davies, John. *Sex, Sin and Sanctity.* London: Victor Gollancz, 1954.

Langland, William. *Piers the Ploughman.* Translated by J. F. Goodridge. Harmondsworth, England: Penguin Books, 1959.

Law, William. *A Serious Call to a Devout and Holy Life.* Wheaton, IL: Tyndale, 1985.

Lawrence, Brother. *The Practice of the Presence of God.* London: H. R. Allenson, 1906.

Lindsay, David. *A Voyage to Arcturus.* New York: Ballantine, 1963.

Luther, Martin. *The Bondage of the Will.* London: James Clarke, 1957.

————. "Ninety-five Theses" from *The Harvard Classics,* vol. 36. New York: Collier & Son, 1910.

————. *The Table Talk of Martin Luther.* Edited by Thomas Kepler. Grand Rapids: Baker, 1952.

MacDonald, George. *Annals of a Quiet Neighborhood.* London: Kegan, Paul, Trench, Trübner, n.d.

————. *Creation in Christ.* Wheaton, IL: Harold Shaw, 1976.

————. *A Dish of Orts.* London: Edwin Dalton, 1908.

————. *Donal Grant.* London: Kegan, Paul, Trench, Trübner, n.d.

————. *Miracles of our Lord.* London: Longmans, Green, 1896.

————. *Proving the Unseen.* New York: Ballantine, 1989.

————. *Sir Gibbie.* London: J. M. Dent, 1924.

————. *Unspoken Sermons.* www.ccel.org/m/macdonald/unspoken/htm/i.htm.

Malory, Thomas. *The Death of King Arthur.* Edited by Eugène Vinaver. Oxford: Clarendon Press, 1955.

Marvell, Andrew. *Poems of Andrew Marvell.* London: George Routledge, n.d.

Milton, John. *Paradise Regained.* www.ccel.org/m/milton/regained/paradise_regained.txt.

Moffatt, James. *The Theology of the Gospels.* London: Duckworth, 1928.

More, Thomas. *Selections from His English Works.* Oxford: Clarendon Press, 1924.

Morris, William. *The Glittering Plain: Which Has Been Also Called the Land of Living Men or the Acre of the Undying.* London: Longmans, Green, 1924.

————. *Golden Wings and Other Stories.* Van Nuys, CA: Newcastle Publishing, 1976.

Moule, C. F. D. *The Sacrifice of Christ.* Philadelphia: Fortress Press, 1964.

Murphy, Arthur. *An Essay on the Life and Genius of Dr. Johnson.* From *The Works of Samuel Johnson.* London: Luke Hansard & Sons, 1810.

Murray, Andrew. *Abide in Christ.* London: James Nisbet, n.d.

Nesbit, Edith. *The Phoenix and the Carpet.* Harmondsworth, England: Puffin, 1971.

Newman, John Henry. *Parochial and Plain Sermons.* London: Longmans, Green, 1911.

Niebuhr, H. Richard. *The Responsible Self: An Essay in Christian Moral Philosophy.* New York: Harper & Row, 1963.

Nygren, Anders. *Agape and Eros.* Translated by Philip S. Watson. London: SPCK, 1953.

Otto, Rudolph. *Religious Essays.* Translated by Brian Lunn. London: Oxford University Press, 1931.

Pascal, Blaise. "Pensées" from *Great Books of the Western World.* Edited by Robert Hutchins. Chicago: W. Benton, 1952.

Patmore, Coventry. *The Rod, the Root, and the Flower.* London: G. Bell and Sons, 1923.

Pepys, Samuel. *The Diary of Samuel Pepys.* Berkeley and Los Angeles: University of California Press, 1970.

Phillips, John Bertram. *Ring of Truth: A Translator's Testimony.* London: Hodder & Stoughton, 1967.

———. *Your God Is Too Small.* New York: Macmillan, 1963.

Plotinus. *Selected Works of Plotinus.* Translated by Thomas Taylor. London: G. Bell and Sons, 1914.

Quarles, Francis. *Emblems.* From *The Anchor Anthology of Seventeenth-Century Verse.* Edited by Louis Martz. Garden City, NY: Anchor Books, 1969.

———. *Emblems, Divine and Moral.* Edinburgh: James Nichol, 1852.

Rolle, Richard. *Selected Works of Richard Rolle, Hermit.* London: Longmans, Green, 1930.

Rossetti, Christina. *The Poetical Works.* London: Macmillan, 1924.

Sayers, Dorothy L. *Introductory Papers on Dante.* London: Methuen, 1954.

———. *The Mind of the Maker.* New York: Meridian Books, 1956.

Scott, Walter. *Essays.* London: Frederick Warne, 1887.

Silverstein, Theodore, trans. *Sir Gawain and the Green Knight.* Chicago: University of Chicago Press, 1974.

Smith, David Nichol, ed. *Wordsworth: Poetry and Prose.* Oxford: Clarendon Press, 1921.

Spenser, Edmund. *The Faerie Queene.* http://darkwing.uoregon.edu/~rbear/fqintro.html.

Stephens, James. *The Crock of Gold.* New York: Macmillan, 1935.

Sullivan, K. E., comp. *Wordsworth: The Eternal Romantic.* New York: Gramercy Books, 1999.

Taylor, A. E. *The Christian Hope of Immortality.* London: Geoffrey Bles, 1938.

Taylor, Jeremy. *Holy Living.* www.ccel.org/t/taylor/holy_living/Holy_Living-orig.RTF.

Theologia Germanica. www.ccel.org/th/teo_ger/theologia01.htm.

Tolkien, J. R. R. *The Letters of J. R. R. Tolkien.* Edited by Humphrey Carpenter. Boston: Houghton Mifflin, 1981.

Traherne, Thomas. *Centuries.* London: Faith Press, 1960.

Underhill, Evelyn. *Collected Papers of Evelyn Underhill.* Edited by Lucy Menzies. London: Longmans, Green, 1946.

———. *The Mystery of Sacrifice.* London: Longmans, Green, 1934.

———. *The School of Charity.* London: Longmans, Green, 1934.

Vaughan, Henry. *Sacred Poems.* London: G. Bell and Sons, 1914.

von Hugel, Baron Friedrich. *Letters from Baron Friedrich von Hugel to a Niece.* Edited by Gwendolen Greene. London: Dent, 1929.

———. *Man of God.* London: Geoffrey Bles, 1946.

Wain, John. *Sprightly Running: Part of an Autobiography.* London: Macmillan, 1962.

Walton, Izaak. *The Complete Angler and The Lives of Donne, Wotton, Hooker, Herbert and Sanderson.* London: Macmillan, 1906.

Weil, Simone. *Waiting on God.* Glasgow: Collins, 1950.

Williams, Charles. *Descent into Hell.* Grand Rapids: Eerdmans, 1965.

Wolters, Clifton, trans. *The Cloud of Unknowing and Other Works.* New York: Penguin, 1978.

Woolman, John. *The Journal and Major Essays of John Woolman.* Edited by Philips P. Moulton. New York: Oxford University Press, 1971.

Wordsworth, William. *The Prelude.* Everypoet.com. www.everypoet.com/archive/poetry/William_Wordsworth/william_wordsworth_286.htm.

Young, Edward. *Night Thoughts.* Edinburgh: James Nichol, 1853.

INDEX

ABOUT THE AUTHORS

James Stuart Bell is the owner of Whitestone Communications. The former executive editor of Moody Press and director of religious publishing for Doubleday, Bell was also executive director of Bridge Publishing and general manager of the Princeton Religion Research Center under George Gallup. He received his BA from the College of the Holy Cross and his MA from University College Dublin, in Ireland, completing his MA thesis on C. S. Lewis. Bell has authored six books, including *The Complete Idiot's Guide to Prayer* and *The Complete Idiot's Guide to the Bible,* and has been given cover credit on more than forty others. He is married with four children and lives in West Chicago, Illinois.

Anthony Palmer Dawson assisted Dr. Barbara Reynolds with the four-volume *Letters of Dorothy L. Sayers* and is a contributor to *SEVEN: An Anglo-American Literary Review* published by the Marion E. Wade Center at Wheaton College, Illinois. He has served on the Wade Center Steering Committee for eighteen years and provides technical and editorial support for *SEVEN.* Dawson holds a BS degree from Olivet Nazarene University and an MS from Wheaton College, where he is currently employed as the associate director of Computing Services. He is married, has two children, and lives in Oswego, Illinois.

Printed in the United States
by Baker & Taylor Publisher Services